Hollywood Made in China

The publisher gratefully acknowledges the generous support of the Ahmanson Foundation Humanities Endowment Fund of the University of California Press Foundation.

Hollywood
Made in China

Aynne Kokas

UNIVERSITY OF CALIFORNIA PRESS

University of California Press, one of the most distinguished university
presses in the United States, enriches lives around the world by
advancing scholarship in the humanities, social sciences, and natural
sciences. Its activities are supported by the UC Press Foundation and by
philanthropic contributions from individuals and institutions. For more
information, visit www.ucpress.edu.

University of California Press
Oakland, California

Library of Congress Cataloging-in-Publication Data

Names: Kokas, Aynne, 1979– author.
Title: Hollywood made in China / Aynne Kokas.
Description: Oakland, California : University of California Press, [2017] |
    Includes bibliographical references and index.
Identifiers: LCCN 2016034601 | ISBN 9780520294011 (cloth : alk. paper) |
    ISBN 9780520294028 (pbk. : alk. paper) | ISBN 9780520967298 (Epub)
Subjects: LCSH: Motion pictures—China. | Motion pictures—United
    States. | Mass media—China. | Mass media—United States. | Mass
    media and globalization.
Classification: LCC PN1993.5.C4 K67 2017 | DDC 791.430951—dc23
LC record available at https://lccn.loc.gov/2016034601

Manufactured in the United States of America

25 24 23 22 21 20 19 18 17
10 9 8 7 6 5 4 3 2 1

For A. M.

Contents

Illustrations

TABLES

Preface

Hollywood's collaborations with China are a living, breathing contemporary phenomenon. As a student at both the Beijing Film Academy and the University of California, Los Angeles (UCLA), and as a media worker in production companies in Los Angeles and Beijing, I participated in the early incarnations of this world. Much of this book draws on my personal experiences for reference or contacts, yet I would be remiss if I did not discuss the biases inherent in my position. At a minimum, I hope that awareness of these biases—economic, gendered, racialized, and nationalized—can offer a valuable perspective to consumers, researchers, and filmmakers working within the Sino-US media industries.

For most of the time during which I conducted research (in Beijing, Shanghai, and Los Angeles), I was a graduate student. Anthropologist Sherry Ortner notes that academics occupy a similar—if not the same—cultural position as many filmmakers and film industry professionals, albeit with several noteworthy differences.[1] Ortner identifies the practice of academics studying the film industry as "studying sideways," which distinguishes it from other power hierarchies of anthropological research—such as "studying down" (in which the anthropologist has a higher status than the subject, usually because of privileged access to resources from Western academia) and "studying up" (in which the scholar attempts to access high-level individuals with greater financial or political clout)—meaning that people with similar cultural backgrounds interact on a study.[2] She describes the different types of cultural backgrounds characterizing people within the film industry, noting that some individuals—such as independent film-makers, film festival directors, and so-called creative producers—view themselves as being part of the cultural vanguard, not dissimilar from an academic in the humanities. In this sense, studying sideways offers the researcher an opportunity to develop a deeper understanding of the topic.

During the course of my research, I had experiences that complicated Ortner's claims about studying sideways with regard to issues of age, gender, and race. The relative significance of these issues emerged differently in Los Angeles and in China. In Los Angeles, because of academic interests held by high-level industry players, I was repeatedly granted frank, relatively lengthy interviews. In one particularly interesting incident, Paul Schwartzman, agent for the Hong Kong–based director Wong Kar-Wai, described research he had conducted for his graduate thesis at length before moving on to the heart of our interview.[3] Schwartzman's academic background gave us a shared scholarly language for discussing films. The late Gareth Wigan, then vice chairman of Columbia TriStar Pictures, reached out to the UCLA Center for Chinese Studies to share his expertise beyond an industry audience as he was nearing the end of his life.[4] I encountered similar references to interest in contributing to media scholarship during at least three other interviews, in which part of my interview focused on the academic interests of the high-level industry player with whom I was speaking.

Although my academic credentials may have facilitated our conversations, my age (under thirty-five) and gender (female) affected the nature of my interactions, encouraging many of my (almost exclusively male, older) interlocutors to take an instructive persona in our discussions. Thus, the practice of studying sideways must consider age and gender in addition to relative social position. Notably, Ortner's theorization drew heavily from her experiences interviewing Christine Vachon, a filmmaker who not only operated within a similar cultural class to Ortner but was also a woman of a similar age.[5]

On at least three occasions when I was introduced to interviewees, the introducer referred to me as some variant of "a nice girl." The inherently gender-inflected context of a young woman interviewing an older, powerful man in some ways re-creates the gender dynamic seen elsewhere in Hollywood's industry circles. I am grateful for the information and access I received. At the same time, I propose that my access was at least partially based on my ability to fit into an established industry gender dynamic—in particular, the culture of young female assistants as described by media industries scholar Erin Hill.[6] My research experience represented an instance in which studying up and studying sideways became intertwined. As in any other ethnographic study, the relationship between the interviewer and the interviewee had a significant impact on the project's overall outcome.

In the People's Republic of China (PRC), while the same issues of age and gender operated during my interviews with older (again, primarily male) industry players, my access was also inflected by my race and nationality. I am a Caucasian researcher from the United States. My racial and national profile supported China's "going out" policy (*zouchuqu zhanlüe*), which focuses on increasing the global influence of Chinese industries, including media, and therefore gave policymakers increased incentive to speak with me in order to advance Chinese policy priorities.[7] I spoke with many of the policymakers cited in this book as a result of a 2013 scholarly exchange between Rice University's James A. Baker III Institute of Public Policy and the Shanghai Institutes for International Studies, a Shanghai city government policymaking institute then led by Yang Jiemian, the brother of China's foreign minister at the time, Yang Jiechi. This position is important to note because it both enhanced my access and embedded my interviews within the Chinese government's globalization efforts. Although assessing the impact of race and nationality on ethnographic interviews is difficult, in the PRC, in my case, these elements shaped the conditions of my access.

In both the United States and the PRC, the circumstances of my research inform the outcome of this study, both enriching and complicating the materials included. Scholars and practitioners entering this world of Sino-US media collaborations must consider their position within the production ecosystem to be able to understand issues of access and bias. As the relative media market sizes of China and Hollywood shift, the relationship between individual identity and access will change. However, an awareness of one's role as a participant in the Sino-US media ecosystem will remain essential for successful engagement.

Acknowledgments

Writing the acknowledgments for this book has been one of the most joyful parts of the process because it has allowed me to reflect on the relationships I have developed, people I have met, and things I have learned over the time during which I researched, wrote, and revised the project. Scholars from both media studies and Asian studies provided insight that helped this book develop into what it is today. I would like to first thank Professors John Caldwell and Ted Huters, for their continuous support and willingness to explore new fields of knowledge with me. John Caldwell's research on media cultures of production offered invaluable tools for developing a new approach to the analysis of Chinese media. Ted Huters's encyclopedic knowledge of everything Shanghai was an astounding resource. I only hope that I can mentor others in the future as they have mentored me. Support from Jack Chen and Seiji Lippit at UCLA was essential to getting to this stage. Michael Curtin has offered kind, steadfast guidance over many years.

At various points throughout this process, different communities contributed essential intellectual and financial support. My work during the East-West Center's Asia-Pacific Leadership Program Fellowship provided the foundation for the idea of this project. Support from the Chinese

Ministry of Education allowed me to study at the Beijing Film Academy and see the Chinese film industry firsthand. The Social Science Research Council Dissertation Proposal Development Visual Culture Fellowship headed by Vanessa Schwartz and Anne Higonnet provided a space to develop my project with a group of mentors and peers, while also supporting my initial foray into the Shanghai media community. The Fulbright US Student Program offered me the chance to devote myself to fieldwork in Shanghai, and to meet some of the most inspiring individuals I have ever had the chance to know. Ted Huters's UCLA-Fudan Translation Institute helped me to build a cohort of China scholars and friends while providing essential support to tie up final questions in the field. Funding from the Connected Viewing Initiative of the UCSB Carsey-Wolf Center's Media Industries Project helped me take my work in new and exciting directions related to distribution. Michael Curtin, Jennifer Holt, and Kevin Sanson provided excellent leadership. Fellow cohort members Josh Braun, Max Dawson, Amanda Lotz, Paul McDonald, Matt Payne, Greg Steirer, Sharon Strover, Chuck Tryon, Ethan Tussey, and Patrick Vonderau offered inspired advice on how to bridge the communities of media studies and area studies. A Prosper.NET grant from the United Nations Institute for Advanced Studies provided an excellent intellectual community within which to work on my project at a formative moment. Rice University's Transnational China Project funded fieldwork during my postdoctoral fellowship. The UVA East Asia Center offered indexing support for the book, as well as a wonderful scholarly community.

The scholarly community at the Getty Research Institute (GRI) was a second intellectual home for me throughout graduate school. I will be forever grateful to Sabine Schlosser for offering me the chance to work at the Getty. Thomas Gaehtgens, Alexa Sekyra, and Katja Zelljadt created an inspiring space of inquiry at the GRI. I remain inspired by the scholars that I worked with there. In particular, Petra Chu, Sarah Fraser, Tom Gunning, and Ding Ning exemplified how to be a wise and generous researcher. I would also like to thank my friends in the GRI community who made the process of writing early drafts of this book as enjoyable as possible.

Many scholars in the field gave me excellent formal and informal guidance along the way. In the field of Asian media studies, Chris Berry, Michael Berry, Nick Browne, Wenhong Chen, Shi Chuan, Stephanie

Donald, Nitin Govil, Michael Keane, Jason McGrath, Toby Miller, Stanley Rosen, Shaoyi Sun, Cara Wallis, Yiman Wang, June Yip, Weiyu Zhang, and Ying Zhu helped me to refine my work with excellent, directed feedback. In Chinese literature, Shu-mei Shih and David Schaberg offered rigorous training.

Assistance from wise reviewers and editors helped to refine the project in ways that I could not have foreseen. The anonymous reviewers for the University of California Press, the University of California Press editorial committee, Mary Francis, Ken Wissoker, and Leslie Mitchner all offered invaluable perspectives on how to develop the book into what it is today. Seamane Flanagan, Emily Park, and Susan Yudt generously helped to refine my prose. Raina Polivka, Dore Brown, and Zuha Khan were sage guides through the process of going from manuscript to book. I am deeply grateful for their support and patience throughout the publishing process.

Numerous communities in the United States and China kindly offered me the chance to share early drafts of my research and thus informed the outcomes of this book. I would like to thank Ding Ning, Li Daoxin and the Peking University School of Art; Chen Dongxiao and the Shanghai Institutes for International Studies; Shi Chuan and the Shanghai University School of Film and Television Technology; and Daisy Yan Du and the Humanities Division at the Hong Kong University of Science and Technology for enabling me to share chapters with scholars in China. In the United States, Sharon Strover and the University of Texas at Austin Department of Radio, Television and Film; Jennifer Thackston Johnson-Cooper and Austin College; Andrea Ballestero and the Rice University Anthropology Colloquium; Alexa Sekyra and the Getty Research Institute; and Colin Agur and Valerie Belair-Gagnon at the Yale University Information Society Project all hosted talks that were formative for the project. Fellow conference panelists and audiences at the annual conferences of the Association for Asian Studies, Society for Cinema and Media Studies, and International Communication Association provided important guidance along the way. In particular, I would like to thank Aymar Jean Christian, Hye Jean Chung, Stephanie DeBoer, Evan Elkins, Tarleton Gillespie, Brian Hu, Ramon Lobato, and Serra Tinic for their guidance. Wenhong Chen and Stephen Reese's "Networked China" workshops provided me with formative opportunities to speak with and listen to others in the field. In addition, "Chinese Cinema: To Hollywood and Beyond," organized at Yale University by Dudley Andrew, Ying Zhu, and Ronald Gregg, offered a rich space in which to refine my ideas.

During my postdoctoral fellowship at Rice University's Chao Center for Asian Studies and as a fellow in Chinese media at Rice University's Baker Institute for Public Policy, I had many wonderful mentors. Tani Barlow and the Chao Center brought me to Rice. Steven Wayne Lewis at the Baker Institute helped to shape the policy vantage point of much of my work through his expertise. Ambassador Edward Djerejian encouraged my scholarly exchange with the Shanghai Institutes for International Studies. My colleagues at the Chao Center for Asian Studies provided daily support. Pauline Bolton, Anne Chao, Kimberly Kay Hoang, and John Hopkins indelibly shaped my work as a scholar through regular discussions. The CEHNS team at Rice, especially Dominic Boyer, Cymene Howe, Tim Morton, Joseph Campana, and Derek Woods, added a rich interdisciplinary perspective to my work. Chris Bronk, Dan Cohen, Anhei Shu, Peiyou Song, Dan Wallach, and Rui Zhang drove me to look at technology in new ways.

I am deeply fortunate to work at an institution that has been ceaselessly supportive of this project. The media studies department at the University of Virignia has been a truly remarkable place to begin my career. In addition to being inspiring senior colleagues, Bruce Williams, Hector Amaya, Jennifer Petersen, and Andrea Press shared invaluable perspectives on the publication process. Siva Vaidhyanathan's research on Google in China helped to inform my thinking about the growth of Chinese media and technology firms in the PRC. Christopher Ali, Andre Cavalcante, and Jack Hamilton are the best co-assistant professors a colleague could ask for. Barbara Gibbons manages the department to ensure time for research. Wyatt Andrews, Aniko Bodroghozy, Shilpa Davé, and William Little all generously share their research, humor, and insights.

My colleagues at the University of Virginia's Jefferson Global Seminars at the Hong Kong University of Science and Technology created a space of inquiry in Hong Kong that I will never forget. I will always be thankful to Martien Halvorson-Taylor for the opportunity. Melissa Thomas-Hunt, Chris Aukstikalnis, Stephen Plaskon, and the students of Brown College have been tireless advocates of my work and lights of optimism during difficult times.

The University of Virginia East Asia Center has provided me with a wealth of wonderful colleagues who generously share their experience and humor. Sylvia Chong, Harry Harding, Charles Laughlin, Jeff Legro, Shiqiao Li, Hsin-hsin Liang, Leonard Schoppa, John Shepherd, Robert Stolz, Brantly Womack, and Dorothy Wong brought me into the community and have been influential in the process of bringing this project to press.

My writing partners have generously offered support, read drafts, and kept me sane throughout the process of researching, writing, and editing. Included in this (by no means comprehensive) list are Christopher Ali, Mike Ananny, Whitney Arnold, Valerie Belair-Gagnon, Josh Braun, Karen Fang, Gökçe Gunel, Andrea Hickerson, Seth Lewis, Jenny Lin, Ling Woo Liu, Benedetta Lomi, Leila Pazargadi, Linda Peché, Elizabeth Peng, Matthew Powers, Jen Schradie, Erin Sullivan, Yurika Tamura, Allison VanDeventer, and Sandra Zalman.

The work of this book would have been impossible without the generous time and resources shared by the people in the Chinese and American film communities I interviewed along the way. My professors and classmates in the directing department at the Beijing Film Academy helped me to understand the Chinese media production community from the inside out. Zhang Yang, Peter Loehr, and Jonah Greenberg kindly introduced me to the world of Chinese commercial film production and inspired the first thoughts about writing a book like this. Liu Zhenyun, Cindy Lin, and Fiona Liang provided me with life-changing experience in production development and marketing in China. I would not have been able to connect with many of the people I spoke with in this book without generous introductions from friends and colleagues. I would like to thank Hanson Chen, Shi Chuan, Wang Fang, Matthew Feitshans, Larry Foster, Catherine Wenxia Fu, Ying Hu, Wang Lei, Cindy Lin, Song Qing, Shaoyi Sun, James Schamus, Jason Siu, Stefano Stella, Janet Yang, and Sen-lun Yu for going far above and beyond the call of duty by not only sharing their own knowledge, but also generously connecting me with members of the media co-production community in China.

My dear friends offered endless support throughout this project. Rania Succar, Steve Paulikas, and Feng Songzi provided stories, ideas, and motivation whenever things got tough. My friends from the Asia-Pacific Arts/ Asia Media community continue to help me refine my understanding about media in East Asia. Tony Luce, Sera Hill, Ryan Adams, and the Trepantech team offered priceless perspectives on the Shanghai social media community while also generously making sure that I could write in a space with lightning-fast wireless Internet access and constant good humor. My fellow East-West Center alumni continuously surprised me with support during travels throughout the globe. In particular, I would like to thank Thinley Choden, Greg Dvorak, Supranee Liang, Yuki Lin, Jenine Mak, Maliwan (Buay) Pattanachaisiri, Iris Prasetyo, and Zhao Zhengge for generously guiding me when I was away from home.

Most importantly, this book would not have been possible without my family. My parents and grandparents instilled a love of learning from a very early age. My sisters are endlessly supportive, even as they ensure that I am always improving and questioning my assumptions. My husband brings me joy every day. As I finish writing these acknowledgments, I am deeply humbled by the support I have received through the process of writing this book. As such, at its core my work is an expression of gratitude.

Abbreviations

BJIFF	Beijing International Film Festival
CEO	chief executive officer
CFCC	China Film Co-production Corporation
CFO	chief financial officer
CFPC	China Film Pitch and Catch
CGI	computer-generated imagery
FDI	foreign direct investment
GATT	General Agreement on Tariffs and Trade
M&A	mergers and acquisitions
MOU	Memorandum of Understanding between the People's Republic of China and the United States of America Regarding Films for Theatrical Release
MPAA	Motion Picture Association of America
PRC	People's Republic of China

SAPPRFT	State Administration of Press, Publication, Radio, Film and Television
SARFT	State Administration of Radio, Film and Television*
UCLA	University of California, Los Angeles
WTO	World Trade Organization

* This became SAPPRFT in 2013 after the Ministry of Press, Publication, Radio, Film and Television and the General Administration of Press and Publication merged.

Introduction

Chinese military ships enter Victoria Harbour in Hong Kong to rein in mass chaos. The defense minister in Beijing assures citizens that he has the situation under control. Is this a tableau depicting the worst fears of protesters in Hong Kong's pro-democracy movement? It could be. In actuality, however, it is a scene in Michael Bay's 2014 film *Transformers: Age of Extinction* (hereafter *Transformers 4*). The movie was released just days before the 500,000-person Occupy Central protests began in the city on July 1, 2014, the seventeenth anniversary of Hong Kong's return to the People's Republic of China (PRC). *Transformers 4*, improbably enough, emphasizes some of the challenges Hollywood studios face in their increasing collaborations with Chinese firms and regulators. The movie is a Sino-US film collaboration, a cultural product at the center of a developing media system driven by the cooperative and competitive interactions of China and Hollywood. In addition to shared filmmaking endeavors, Hollywood and China are beginning to cooperate in larger media ventures. In 2012, DreamWorks Animation founded Oriental DreamWorks, a Sino-US film production studio joint venture in Shanghai. China's Wanda Group acquired American studio Legendary Pictures in 2016. The Walt Disney Company opened its Shanghai Disney Resort in the same year. All three firms are planning film slates to take advantage of China's booming film market, which estimates project will rapidly overtake that of the United States.[1]

Chinese government regulations on importing films and investing in media encourage Hollywood conglomerates to collaborate with domestic Chinese firms to access the Chinese market. And the Chinese box office is becoming ever more essential for recuperating the costs of global blockbuster production. *Jurassic World* broke opening weekend records for June 2015 in large part because of the contribution of Chinese box-office receipts.[2] In addition to film exports to China, joint film production and infrastructure investment allow Hollywood media conglomerates to build their brands in the PRC. Brand-building investments in China are shifting the balance of global media capital, so that Hollywood is increasingly building its products in China and for the Chinese market first.

Collaborative ventures highlight a movement by the Chinese central government to overcome its perceived lack of influence on global commercial culture, known in Chinese policy circles as a "cultural trade deficit."[3] These joint projects are part of a systematic, policy-driven attempt to enhance investment in the Chinese culture industries as a way of increasing the PRC's international influence. Such policies counter the assertion made by sociologist John Foster and communications scholar Robert McChesney, among others, that China is merely an assembly factory.[4] Chinese media production thus becomes part of what international affairs expert David Shambaugh refers to as a "discourse war" between China and the West.[5] As both China and Hollywood push global brand-building efforts forward, analyzing shared film and branded content production becomes an essential way of understanding these competing discourses.

In explaining China's media industry growth, film scholar Darrell Davis describes a "'Chinawood' aspiring to match Hollywood internationally while continuing to serve the Party at the national level."[6] The aspiration toward Chinawood informs the growth of the Chinese media industries, but it is only one part of China's media globalization endeavors. Increased Sino-US cooperation expands China's industrial and soft-power reach while simultaneously advancing Hollywood's branding efforts. Hollywood and China are working together to create global products, constrained by Chinese regulatory regimes and the need for reliable quarterly earnings on the part of the publicly held studios.

THINKING ABOUT THE RELATIONSHIP BETWEEN FILM, MEDIA, AND BRANDS

The intersection of China's cultural trade deficit and Hollywood's thirst for an expanding global market share underscores both China's and Hollywood's search for dominance in the global media industries, which now hinges on successful investment with Chinese partners. By investing in commercial filmmaking in China, media conglomerates can build ever-more-powerful global brands. The names of major China-Hollywood productions in China only accentuate the significance of marketing efforts as central to the collaborations. Many are sequels relying on a preexisting narrative world, as in the case of *The Mummy: Tomb of the Dragon Emperor* (2008, hereafter *The Mummy 3*), *Iron Man 3* (2013), *Transformers 4* (2014), and *Kung Fu Panda 3* (2016). Others draw on the global recognition of Chinese place names, like *Shanghai* (2010) and *The Great Wall* (2016). Similarly, entertainment complexes such as the Shanghai DreamCenter (the home of Oriental DreamWorks) and Disney's Shanghai Disney Resort build on preexisting intellectual property to move corporate brands forward.

Examining China-Hollywood collaboration in terms of global media brands, events, and merchandise introduces a new way to approach this important relationship. However, the way in which the branding process situates commercial media content as part of a broader media experience harks back to early cinematic practices. Cinema scholar and art historian Tom Gunning links early twentieth-century viewing experiences more "to the attractions of the fairground than the traditions of the legitimate theater."[7] By identifying the role of media as part of a larger spectacle, Gunning's work underscores cinema's standing as just one attraction among many in an interconnected media landscape. Much like the tradition Gunning describes, twenty-first-century media conglomerates create transnational branded media spectacles within which films are one piece of a multidimensional culture of media consumption and exhibition. Brands act as the fiber connecting media content with theme parks and new production studios with industry events.

At Hollywood studios, marketing on average accounts for more than 50 percent of a project's total budget, thereby rendering film studios more marketing companies than production companies on a dollar-for-dollar basis.[8] Rather than only film, Hollywood's presence in China is about the expansion of vertically and horizontally integrated media conglomerates.[9] As marketing-driven companies, Hollywood studios increasingly rely on such revenue streams as merchandise, theme parks, licensing, and other ancillary income.[10] Establishing a brand identity becomes the larger goal for media conglomerates producing and distributing films in global markets, because their share prices depend on consistent financial success across multiple platforms.[11]

In China, similar pressure exists to maximize additional revenue streams from content. Peter Li, the managing director of China Media Capital, a media investment firm backed by the Chinese government but with financial investment by American media conglomerates, explained the firm's media investment strategy as using resources in media and entertainment to drive value creation in other parts of the business to ultimately promote brands.[12] As a result, although this book may appear to be about movies, it is more fundamentally about competition between global media brands—specifically, the brands of "Hollywood" and "Made in China."

In conjunction with an exploration of Hollywood's expansion into China, this book explores how Chinese president Xi Jinping's guiding ideal, the "Chinese Dream" (Zhongguo Meng), asserts a vision of China's global power through media branding. Much ink has been spilled regarding the meaning of the Chinese Dream, most focusing on the concept of enhancing global perception of the country's domestic growth.[13] But "Chinese dreaming" is also a branding strategy that actually has a lot in common with the mythology of Southern California. In 1951, anthropologist Hortense Powdermaker described Hollywood as a "dream factory," a notion that has only intensified with time.[14] When trying to build a global vision of the Chinese Dream, what could be better than turning to the *original* dream factory?

Chinese regulators therefore have an incentive to accommodate foreign media capital. Promoting the location of a project's production is of deep import for a country with an ascending global position, as well as for one attempting to compete in a broad range of new creative industries. Foreign media investment offers capital infusions to the local economy.[15] Investment in China also leverages Hollywood's technical expertise to promote China's entertainment industry and to disseminate images of con-

temporary China throughout the rest of the world.[16] The practical outcomes of a Chinese media policy that allows certain forms of foreign
investment are substantial. The Shanghai Disney Resort has the largest of
all Disney castles globally. The total investment for the park will exceed
USD 5.5 billion.[17] *Transformers 4*, which was partially shot in the PRC,
had larger box-office receipts in that country than in the United States in
2014, infusing USD 320 million into the Chinese theatrical box office,
according to the entertainment trade website Box Office Mojo.

Leveraging foreign capital and expertise to generate domestic capital
and expertise is an economic development strategy that Chinese policymakers have successfully deployed in other industries—media and entertainment is just the most recent. Scholars have documented that foreign
direct investment (FDI) in the PRC in a range of industrial sectors has led
to domestic development, creating a so-called spillover effect of innovation capacity.[18] In particular, technology-focused FDI, in areas such as
media industries, has a comparatively high level of benefit from foreign
capital infusions, particularly when local firms operate in an environment
supported by government policy.[19] As content production becomes more
technologically intensive, these same benefits accrue to the Chinese media
industries. Since the first decade of the 2000s, Chinese policymakers have
focused on driving the growth of the country's media industries as a way
to expand China's cultural influence, from the central government down
to the municipal government.[20] (See figures 1 and 2.) As a result, Chinese
policymakers and, by extension, foreign filmmakers seeking to distribute
their films in the PRC have an incentive to foster collaboration as a way of
advancing Chinese global cultural expansion.

WHAT IS "CHINA"? WHAT IS "HOLLYWOOD"?

Both Hollywood and China are places on a map, yet their names also con-
jure rich non-geographic images. As geographer Allen J. Scott argues, a
significant concentration of production facilities remains in and around
the city of Los Angeles, thereby literally grounding the US film industry in
Southern California. Hollywood production also extends beyond geographic boundaries and actually drives the larger global film industry.[21]

Figure 1. Slogan at entry to Shanghai Media Group that reads "Become an International First-Class Culture and Media Production Group." (Photo by Aynne Kokas, Shanghai, PRC, July 2, 2013)

Hollywood is much more than physical production space or even the American film industry's global power. Film and television scholar Paul Grainge has argued that Hollywood is as much a brand as it is a place or an industry.[22] To parse the distinctions between Hollywood as a place, as an industry, and as a brand, I will use "Hollywood" in this text to denote the brand of US commercial media production. The choice to use the term "Hollywood" to refer to US commercial filmmaking draws from Chinese entertainment journalism and industry forums, which tend to equate American commercial filmmaking with Hollywood, despite the existence of rich filmmaking traditions in other parts of the United States. In trying to understand the relationship between the film industry in the United

Figure 2. Shanghai Cangcheng Film and Television Cultural Industry Park, a product of the PRC's investment in the media industries. (Photo by Aynne Kokas, Shanghai, PRC, June 13, 2013)

States and that in the PRC, one must seriously consider how the industries refer to each other. In this text, the names of specific cities or regions—such as Los Angeles, New York City, and Southern California—refer to the geographic locations involved in American commercial media production.

"China," like "Hollywood," is a contested term. The PRC and Taiwan disagree on their political relationship, with the PRC pursuing a "One China" policy that designates Taiwan as part of the PRC.[23] Meanwhile, Hong Kong has been actively testing the boundaries of what it means to be a special administrative region of the PRC through demonstrations, most notably the Umbrella Movement and Occupy Central.[24] And demographic diversity in ethnicity, age, and religion further complicate discussions of "China" as a monolith. How different groups understand China, particularly as an agent of media and brand production, is therefore contextual.

When talking about China in this book, I refer to it as a conceptual framework, specifically as a market and as a cultural production industry, in much the same way that Hollywood has become synonymous with American commercial filmmaking. When discussing China as a media production brand, the text critically draws from language common to English-language trade publications and corporate communications, which emphasize economic and cultural production in trying to understand the growth of an alternative global mega-industry. I therefore refer to the Chinese media industries as the trade publications and English-language corporate communications do. The rationale behind speaking about China this way is not to occlude the specific production conditions of Shanghai, Beijing, or other production centers but rather to engage with the discursive structure of "China" already used in both Chinese and Western trade media. To differentiate China the political entity from China the brand, the text uses the term "PRC" when referring to specific policymaking bodies and the country's physical landscape.

Similar challenges exist in discussing the special administrative regions of Hong Kong and Macau. When referring to the space of the PRC exclusive of Hong Kong and Macau, I use the term "mainland China" to account for the distinct current and historical conditions of media production in each of these locations. The phrase "Greater China region" pertains to the overall market for Chinese-language films, including the special administrative regions of Hong Kong and Macau, as well as Taiwan, irrespective of political designation. Again, using the term "China" in this case is intended to engage with current industrial discourse, rather than to reassert PRC political authority.

Finally, there is the question of what the term "Sino-US" means in discussions of media, given that it can signify collaboration as well as contention. As with the economic and security concerns in the relationship between the United States and the PRC, China and Hollywood have clear incentive to cooperate as well as to compete. At its root, however, the term suggests the constant interaction and variability that characterize the contemporary Sino-US media relationship. Hollywood is a recognized brand in global media, and China is maturing as a global media brand. Showing how Hollywood is made in (and with) China demonstrates the way in which studies of global media brands and production inform our understanding of the relationship between the world's two largest economies.

2001: A TRADE ODYSSEY

For nearly twenty years, the PRC has been a major site of global production for the automotive, engineering, and consumer products industries. Yet significant legal pressures to globalize the PRC's international film and media production infrastructure began only after the nation's accession to the WTO in 2001.[25] As media expert Ting Wang argues, WTO accession marked a major shift in how films could be financed in mainland China by liberalizing the type of legal FDI allowed in the market.[26] Since 2001, Chinese and US media corporations have been increasingly open to joint investment.[27] Because of their prominent role in public discourse in both the PRC and the United States, the media industries are the perfect place to begin understanding the multilayered systems that unite the American and Chinese economies.[28] Within the context of the changing Sino-US relationship, media is also one of the prominent US industries most affected by the Chinese market. By focusing on the post-WTO period, this book explains what has driven—and continues to drive—the growth of Sino-US media industries, the intersection of the Chinese and US economies, and the global reality of the twenty-first century.

As the PRC overtakes the United States as the world's largest economy, understanding how the two countries' industries relate to each other becomes more and more essential.[29] Whether the United States is "pivoting" to Asia, as political scientist Kenneth Lieberthal argues, or "rebalancing" its relationship, the PRC's increasing prominence in relation to US industries is clear.[30] But the two countries' industries are—and will likely remain—inextricably linked in a system where any trade antagonism occurs within a context of economic interdependence. Thus, an examination of the recent history of Sino-US media brand collaboration not only gives important insight into the past but also is essential for understanding the future of the global media industries.

The Chinese theatrical box-office distribution market totaled USD 6.8 billion in 2015.[31] The country's box office is slated to become the world's largest in the near term.[32] From 2012 to 2015, the Chinese film market grew 33 percent, from USD 2.7 billion to USD 6.8 billion.[33] China's rapid box-office growth dwarfs that of North America, which only grew from

USD 10.8 billion to USD 11.1 billion during the same period.[34] Examining
the interaction between the Chinese and US media industries further
underscores the significance of the shift in the balance of market power
between these industries.

By virtue of their popular appeal, media projects offer a comparatively
rich trove of public information. As celebrity-driven vehicles, collaborative
film projects garner popular press in addition to trade coverage. At the
same time, the Sino-US media relationship has become a policy priority
for the US federal government.[35] Thus, although the media industries
may not constitute the largest financial relationship between the two
countries, they are, quite literally, the most visible.

While the number of China's connections to Hollywood increases
through various types of investment, Sino-US collaborations led by global
media conglomerates offer the largest-scale insights into how Hollywood
and China work together. China-Hollywood collaborations are particularly important because they affect how everyday people see and understand their world. US trade writers focused on China, such as *The
Hollywood Reporter's* Clifford Coonan and *Variety's* Patrick Frater, regularly point to how Sino-US media co-ventures are shaping the growth of
global media industries in ways that are changing media in both the PRC
and the United States. US corporate forecasters, such as the professional
services firm Ernst & Young, call attention to China's media market potential.[36] Figures such as former Connecticut senator Christopher Dodd, now
chairman and chief executive officer of the Motion Picture Association of
America, assert the centrality of the Chinese market in policy speeches
directed at Chinese government officials and industry elites.[37] All these
groups, as media scholar Michael Curtin argues, are seeking a way to
access the world's biggest audience.[38] *Hollywood Made in China* explores
how China and Hollywood collaborate and compete to expand audiences,
produce content, and leverage their brands.[39]

BRANDS AT WORK

So, how *do* China and Hollywood collaborate in media brand investment?
Trade publications are already alerting their readership to the ways in

which the growth of China's film market will ultimately shape the branding of and within Hollywood films. In a February 24, 2014, *Adweek* article entitled "A By-the-Numbers Look at Hollywood's Marketing Machine" by Gabriel Beltrone, the "expert opinion" at the article's end concludes that as China's importance grows, Hollywood will increasingly incorporate Chinese brands. The article, while focusing on the anticipated gains for advertisers and Hollywood studios, never mentions the implications for the expanding global presence of China's brand and the accompanying long-term political impact. In other words, Hollywood's central focus in China is on the potential upside for Hollywood.

But by expanding the capacity of China's culture industries through FDI, Hollywood is advancing the Chinese Dream. Thinking of action director Michael Bay as furthering Chinese government strategic objectives sounds much more like the stuff of farce than the reality of the global motion picture industry. But, as chapter 1 of this book will demonstrate, *Transformers 4* offered the PRC government a major promotion opportunity through its depiction of the Chinese Ministry of Defense and the relationship between mainland China and Hong Kong.

But collaboration is not without its downsides for Chinese partners. Sino-US collaborations also constrain some Chinese brands. As Chinese regulators are overseeing the production of Hollywood commercial blockbusters to advance the PRC's commercial film interests, the films present stiff competition for the PRC's new mainstream cinema (*xin zhuliu dianying*)—state-supported films that advance social goals but approach production and marketing in a manner similar to commercial productions.[40] Films such as the PRC's fiftieth-anniversary film, *The Founding of a Republic* (2009), directed by Han Sanping (then president of the state-run China Film Group Corporation) and Huang Jianxin (China Film Group Corporation's production manager), as well as 2011's *The Founding of a Party*, also directed by Han and Huang, directly competed with Hollywood films at the Chinese box office. Independent Chinese filmmakers, dubbed the "urban generation," who seek to tell local stories about life in contemporary China also face competition from Sino-US collaborations.[41] Whether independent or supported by the government, domestic Chinese filmmakers face a more cutthroat market as a result of foreign film collaborations and imports.

Perhaps the most visible example of the PRC government's ambivalence about the competition between China's growing international commercial film brand and a domestic Chinese film production involves James Cameron's *Avatar* (2009) and Hu Mei's *Confucius* (2010). The commercial hit *Avatar* broke Chinese box-office records, but it was pulled from 2-D (though not from 3-D) screens after less than two weeks.[42] This was done to increase box-office numbers for the state-supported Chinese film *Confucius*, a domestic period piece depicting the virtuous life of the eponymous Chinese sage.[43] However, Cameron remained in the market as an investor. His Cameron Pace Group, a company that specializes in 3-D technology and production services, established the Cameron Pace Group China in the northern port city of Tianjin to contribute technology to productions in China and further afield.[44] Cameron's uneasy coexistence with production in China calls attention to the ways in which Hollywood brands can both expand and be limited by Chinese government regulations. The case further highlights how accommodating foreign capital can not only plunder Chinese box offices but also infuse new technologies into the market.

In addition to Hollywood media investment and Chinese government policymaking, the interstitial relationships between Chinese industrialists, bilingual local workers, expatriate production labor, and even farmers-turned-production-assistants mediate between Hollywood's and China's brands. Hollywood's industrial aspirations and China's policy incentives extend beyond the binary relationship described by media scholars Michael Keane, Anthony Y. H. Fung, and Albert Moran in *New Television, Globalisation, and the East Asian Cultural Imagination* and by Fung in *Global Capital, Local Culture: Transnational Media Corporations in China*.[45] Through increasingly intimate production relationships with Hollywood's institutions, Chinese policymakers and media producers are deepening the country's soft power.[46] But in addition to institutional-level work, media industry forums, fans, and below-the-line workers all contribute to the growth of Sino-US collaboration. Rather than one new, dominant force emerging, an ever-increasing list of projects that offer new blends of mass media culture, production practices, and brands is expanding beyond the complete control of either industrial or regulatory masters.

Further, spurred by central government efforts to expand China's cultural soft power, Chinese media industry leaders have begun examining ways to leverage relationships with Hollywood into expanded Chinese investments in Hollywood. Starting with Wanda Group's acquisition of AMC Theaters, Chinese investment in Hollywood has continued, with Chinese media companies opening US offices, taking majority stakes in US production companies, and even purchasing entire Hollywood studios.[47] China-Hollywood collaborations in the United States are an important growing trend in Chinese media investment, but the focus of the following pages is the more mature phenomenon of Hollywood's investments in China.

Hollywood Made in China focuses on how China's relationship with Hollywood changed during the formative period between China's December 2001 accession to the WTO and the June 2016 opening of Shanghai Disney. Drawing on this formative period, the text offers a foundation for understanding the future of China-Hollywood relations. By using China- and US-based industry ethnography in parallel with textual analysis of policies, co-ventures, and paratextual brand materials, the resulting text simultaneously provides a top-down and a bottom-up assessment of the radical changes in Sino-US media production. Interviews and firsthand research with policymakers and industry insiders in the PRC, Hong Kong, and Southern California help answer the following questions: How does China influence Hollywood? How does Hollywood influence China? How is the intersection between these two brands changing the way we see the world?

CENTRAL ARGUMENT

Sino-US media brand collaborations emerge from self-aggrandizing motives but constitute a new global media order. Chinese policymakers are trying to broaden the influence of the country's cultural products. Hollywood executives are seeking ways to generate revenue beyond mature US theatrical sales. China's impulse to decrease its cultural production deficit, combined with Hollywood's desire to expand its global market share, is at once symbiotic and competitive.

Chinese cooperation with Hollywood portends the surprising ways in which US and Chinese industries intersect as the fates of the two countries become more entwined. This book enhances understanding of Sino-US relations by examining how and why stakeholders at all levels—production workers, industry executives, and government policymakers—are creating new, blended Sino-US media content and brands. Co-ventures between Hollywood and China range from studio film collaborations to shared brandscapes, what Anna Klingmann refers to as "the demarcation of territory by brands" manifested in production studios, entertainment centers, theme parks, and English-language schools.[48] The most "Hollywood" of Hollywood—the Walt Disney Company, DreamWorks Animation, and director James Cameron—are becoming part of the Chinese media industries through their investments in both films and brandscapes in the PRC. Key players in the Chinese media industries—the China Film Group Corporation (Zhongguo Dianying Jituan Youxian Gongsi), Hengdian World Studios (Hengdian Yingshi Cheng), and the Shanghai Media Group (Shanghai Dongfang Chuanmei Jituan Youxian Gongsi)—are partnering with Hollywood players to expand their capacity.

Examining Sino-US media brand collaborations highlights new analytical approaches through which to understand global media industry intersections at the levels of labor, policy, investment, and marketing. From below-the-line workers who leverage their cultural literacy, to policymakers driving collaboration through central government interventions, to new brandscapes that blend Chinese and US media industry resources, Sino-US media has become a significant system composed of, yet distinct from, that of Hollywood and China.

CULTURAL POWER AS MULTIDIRECTIONAL

With a few notable exceptions that also examine the global power of Asian media, studies of Hollywood's expansion in Asia portray the industry's role as an imperialist media power.[49] China's mighty market has shifted power eastward.[50] The increasing necessity of a broad range of income streams to recuperate investments in corporate media brands, Sino-US production facilities, theme parks, and other branded ancillary collaborations relies on success in China.[51] The multilingual crafts workers based in China commonly known as below-the-line laborers and the cosmopolitan above-the-line workers with connections across the Pacific further con-

tribute to the rise of a new industrial culture at the intersection of
Hollywood and China. Media forums in both China and Hollywood bring
together a mix of journalists, fans, insiders, and experts to facilitate media
industry development across the Pacific. Together, these diverse layers of
people, projects, policies, and infrastructure build dynamic Sino-US
media industries.

In the case of China and Hollywood, media power is neither a one-way
flow nor a polite, tepid pressure coming from both sides. Considering
Hollywood's cultural imperialism in China as a unidirectional phenomenon would offer an inaccurate and limited perspective on the Chinese government and industry's influence.[52] Similarly, seeing Hollywood's investments in China as solely benefiting the Chinese government overlooks the
access to the protected Chinese media market those investments require.
Both China and Hollywood have access to rich resources to project their
influence. Major Hollywood investments in China in the first two decades
of the twenty-first century form an important foundation to understanding the Hollywood-China relationship. The stories presented in this book
focus on Hollywood as it is made in China to facilitate a foundational
understanding of Sino-US media relations as they have been and as they
may become.

BOOK STRUCTURE

Hollywood Made in China begins with a macro-level examination of the
policies, processes, and brands that support the growth of Sino-US media
systems. The book then progresses to a micro-level exploration of how
these systems operate in individual co-ventures, through industry forums,
and within labor networks. The text concludes by exploring these concerns with regard to the television, streaming video, and animation industries and ultimately proposes key issues to watch for in the future.

Chapter 1, "Policy and Superheroes: China and Hollywood in Sino-US
Relations," articulates the role of media, technology, and trade policy in the
creation of a new system of Sino-US media, one with its own parts and players. It examines how policymaking influences these two global media
brands, and vice versa. Using case studies of recent film collaborations—

Iron Man 3 (2013) and *Transformers 4* (2014)—the chapter argues that understanding how Hollywood and China co-create media teaches us about the maturing political dynamic between the PRC and the United States.

Chapter 2, "Hollywood's China: Mickey Mouse, *Kung Fu Panda*, and the Rise of Sino-US Brandscapes," asserts the importance of diversified media brands in Sino-US collaborations. Focusing on Disney's involvement in the Chinese market, the chapter examines how branded real estate ventures generate parallel revenue streams and improve political relationships to facilitate Hollywood's China investments. It also explores the case of Shanghai Disney Resort, the largest Sino-foreign joint venture in the PRC's modern service industry, as well as related projects, such as the company's English-language school empire in China. Ultimately, the chapter argues that Hollywood studios are trying—and, to a degree, succeeding—in staking their claim within China's brand landscape through real estate ventures and other branded spaces. However, Sino-US joint venture ownership structures mean that what first appears as an extension of Hollywood's global ambitions also represents a major advancement of China's global brand. And, taken together, China-Hollywood brandscapes also create new blended Sino-US spaces, not fully compatible with either Chinese or Hollywood interests.

Chapter 3, "Soft Power Plays: How Chinese Film Policy Influences Hollywood," explores how Chinese media policy shapes Sino-US industry relations and how production regulations affect brand and industry growth. It examines a broad range of Sino-US film collaborations, including Chinese government–sanctioned film co-productions (films treated by the PRC government as Chinese but released as Hollywood films in other markets). At its most pragmatic, the chapter parses the complex definitions of the range of co-production activities that can occur between China and the United States. It argues that, despite regulations that currently allow Hollywood films access to the Chinese market, the degree of regulation grants the PRC government a considerable amount of control over how much to accommodate foreign capital in the PRC theatrical exhibition market and a considerable amount of control over the content of Hollywood productions distributed in China.

Chapter 4, "Whispers in the Gallery: How Industry Forums Build Sino-US Media Collaboration," examines how industry production forums both practically and discursively articulate the norms of Sino-US media collaboration. Using ethnography and industry videos from China and Hollywood, it asserts that industry forums circulate strategic narratives that explain the industrial culture of Sino-US media production to insiders and newcomers. The chapter also uses industry forums to explore how China and Hollywood define themselves both in collaboration with and in opposition to each other in the context of increased Hollywood media investment in China.

Chapter 5, "Compradors: How Above-the-Line Workers Brand Sino-US Film Production," looks at how above-the-line cultural intermediaries shape the global image of Sino-US film industries. This book uses the phrase "above the line," as defined by economic geographers Susan Christopherson and Michael Storper (1989), to mean media workers— including directors, actors, writers, and producers—as creative talent.[53] By analyzing Ang Lee's 2007 Sino-US film co-production *Lust, Caution*, the chapter focuses on the role these intermediaries play in shaping the film co-production process, as well as perceptions of the process after the fact. It examines the cultural translation work of writers, directors, producers, and regulators in the creation of collaborative productions between China and Hollywood. To make its case, the chapter draws on the extensive paratextual materials released with the film, as well as on interviews with above-the-line workers such as producer James Schamus. Ultimately, it looks at the ways above-the-line workers promote both the China and Hollywood brands.

Chapter 6, "Farm Labor, Film Labor: How Below-the-Line Workers Shape Sino-US Film Production," examines the role of below-the-line film laborers in guiding China and Hollywood during the production and pre-production processes. The text uses Christopherson and Storper's definition of "below-the-line" workers, which refers to skilled craft labor in Hollywood productions. This is also the definition of "below the line" used in other chapters of this book.[54] "Farm Labor, Film Labor" draws on the case studies of two 2008 Sino-US productions—*The Mummy 3* and *The Forbidden Kingdom*—to examine how crew members from the United States, China, Malaysia, Australia, and New Zealand frame the Sino-US film collaboration process for their colleagues from other countries during the formative years of contemporary Sino-US film collaboration.

The conclusion envisions what the future holds for shared Sino-US media ventures. The final chapter provides a broad overview of how the frameworks presented within this book contribute to understanding Sino-US collaboration in animation, television, and streaming video. Ultimately, the chapter examines how the industrial relationship between the Chinese and US media industries is changing as China becomes the world's largest media market.

Hollywood Made in China explains the complex systems that exist in Sino-US media relations and how phenomena such as media co-ventures will shape the future of the media industries in the United States and China, as well as throughout the rest of the world. Chinese and US leaders are already meeting to discuss global media industry policies. China's market size and Hollywood's global media power are rapidly increasing both competition and collaboration, as each projects its media production brand outward into the world. What emerges from this book is a trans-Pacific map of links between financial, production, policy, and marketing entities connecting China and Hollywood. Here is an early look at what is undoubtedly one of the most formative media transitions of the twenty-first century.

1 Policy and Superheroes

CHINA AND HOLLYWOOD IN SINO-US RELATIONS

The PRC market has become a powerful force in the global media industries, and Hollywood has noticed. Demand for market expansion by Hollywood media conglomerates, combined with China's thirst for global soft power, has caused the Sino-US industrial relationship to expand. In an era of increasing interaction between China and Hollywood, Sino-US film collaborations reveal the role of policy in joint media production. Hollywood studios and the blockbusters they create with Chinese partners amplify global Chinese media production, while at the same time extending the reach of Chinese soft power. In *Iron Man 3*, Chinese doctors in Beijing perform lifesaving surgery on a beloved American superhero, using traditional Chinese medicine. In *Transformers 4*, CGI (computer-generated imagery) robots rebooted from American cartoons tromp through Guangdong Province and Hong Kong. As this chapter will show, the rise of Sino-US joint production activity in the PRC aligns closely with the country's financial, technological, and policy priorities.

The role of soft power in China has a long historical trajectory in Chinese media policy. Although the importance of the term "soft power" has been much debated in policy circles since political scientist Joseph Nye's seminal 1990 article, the concept remains central to how Chinese policymakers think about media.[1] When I was a visiting fellow at the Shanghai Institutes for International Studies in the summer of 2013, the idea of soft power guided policymakers' lecture questions throughout my residency. Soft power offers what Chinese policymakers term "cultural security."[2] Former president of the People's Republic of China Hu Jintao observed in the Seventeenth Party Congress in 2007 the need to "enhance the state's cultural soft power."[3] In 2014, Premier Li Keqiang promoted the development of the cultural sector in his *Report on the Work of the Government* at the Twelfth National People's Congress on March 5, saying: "We promoted the sound development of the cultural sector. A number of high-quality cultural works were produced, and more public cultural facilities were opened free of charge. We deepened reform of the cultural management system and developed the market for cultural products."[4] Chinese media scholar Wendy Su argues that China's cultural policy has led to a complete reformulation of the state's global communication practices.[5] The high profile of the cultural sector underscores its centrality in China's global development.

Soft power is a feature of China's foreign policy at the very highest levels. A January 1, 2014, article in the *People's Daily* newspaper, entitled "Build Socialist Culture to Strengthen the Nation, Focus on Improving the Country's Cultural Soft Power" (*Jianshe Shehuizhuyi Wenhua Qiangguo, Zhuoli Tigao Guojia Wenhua Ruanshili*), profiled comments by President Xi Jinping encouraging politburo members to "increase the nation's cultural soft power."[6] In this same article, Xi further advocated for efforts to "strengthen construction of international broadcasting capacity, meticulously construct external discourse, exhibit up-and-coming media activity, increase the creativity, inspiration, and accountability of external discourse, tell Chinese stories well, broadcast Chinese voices, and explain Chinese characteristics properly."[7] Xi's exhortations in a newspaper that is commonly considered one of the key mouthpieces of the Chinese Communist Party directly linked foreign projection of Chinese international relations discourse to the flowering of the media industries and the rise of the Chinese Dream. (See figure 3.) As Hollywood studios share China's global trade in media, China, in turn, bolsters its media production capabilities. The Hollywood dream factory and the Chinese Dream work together, while mired in a state of perpetual negotiation.

Figure 3. Public advertising advocating the Chinese Dream that reads "Chinese Spirit, Chinese Images, Chinese Culture, Chinese Representation." (Photo by Aynne Kokas, Shanghai, PRC, July 12, 2013)

THE INTERSECTIONS OF POLICY AND PRODUCT

China

When the People's Republic of China (PRC) joined the World Trade Organization (WTO) in 2001, the country agreed to open its media markets.[8] Yet rather than smoothly increasing trade, the opening of the PRC's media markets has exacerbated tensions between the PRC and the United States. In 2007, the United States issued a formal complaint to the WTO, stating that the PRC was not following its commitment to opening its audiovisual markets as outlined in its WTO accession protocol, in the General Agreement on Tariffs and Trade (GATT), and in the General Agreement on Trade in Services (a separate trade agreement).[9] The United States won the WTO dispute in 2009, but implementation took three years and required eighteen different WTO status reports issued by the PRC; agreements on film distribution in the PRC were left to bilateral negotiations.[10] The resulting 2012 "Memorandum of Understanding between the People's Republic of China and the United States of America Regarding Films for Theatrical Release" (MOU), also known as the US-China Film Agreement, required an increase in China's revenue-sharing import quota to include fourteen special-format films (3-D, IMAX) in addition to the twenty films already permitted by Chinese law, for a total of thirty-four imported films in the Chinese market.[11] It further stipulated a review of enforcement in 2017, five years after the initial MOU agreement, emphasizing the long-term nature of policy negotiations surrounding Hollywood's influence in China.[12]

The 2014 *Report to Congress on China's WTO Compliance* underscored that China had "not yet fully implemented its MOU commitments."[13] In a public hearing before the Trade Policy Staff Committee on China's WTO Compliance, the Office of the United States Trade Representative further elaborated by explaining that few films could secure import quota slots. Additional distribution options were limited because of the power of Chinese state-owned enterprises, opaque censorship processes, and special protected periods for the distribution of local films, with each of these practices violating the US-China Film Agreement of 2012.[14]

In China, the film import "master contract," or the agreement outlining policies for the importing of foreign films into China, is reportedly under negotiation to more accurately reflect WTO commitments.[15] China's State Administration of Radio, Film and Television (SARFT) (Guojia Guangbo Dianying Dianshi Zongju) first established co-production regulations, outlined in "The Stipulation of the Administration of Chinese-Foreign Film Co-production," at an executive meeting on June 15, 2004, three years after China's accession to the WTO. In 2013, the newly formed State Administration of Press, Publication, Radio, Film and Television (SAPPRFT) (Guojia Xinwen Chuban Guangbo Dianying Dianshi Zongju) absorbed SARFT and adopted its existing policies. However, through July 2015, the imported film master contract on the official SAPPRFT website reflected a policy written in 2009, which stipulated specific domestic Chinese film distributors for foreign and coproduced films, in opposition to the 2012 ruling. Given that SARFT was absorbed into SAPPRFT in 2013, this indicates that the website had been updated since the 2012 decision was issued but still included the 2009 policy, rather than the 2012 ruling. The tension caused by increasing access to the Chinese market despite ambivalence about opening the market epitomizes the types of challenges the PRC faces in working with the United States, and vice versa.

In addition to China's film import regulations, central government media policy informs the rise of other types of Sino-US media collaborations. The Chinese government's film co-production policy allows foreign films with sufficient Chinese talent and financing to be treated as "local" films for the purpose of distribution and to circumvent the country's thirty-four-film import quota.[16] The quota on imported films restricts foreign access to a market that was worth USD 6.8 billion in 2015.[17] PRC co-production policy allows films to apply for approval at the preproduction, rather than the postproduction, stage. Hollywood producers therefore have strong market incentives to follow Chinese co-production policy from the beginning of a project to secure market access. Although co-productions provide US film companies an important entry point into the PRC's market, the SAPPRFT (and, by extension, the central government) has final-cut and distribution approval of any film that is considered an official PRC product—including co-productions. Any films produced within the context of the Sino-US film co-production policy are thus beholden to a complex political approval landscape for distribution in the PRC, which begins during preproduction. Through co-production policy, the PRC can leverage Hollywood expertise in developing its domestic media industries and national brand.

Still, Chinese policymakers have reason to be concerned about foreign investment in a changing domestic industry. Protecting culture industries from Hollywood has been the subject of multilateral negotiations around the world, including negotiations in the Uruguay Round of the GATT from 1986 to 1994, WTO negotiations, and the UNESCO Convention on the Protection and Promotion of the Diversity of Cultural Expressions in 2005.[18] Pushback from WTO member countries against Hollywood's influence led to a cultural exception to protect domestic culture industries.[19] At the same time, China's state-owned media industries—and its film studios in particular—wield a huge amount of power. As film scholars Emilie Yueh-yu Yeh and Darrell William Davis compellingly argue, state-owned film groups broker between the pressure to expand the market and the pressure to protect the national screen industry.[20] Even as state-owned film groups privatize, the inertia behind long histories of government involvement continue to protect domestic industries. When extended to the role of media in China's larger economic plan, these tensions become even more acute.

The PRC's twelfth five-year plan, released in 2011, identified the country's media industries as a major pillar for economic growth that should therefore receive central government support. Within the policy context of the PRC's twelfth five-year plan, Sino-US media are an extension of the PRC central government's role as a media industry stakeholder. The plan discusses the growth of media industries in terms of the development of hard infrastructure (physical spaces for industrial development) and soft infrastructure (workforce skills development).[21] Brandscapes—what architect, academic, and branding expert Anna Klingmann refers to as "the demarcation of territory by brands"—demand both hard infrastructure (as in the case of the production studio Oriental DreamWorks) and soft infrastructure (as with the requirements for Chinese talent to be used in Sino-US film co-productions).[22] China's cultural policy demands growth, which not only stimulates the Chinese media economy, but also creates an opportunity for Hollywood media conglomerates that can amplify domestic capabilities.

Films such as the Sino-US collaborative productions *Iron Man 3* and *Transformers 4* demonstrate how blockbuster production in the PRC can train Chinese media industry labor. Intense special effects meet the demands for infrastructure innovation outlined in the twelfth five-year plan, which stipulates "cultural innovation, video production, publication, printing and reproduction, performing and entertaining arts, digital contents, and animation."[23] The plan articulates "a need to implement . . . major cultural industrial projects, and [to] enhance the construction of cultural industrial bases and the building of cultural industrial clusters with special regional characteristics."[24] The growth of co-ventures—think of projects like Shanghai Disney Resort and Oriental DreamWorks that build hard and soft infrastructures—drives cultural production in the Chinese and US media industries.

Similarly, the twelfth five-year plan also underscored the importance of international trade in reaching China's media industry development goals. Explicitly, it "encourage[d] cultural enterprises to engage in cross-region,

cross-trade, cross-ownership operations and reorganizations; and raise
the scale, intensification, and professional level of the cultural industry."[25]
The plan emphasized the high-level policy- and decision-making that
back film and media collaborations, from major blockbusters to media
production parks, between the PRC and the United States.

There is reason to follow this strategy: Chinese central planning in the
1990s and early 2000s was effective in developing the country's industrial
landscape. The number of buildings for Chinese creative-industry clusters
is increasing throughout the country, with government support.[26]
Communications scholar Wendy Su argues that, through central planning, China has effectively harnessed the power of Hollywood to do
China's soft power work.[27] Even so, Hollywood and China continue to
negotiate the terms of the balance of global media power with each new
deal creating uncertainty for both sides.

Hollywood

The Chinese government's approach to regulation of the film industry is
very different from the inconsistent intervention of the US federal government in Hollywood.[28] Blockbusters made in the United States, such as
Independence Day (1996), and military-themed superhero films, such as
the *Captain America* series (2011 to 2016) and the *Iron Man* series (2008
to 2013), are produced with ad hoc cooperation from the US federal government via the public affairs offices of specific military branches, including the Marine Corps Motion Picture and TV Liaison Office, the Air Force
Entertainment Liaison Office, the US Army Community Relations Office–
West, and the Navy Office of Information–West. According to these
organizations' websites, filmmakers can choose to use these resources, just
as the offices can choose to support or not support certain films.
Policymakers advocate for the industry as a whole more rarely, usually in
conjunction with trade groups and industry representatives.

Feature film production in Hollywood has never been an official state-
run enterprise, unlike large portions of the PRC's film industry. However,
this does not mean that censorship, albeit industry driven, has not played
an important role in shaping both Hollywood itself and Hollywood's
global influence. The Motion Picture Producers and Distributors of

America established the Motion Picture Production Code of 1930 (also known as the Hays Code) in March 1930. The group changed its name to the Motion Picture Association of America (MPAA) in 1945. Industry partners established the Hays Code via collusive industry efforts to consolidate power.[29] However, like China's censorship practices, the Hays Code influenced the types of films produced in Hollywood until the code fell out of favor in the period from the mid-1950s to the mid-1960s.[30] The Motion Picture Association of America remains the dominant trade organization for the United States and still provides content ratings for films.

Despite a lack of official authority over each other, Hollywood and Washington, DC, have historically been mutually influential.[31] Nongovernmental lobbying organizations contribute to larger policy debates regarding the growth of Sino-US media. Washington, DC, insiders have run the MPAA since 1966. Jack Valenti, a former advisor to US president Lyndon B. Johnson, was the organization's head from 1966 to 2004. Dan Glickman, who succeeded Valenti, was previously secretary of the United States Department of Agriculture and a congressman from Kansas.[32] Starting in 2011, Christopher Dodd, a former Connecticut senator, assumed the role of MPAA chairman and CEO.[33] Because of its significance in setting US policy and circulating images of the United States around the world, the MPAA has long held the nickname the "Little State Department."[34] The movement of high-level US government officials into positions of leadership with the MPAA demonstrates the importance of the US federal government's influence in Hollywood's relationship with Chinese regulators.

In 2011 the Motion Picture Association of America began hosting screenings of Chinese film co-productions each November. Chinese film regulators are typically the special invited guests or official partners, and American industry partners cohost. This type of event calls attention to the type of joint efforts between the US trade association and the Chinese government that create the conditions for media collaboration. Yet cooperation also presents the downsides of the globalization of Chinese media policy. If films can enter the Chinese market only after Chinese censors have approved them, then the US efforts to increase market quotas in the PRC stand as an example of exchanging freedom of expression for market-access opportunities. The MPAA lobbies heavily for access to the Chinese market, even while turning a blind eye to the concessions US filmmakers may have to make to the Chinese SAPPRFT to get their films approved for Chinese distribution.

The lack of a comprehensive US state-level media policy, combined with Hollywood's lobbying power in the nation's capital, has created a dynamic in which Hollywood's economic needs are at the forefront of the US side of Sino-US media industry development. This produces twin outcomes: first, the US government supports the growth of Hollywood blockbusters in the Chinese market, and second, major US media products are beholden to the content restrictions placed on Chinese media productions. That Hollywood and China would collaborate to meet their joint goals of cultural export (China) and expanded market share (Hollywood) makes sense, but the landscape becomes much more complicated when we consider the role of US trade policy in bringing these goals to fruition. Further, the implication is that Hollywood studios that have long been self-regulating through US trade organizations must now rely on approval from the SAPPRFT to distribute films in a key market. By contrast, within the Chinese context, there is more formal policy dialogue at the central government level discussing the outward, global expansion of the PRC's media industries.[35]

The incongruity between China's and America's approaches to managing the media industries at the highest levels demonstrates the fundamental challenges in developing sustained industrial collaboration. In the PRC, government intervention drives the media industries, whereas in the United States, the media industries, in large part, drive the government. This distinction has led to strange bedfellows, with Hollywood and China negotiating what global consumers can access and how. The outcome is the creation of models in which Chinese government officials are poised to have final-cut approval of major blockbusters and other transnational cultural products. Chinese government oversight over the production process precipitates a watershed moment that is changing the nature of global media for everyone, from leaders of global media capitals to the most casual of movie fans.

The following vignettes further illustrate how the US and Chinese governments influence policymaking related to Sino-US collaborations.

CHINESE AND US POLICYMAKERS IN THE GLOBAL
MEDIA INDUSTRIES

The February 2012 meeting in Washington, DC, between then Chinese vice president Xi Jinping and US vice president Joe Biden to discuss boosting the PRC's quotas for importing films underscored the Sino-US media policy priorities at the highest levels of government. The 2012 Xi-Biden meeting and related WTO action led the PRC to increase its foreign film import quota from twenty to thirty-four films per year.[36] The fourteen films added to the quota were slated to be "special-format" productions in platforms ranging from IMAX to 3-D, thereby linking Hollywood's technology advantage with the PRC's media policy to expand the country's digital theatrical footprint and product range.[37] The increase offered additional opportunities for Hollywood studios to access the Chinese market. Special-format film distribution relies heavily on theater-based technologies that cannot be replicated in a home setting. In the context of Sino-US film, this both reduces piracy risk and drives revenue to Chinese theaters.

Additional distribution of 3-D and other types of special-format American films increases digital theatrical content in China while protecting Chinese domestic filmmakers working in 2-D from foreign competition. The Chinese market's rapid special-format growth has also supported the development of new filmmaking practices. IMAX now converts both imported and Chinese films into the IMAX format for the Chinese market—focusing on Chinese films that might not otherwise be altered in this way—during summer blackout periods when foreign films cannot be released in the Chinese market.[38] IMAX's conversion strategy has been so successful in the Chinese market that it established an IMAX China subsidiary that trades publicly on the Hong Kong stock exchange. The special-format distribution quota increase is an example of a comparatively successful negotiation between Chinese and US interests for the growth of both media industries.

Although government intervention in the media industry is consistent with China's planned economy, the practice is somewhat of an anomaly for the United States. For example, during Xi's February 2012 visit with Biden, the two men worked with Hollywood film executive and producer

Jeffrey Katzenberg to agree on the establishment of Oriental DreamWorks —a joint venture to create family branded entertainment in China backed by Chinese investors China Media Capital, Shanghai Media Group, Shanghai Alliance Investment Limited, and Hollywood's DreamWorks Animation SKG.[39] Katzenberg was seated next to Xi at a February 2012 State Department Luncheon in Xi's honor in Washington, DC. Xi Jinping also attended a Los Angeles Lakers basketball game accompanied by none other than Katzenberg during his 2012 visit.[40] That Biden, Xi, and Katzenberg brokered one of the milestone industrial collaborations between a major US corporation and Chinese government and private-sector partners underscores the complex public-private collaboration between the PRC and the United States. Media collaborations draw US politicians and industry leaders together in a way that evokes the close relationships among Chinese politicians and executives in other sectors.[41]

In August 2012, Katzenberg's DreamWorks Animation announced on its website that it was planning to open a new co-venture, Oriental DreamWorks, in the Xuhui District of Shanghai. The intersection of the highest levels of Chinese and US leadership and the participation of key Hollywood players offer a view of how important the media industries are to the Sino-US relationship.

As the Chinese media market grew, the relationship between the US and Chinese media policy also evolved. Negotiations structure Sino-US media industry collaboration while presenting opportunities to assert authority as the relative sizes of the Chinese and US media markets change. With the proliferation of major international productions and brandscapes, the significance of Sino-US relations in both countries' media and cultural products increases. Leaders on both sides of the Pacific actively bridge policy gaps to expand China's market influence and Hollywood's market share.

Xi Jinping's first visit to the United States as the PRC's president had links to the media industries. The June 2013 Sunnyland Summit was the first face-to-face meeting between US president Barack Obama and after Xi became president in March 2013.[42] The summit was strategically located at the Annenberg Foundation Trust residence at Sunnylands in Southern California, owned by the same foundation that funds the School of Communication at both the University of Southern California and the

University of Pennsylvania. Although the event's focus was not Sino-US media policy, the entire region surrounding the summit was steeped in the industry. The Southern California backdrop to this historic meeting between the two leaders foreshadowed the strong media and communication emphasis of future meetings between Obama and Xi.

In September 2015, Chinese president Xi Jinping visited Washington, DC; Seattle; and New York City for meetings with US industry leaders. This visit, like Xi's earlier visits to the United States, coincided with a rash of Sino-US deal making and networking with US media industry leaders. Warner Bros. and the Chinese media investment firm China Media Capital announced the opening of Flagship Entertainment, a new co-venture based in Hong Kong and designed, like Oriental DreamWorks, to produce English- and Chinese-language content.[43] The announcement of the agreement between China Media Capital and Warner Bros., in conjunction with Xi Jinping's visit, continued the trend established in 2012, when Xi's visit to the United States coincided with negotiations about Oriental DreamWorks. State-level diplomacy is thus closely tied to the business of the global entertainment brands of China and Hollywood.

The guest list for the state dinner hosted by President Barack Obama during the visit further reinforced the media and technology emphasis of President Xi Jinping's trip. Of roughly two hundred people from both countries, eighteen were representatives of entertainment companies or their guests.[44] Another eighteen US guests were media personalities or their guests. Twelve additional attendees were leaders in the technology industries.[45] Judy Chu, one of the four members of the United States House of Representatives at the event, represents Los Angeles, and the following week opened the 2015 US China Film and Television Industry Expo.[46] Also present was Christopher Dodd, former US senator and the chairman and CEO of the Motion Picture Association of America.[47] A total of fifty-two American guests at the 2015 state dinner for Xi Jinping were involved in the media and technology industries, dwarfing representation from any other industrial sector and roughly equivalent to the number of US government officials. Significantly, Walt Disney Company CEO Robert Iger, DreamWorks CEO Jeffrey Katzenberg, and their guests were reportedly four of the eighteen people at the dinner's head table.[48] The outsized presence of figures from the media and technology industries underscores the significance of these industries in the relationship between the two countries. Yet the presence of US CEOs of media and technology companies that still cannot legally operate all their business units in China, such as Netflix and Facebook, points to the precariousness of Hollywood's investments in China.

As Xi Jinping's US meetings suggest, one of the most remarkable aspects of Sino-US media joint ventures in the twenty-first century is that they have been spearheaded by industry leaders and policymakers in both countries. This dynamic is made all the more provocative by the mythology surrounding both Hollywood producers and Chinese political leaders.[49] The US government does not have direct authority over Hollywood, though Peter Decherney, among others, asserts that this has not always been the case; meanwhile, the Chinese government does have substantial authority over its media industries. Indeed, the incongruity in the level of influence that government officials in China and the United States have over the media industries leads to a particularly complex bilateral media policymaking environment.

MEDIA POLICY ON SCREEN

Chinese and US trade policy have infiltrated the narratives and production practices of Sino-US film collaborations. The following sections use two of the first big-budget Sino-US blockbuster collaborations to examine how stakeholders broker the changing relationship between Chinese and US media industries in the products that emerge from these policies. Released in May 2013, *Iron Man 3* was the third in a series of comic book adaptations about American military contractor Tony Stark, whose alter ego is the title character Iron Man. In the film, a terrorist attacks Stark's home, his best friend, and his cache of wearable robotics. At the time of its worldwide release in 2013, the movie became the fifth-highest-grossing film ever, with a total global revenue of USD 1.215 billion, including more than USD 121 million in the PRC, according to the trade website Box Office Mojo. The success of *Iron Man 3* in the Chinese market signaled a turning point in the intersection of Chinese media policy, US media investment, and Sino-US media culture.

Iron Man 3 debuted in the PRC before its release in the United States, and it broke opening-day records there.[50] Producers released the film in China before the United States in an attempt to avoid piracy in the PRC.[51] The practice mirrored troubleshooting tactics for intellectual property protection exercised by other US industries operating in the market. By releasing a blockbuster of *Iron Man 3*'s scale in the Chinese market first, the film demonstrated the influence of the Chinese market on the global media industries.

Iron Man 3 started its life as an official Sino-US co-production between the Walt Disney Company, Marvel Studios, and American-run, Chinese-licensed DMG Entertainment, according to the Marvel Studios website on May 29, 2012. The film production was the outcome of policy processes—neither a film co-production nor exclusively an imported film, *Iron Man 3* is an example of what I term a "faux-production" in this text. All films that attempt to get co-production approval in the PRC bear the bureaucratic imprint of Chinese regulators from the beginning of the production process. Faux-productions, by contrast, occur when either the producer or the Chinese government declines to complete the co-production process after having received co-production approval for at least part of the film's production process. In other words, faux-productions are a product of policy negotiations between stakeholders over co-production policy. The faux-production process can shift the content of a production without providing a guarantee of distribution in the Chinese market. In an interview about the 2012 Sino-US faux-production *Looper,* director Rian Johnson stated that he decided to shoot his film in Shanghai rather than in Paris to take advantage of Chinese film co-production policy.[52] The film, despite beginning as a co-production, was released in the Chinese market as an import, rather than as a co-production. Faux-productions—essentially partial co-productions—reflect how Chinese media policy and Hollywood interests draw attention to the limitations of US federal government lobbying on behalf of Hollywood in the Chinese market. *Iron Man 3* was ultimately subject to multiple stages of Chinese government review, both as a co-production and as an imported film.

The complexity of the Chinese film co-production process also belies the unpredictability of Sino-US media collaborations. Indeed, after Laurie Burkitt of the *Wall Street Journal* proclaimed on March 8, 2013, that *Iron Man 3* "blasts away the China co-production myth," the film's producers revealed that two different versions would be released—one in the United States and one in the PRC. The Chinese version was treated as one of the films in the PRC's thirty-four-film import quota rather than as a co-production. The time, effort, and access provided to the state-run China Film Co-production Corporation (CFCC) (Zhongguo Dianying Hezuo Zhipian Gongsi), China's official co-production company, and to the SAPPRFT were also unprecedented for a major Hollywood film that ultimately became part of the PRC's foreign import quota. During production, Chinese censors regularly visited the *Iron Man 3* set and gave notes on the script.[53] This practice of censorship during production is common with film co-productions, which are treated like domestic Chinese films in the PRC market, but *Iron Man 3* was officially an imported foreign film.[54] The SAPPRFT thus both influenced the content of this major Hollywood release and required that the film be subject to the comparative unpredictability of film import rules. As a result, the co-production process and related co-production policy frameworks influenced a product that extended beyond the policy's official reach.

Although for *Iron Man 3*, Marvel Studios did not meet the preconditions for a film co-production release, it accommodated the Chinese market by creating a special version of the movie specifically for PRC distribution. Chinese audiences reacted negatively to the scenes that were added specifically for the film's Chinese version, suggesting that influence over the production process does not immediately translate to gains in cultural soft power.[55] In Chinese online forums, domestic viewers criticized the differences between the international and Chinese versions of the film. One of the most excoriated moments was an advertisement inserted into the Chinese version for an energy drink from milk manufacturer Yili, a drink that ostensibly helped bring Iron Man back to life. Other largely lambasted sequences included a scene of small talk between Chinese doctors in charge of conducting a risky surgery (aided by acupuncture, of course) on the body of Iron Man's human alter ego, Tony Stark. Despite audience disapproval, the ceding of control in a Hollywood blockbuster to Chinese regulators and distributors marked a moment of transformation in Hollywood's relationship with China.

But it was not only the images on screen that demonstrate China's role. Publicity stills from production in Beijing circulated in the global trade press during the film's production.[56] The final version of the film contained no exterior shots of Beijing, but the production stills communicated China's importance as a shooting location by sharing Chinese location images with industry observers, even if not directly with audiences. Leaked production stills show Chinese actor Wang Xueqi and the character of Iron Man in front of Beijing's iconic Yongding Gate, though this image did not make the final cut. American reporting on the filming of blockbusters in the PRC offers industry publicity for China's media production brand even for scenes that audiences never actually see.

Through *Iron Man 3* the SAPPRFT flexed its regulatory muscles in the context of the release of a major global blockbuster. In exchange for being vetted by Chinese censors at nearly every stage of production and featuring special (albeit poorly received) Chinese scenes, the filmmakers received a greater measure of certainty that they could advance their brand within the unpredictable Chinese market. This ultimately resulted in huge box-office revenue in the PRC. The choice to release the film in China first paid off financially; the PRC, where it had box-office records of USD 63.5 million in its first five days, was the film's largest international market.[57]

Beyond *Iron Man 3*'s production process, an important message about the change in the balance of global power is embedded within the film's narrative. The film is the tale of Tony Stark, a defense company CEO trained at the Massachusetts Institute of Technology, who transforms himself into a superhero using his engineering acumen, ultimately saving the world from a corrupt US politician. The film follows Stark (aka Iron Man) as he battles Aldrich Killian, a villainous technology entrepreneur secretly backed by the US vice president, who seeks to mainstream eugenically altered fighters. In the film's Chinese version, Stark's international collaborators are Chinese physician-scientists in Beijing, albeit in roles reduced from those in the film's original script.[58] The film valorizes collaborative investment in advanced technology while simultaneously casting doubt on US government motives. In the film's American version, the role of the Chinese scientists was excised, hiding traces of international collaboration, lest this story element create any cognitive dissonance for American viewers.

Even throwaway gags in *Iron Man 3* illustrate the numerous ways in which media is essential to shaping state-level policy. For example, after experiencing an embarrassing debacle in *Iron Man 2* (2010), US government bureaucrats in *Iron Man 3* rebrand Tony Starks's Iron Man clone for the US government from "War Machine" to "Iron Patriot" to improve press coverage. In the movie, the repeated diegetic reports about the rebranding of the machine emphasize the importance of the media industries in a movie that is promoting American interests abroad. The front for the US vice president's treachery is an actor whose character is called the "Mandarin" and whose fearsomeness is bolstered by the high production value of the propaganda videos he makes in his own studio. Notably, the ethnicity of the villainous Mandarin was Chinese in the Iron Man comic book series, but not in the film, in recognition of the importance of the Chinese market. Much like in *Iron Man 3*, in the Marvel film adaptation of *Doctor Strange* (dir. Scott Derrickson 2016), a character that was originally Tibetan in the *Doctor Strange* comic book series is played by Tilda Swinton, a Caucasian actor.[59] The choice to change the ethnicity of a member of a minority group with a contested relationship to the PRC government at a minimum raises questions, despite denials by the studio, Marvel, that the move had creative motivations.[60] The casting choices suggest a strategic whitewashing of Hollywood films, one that avoids casting Chinese people as unlikable villains or drawing attention to hot-button political issues like Tibet.

Iron Man 3's narrative also contextualizes the major historical changes in US, Chinese, and global trade policy that facilitated the production of this Sino-US blockbuster. The movie's plot begins in the first moments of the year 2000, the same year the US Congress enacted legislation (H.R. 4444) granting the PRC permanent natural trade status upon its entrance into the WTO. The PRC's new trade status and WTO entry marked a significant moment in the country's meteoric rise to global economic prominence. After the PRC's WTO accession, film policy was one of the first cultural policies that focused on developing joint financing and technology transfer. It is therefore no coincidence that dialogue in this megablockbuster, penned by Western screenwriters Shane Black and Drew Pearce, referred to the last moments of the twentieth century as "the good old days," a time when Hollywood reigned.[61]

Apropos of the *Iron Man 3* narrative, the PRC central government's policy for growth supports the intersection of the media and technology industries. The country's twelfth five-year plan supported "the innovation of culture, science and technology."[62] The rise of the media industry in parallel with increased technological innovation suggests how the PRC's cultural policy seeps into essential parts of the country's trade relations with the United States. The question is not just about the co-creation of culture but also about the resulting joining of broad industries, from technology to media to science. *Iron Man 3* drew these issues together in its narrative and provided a global pop culture representation of how technology, entertainment, science, and industry work together.

Iron Man 3, despite being successful financially, was neither a full soft power nor a policy win for China. The film tested, but then ultimately circumvented, the co-production process. The "Chinese elements" added to the film were visibly forced into the narrative. Marvel Studios claimed a share of the Chinese box office that might otherwise have gone to local Chinese films. At the same time, the PRC's media and trade policy demonstrated the beginnings of Chinese soft power in Hollywood. The film was a big-budget parable, and Chinese distributors profited from its success. The give-and-take involved in faux-productions such as *Iron Man 3* draws attention to the ways in which policy drives Chinese and US film industries to become more entwined, demanding compromises from both.

The relationship between policy and economic demands in the production of Chinese and American visual culture became even more complex in 2014, when the release of *Transformers 4* actually anticipated mass political action in Hong Kong. July 1 is a public holiday in Hong Kong, commemorating the territory's 1997 return to mainland China, a day historically marked by protests in Hong Kong. Paramount Studios and the SAPPRFT jointly decided at a 2013 meeting in Beijing on a release date for the *Transformers 4* movie of Friday, June 27, 2014, the weekend immediately preceding the July 1 holiday.[63] *Transformers 4* includes prominent scenes of a fictional PRC minister of defense sending ships into Hong Kong's harbor. The images appeared on screens around Hong Kong the weekend before the mass protests there against PRC government authority, which involved more than 500,000 protesters (of Hong Kong's seven million residents) and marked the beginning of a series of democracy protests in Hong Kong eventually referred to as the Umbrella Movement.[64] The presence of the Chinese military in Hong Kong's Victoria Harbour in the film visually extends its power in a way that would be politically unfeasible in real-world Hong Kong. The film also included images of a dominant police presence in Hong Kong, which foreshadowed images of the police presence on the streets on July 1. As protests raged in Hong Kong, *Transformers 4* bested previous Chinese box-office receipts, according to the trade website Box Office Mojo in July 2014.

Transformers 4 offers a startling example of the commingling of the Hollywood dream factory and the Chinese Dream. First, the film demonstrates the movement toward horizontally integrated media conglomerates described by communications scholar Robert McChesney and media analyst Edward S. Herman (2004). It promotes a major US commercial brand property—*Transformers*—that carries both box-office potential and a proven record of success as a branded property in television, merchandise, and video games, as well as high potential for future theme park investment. The film created ancillary media-branding opportunities not only for horizontally integrated Hollywood media conglomerates, but also for Chinese media companies. In preparation for shooting the film, New China TV—the digital video arm of the Chinese state news agency Xinhua— reported on August 27, 2013, that a reality show on Chinese TV would recruit new Chinese actors to take part in *Transformers 4*. A promotional clip shows *Transformers 4* director Michael Bay introducing the reality show to Chinese audiences and depicts producer Lorenzo di Bonaventura and Paramount Pictures president of worldwide distribution and marketing Megan Colligan as judges.

The reality show clip reveals several ways in which the trade in blockbusters advances Chinese domestic cultural policy. First, the new show generated domestic television content. Second, the "talent search" aspect of the show furthered the goal of domestic media talent development through Hollywood film investment. Finally, the clip (and related production news surrounding *Transformers 4*) spotlights the rise of China's domestic media industry. Far from representing one-way cultural imperialism, Sino-US blockbusters such as *Transformers 4* involve a constant back-and-forth of branding efforts between Chinese and Hollywood partners that reflect the demands of both US trade and investment and Chinese soft power.

Transformers 4 asserts China's worldwide importance as a film location, a fact that was magnified by the film's global box-office success. A US-based special effects trade publication released production stills of Michael Bay shooting on the Great Wall of China even though that footage was never incorporated into the film.[65] Additional supplementary production footage, or B-roll, featuring the shooting process, includes footage taken at the Great Wall that was released on the US website YouTube on June 21, 2014, with the title *TRANSFORMERS 4 (Making of Video)*. Although this footage of China's greatest historical architectural achievement did not make the film's final cut, the fact that the *Transformers 4* crew received permission to shoot at such a significant landmark demonstrates the ways in which the Sino-US media relationship is growing, and fuels a perception on the part of Chinese regulators that Hollywood films offer China the opportunity to further project its cultural power. As in the case of *Iron Man 3,* the stills of shooting in China, despite appearing primarily in trade materials rather than in multiplexes, signal to professionals the type of productions that have been successfully made in the PRC.

The changing relationship between China and Hollywood has important policy implications that influence both countries' media industries. Global popular culture is increasingly becoming an output of the overlapping industrial and policy interests in both countries. However fanciful they may seem, superhero blockbusters about national defense reveal how media industry leaders and policymakers broker the PRC's and the United States' changing positions in the global order.

Media industry collaboration between the PRC and the United States is a key factor in trade relations between the two countries. The financial success of blockbuster collaborations and related products demonstrates that media brand co-ventures influence both trade and global entertainment. For example, *Transformers 4* box-office grosses, excluding ancillary income, reached nearly the USD 1 billion mark according to trade website Box Office Mojo. Collaboration does not come naturally, but trade policy partially accommodates collaboration in two key ways. The first approach to managing collaboration is pressure through such international organizations as the WTO. By enforcing China's WTO accession agreement and subsequent related decisions, the WTO resists limits on access to the PRC media market. Second, as China's media industry continues to develop, in part through collaborative projects and foreign direct investment stimulated by domestic policies, Chinese products and firms become more competitive in the market. The role of policy and related issues of soft power and cultural sovereignty in the Sino-US relationship is complex. Fortunately, blockbusters are revealing how Sino-US relations are changing, if the audiences of the world know how to look.

2 Hollywood's China

MICKEY MOUSE, *KUNG FU PANDA*, AND THE
RISE OF SINO-US BRANDSCAPES

Imagine an English-language school with classrooms arranged like stages and a Mickey Mouse statue at its entrance. Envision a 54,000-square-foot Disney retail space, the largest in the world, closing its doors after just one hour because of fears of overcrowding.[1] Now think of families walking together into a Disney-branded castle in Shanghai. Hollywood's expansion into China extends beyond media content into the creation of new landscapes for consumption and engagement with brands. In their work on the experience economy, marketing experts B. Joseph Pine II and James H. Gilmore argue that *"goods and services are no longer enough* to foster economic growth, create new jobs and ensure economic security" (emphasis in original).[2] They assert that, instead, the most important goal is to "stage experiences."[3] Brands are essential to the experience economy.[4] Generating experiences, in turn, is an increasingly important part of the marketing-driven blockbuster film industry. Already-popular intellectual property (IP) drives consumption at theme parks more effectively than new content.[5] This chapter uses the Walt Disney Company's expansion into the Shanghai region through branded physical landscapes to examine the territorial dimension of how Hollywood's and China's brands collaborate and compete within the Chinese market.

The Walt Disney Company both pioneered the experience economy and led the investment of US corporate assets abroad.[6] By building "brand-scapes" related to film production and distribution activities in China, or what architectural theorist Anna Klingmann calls "the demarcation of a territory by a given brand," such as theme parks and entertainment centers, Disney is shaping China-Hollywood economies of experience to stir warm childhood-related feelings and dreams in the world's largest market.[7] Appropriately, Pine and Gilmore refer to the experience economy as the "Dream Economy," a term of art that helps us further understand the symbiosis of the Hollywood dream factory and the Chinese Dream.[8] In bringing China and Hollywood together via media brands that specialize in combining content with experiences, Sino-US brandscapes in China further entwine the fates of China and Hollywood in the global media industries.

WHAT IS A BRANDSCAPE?

To fully understand the meaning of "brandscape," one must first define what a brand is. Marketing researchers David Aaker and Alexander Biel assert that a brand consists of three essential components: "a) the image of the provider of the product/service, or corporate image; b) the image of the user; and c) the image of the product/service itself."[9] The development of brands in China relies on all three of these components. As China's media industries have transitioned from state-owned enterprises to privatized local firms to global players, media brands in China have changed in parallel. Hollywood's media investments, by contrast, have long been projections of a brand. While there has been much discussion in the PRC about the importance of improving China's film-production capabilities in order to compete with Hollywood, the shared long-term capital investment between public-sector and newly privatizing Chinese companies in conjunction with long-private Hollywood firms is arguably an even greater difference. New Sino-US media brandscapes are capital-driven, real estate–intensive projects that accelerate the growth of marketing infrastructure in China.

Immersive branded real estate investment raises the stakes of technology transfer between China and Hollywood beyond those established in short-term film production projects. Klingmann defines brandscapes as "the physical manifestations of synthetically conceived identities transposed onto synthetically conceived places, demarcating culturally independent sites where corporate value systems materialize into physical territories."[10] Because Klingmann's study primarily focused on a Western context, with substantially lower state land ownership and real estate investment than in China, this definition applies to both corporate and state value systems. Brandscapes also emphasize control via ideology, also called "brand evangelism" by some.[11] The spaces must operate with carefully sealed façades designed to maintain illusions for consumers.[12] Infrastructure investment in brandscapes enhances China's media brands, drives awareness of American brands in China, and facilitates China-Hollywood collaboration intended to raise the profile of Hollywood and China, both individually and together.

Focusing on brandscapes extends research on media revenue streams as the media industries become ever more reliant on revenue generated from experiences.[13] The change from Hollywood studio to corporate media conglomerate has altered how horizontally integrated media manufacturing systems operate.[14] Media brandscapes, such as theme parks, studios, and merchandise stores, blend the physical space of production and consumption while extending the revenue streams for preexisting intellectual property.

Media studies researchers have examined media production in detail, but largely separate from corporate branding efforts like theme parks. Michael Curtin analyzes the urban agglomeration of media capital at the city and regional levels.[15] Other studies have explored the role of studios separate from other corporate infrastructure, but not the role international studio space plays in branding the media conglomerate.[16] Allen J. Scott and Naomi E. Pope look at the concentration of individual companies that constitute Hollywood but do so by considering the space occupied by real estate that is notable for its anonymity rather than its brandedness.[17] Daragh O'Reilly and Finola Kerrigan discuss film franchises in terms of brandscapes but focus on marketing and branding as abstract practices rather than on the physical spaces of brand production.[18] Theme park researchers typically analyze brandscapes apart from production.[19] But in light of the industrial competition between the United States and the PRC, the role of production infrastructure must be considered in conjunction with the brandscape in order to fully understand the complexity of Hollywood's engagement in China.

Anthropologist and geographer David Harvey argues that global sites of capital surplus, such as China after the 2008 global financial crisis, absorb capital as a "spatio-temporal fix."[20] The spatio-temporal fix transfers investment capital to a new geographic landscape but also provides a potential resolution for the overaccumulation of capital in one market (in this case, in the coffers of the Chinese government, media corporations, and consumers). Brandscapes therefore create a space for Chinese financiers to invest their capital, a site to absorb the wealth of Chinese consumers, and a location for Hollywood content providers to expand the presence of their media brands within an important global market. This chapter focuses on Disney brandscapes, but Klingmann's words are also salient when talking about production studios, industry forums, and even film sets. Hollywood's China investments are, most significantly, projections of a brand.

THE MONEY AND THE POWER: HOW HOLLYWOOD AND CHINA BUILD BRANDSCAPES

A good way to understand how China and Hollywood collaborate to maximize each other's brands is by considering the single-largest China-Hollywood real estate co-venture to date: Shanghai Disney Resort. The Walt Disney Company's engagement with China presents a new level of joint branding, one in which the majority of marketing power rests with Disney while much of the financial control rests with the company's Chinese partners. The Shanghai Shendi Group, a state-owned joint venture investment holding company, owns 57 percent of the park, compared with Disney's 43 percent.[21] Shanghai Disney Resort houses the largest Disney park outside the United States and one of Disney's largest-ever capital investments. In other words, a Chinese company controls the site, but a Hollywood media conglomerate owns the brand. This chapter demonstrates how Sino-US joint ventures in media-related real estate investment negotiate between Hollywood and China through the development of shared brandscapes.

Of Sino-US media real estate investments, Disney's are by far the most substantial. The overall initial investment in Shanghai Disney Resort was USD 5.5 billion, making it one of the largest foreign investments in the PRC in any sector when the park opened in June 2016.[22] By examining Disney's capital investment in the PRC after the country's 2001 WTO accession, this chapter explores how Chinese industrial-development policies have facilitated both branded Chinese media investment and new, brand-driven market development for Hollywood studios, often with conflicting objectives.

Hollywood has a clear motive for establishing branded real estate investments in China: expansion. In the PRC, the relative stability of long-term investments is as important as market opportunity.[23] As cultural studies scholar Laikwan Pang notes, Disney's theme park investment in Shanghai emerged from an increased emphasis on protecting intellectual property rights.[24] Thus, a stable environment for major theme park investment portends stable investment in other projects, such as production studios.

Other global media conglomerates are also building physical structures to grow into the world's largest market. With local partners, DreamWorks Animation established Oriental DreamWorks, a production studio collaboration, as well as the Shanghai DreamCenter (Meng Zhongxin), an entertainment center in Shanghai's Xuhui District.[25] These projects anchor the West Bund Media Port (Xian Chuanmei Gang), a Shanghai city government–authorized effort to bring media, art, fashion, innovation, and finance together in a site reminiscent of the cultural milieu of Paris's Left Bank.[26] Director James Cameron's Cameron Pace Group offers production services specializing in 3-D technology services in the Chinese city of Tianjin.[27] China's Wanda Group has planned major capital infrastructure investments in hopes of driving global investment in Chinese media brands. At 200 hectares, the Wanda Group's Qingdao studio would be the largest of its kind in the world. The firm's press release also emphasized that funding provided by both the Wanda Group and the Qingdao municipal government would make the studio competitive for international projects. The Wanda Group further extended its global production ambitions in January 2016 when the firm acquired American studio Legendary Entertainment for USD 3.5 billion.[28] Shared investments in the brandscape advance the growth of Hollywood in China, private Chinese firms, and Chinese central and local government policies to enhance soft power.

China's political landscape provided further incentive to accommodate global media capital. As early as 1998, the Chinese government was focused on creating competitive culture industries.[29] In its twelfth five-year plan (2011–2015), the Chinese government stated a goal of bolstering its culture industries; given that these are pillar industries, doing so would in turn bolster economic activity—not just in sectors such as film production, but also in related sectors such as television production, digital media, tourism, and merchandising.[30] In keeping with China's twelfth five-year plan, the Disney brandscape helps provide long-term grounding for China's place in the global experience economy, as well as additional revenue streams.

Projects such as Shanghai Disney Resort create new infrastructure for economic activity in the experience economy. Infrastructure-based analysis of Sino-US media projects draws on the premise that infrastructure growth is the foundation of industrial growth in developing countries.[31] World Bank economist Rémy Prud'Homme contextualized the value of infrastructure-based development: "Why and how does infrastructure contribute to development? It is a space shrinker, it enlarges markets, and it operates like the lowering of trade barriers. In urban areas, it can be shown that infrastructure contributes to enlarge the effective size of the labor market and of the goods or ideas markets, thus increasing productivity and output."[32]

Disney's urban brandscapes operate precisely in the terms Prud'Homme describes. The Chinese government has implemented major physical infrastructure projects that enhance the economic utility of the investment, such as the municipal metro line that runs to the park to support the expansion of the project.[33] (See figure 4.) In parallel, the Walt Disney Company opened Disney Research China, a laboratory in the PRC that focuses on urban design innovation as well as on maximizing the efficiency of urban infrastructure systems.[34] The strategies it identifies can be applied not only at Shanghai Disney Resort but also at other high-density urban environments throughout China. Investment in Shanghai Disney Resort catalyzed research and transportation improvements that expand China's capacity beyond the media industries.

Figure 4. Futuristic Shanghai Disney metro station steps away from the Shanghai Disney Resort's entrance. (Photo by Aynne Kokas, Shanghai, PRC, June 20, 2016)

Infrastructure development does not serve all equally. The park's rapid development has drawn criticism. Shanghai Disney Resort developed land previously occupied by farmers (*nongmin*). In 2013, some of these farmers refused to leave their homes and, by using signs draped across their residences, challenged Chinese premier Wen Jiabao to protect their land. (See figures 5 and 6.) In the same location, the Shanghai International Tourism and Resorts Zone (Shanghai Guoji Lüyou Dujiaqu) proudly set up its Construction Command Center, asserting a proud vision of new real estate developments. (See figure 7.) The human displacement caused by global brand development calls attention to those who are left behind in the process of media globalization.

Often competing with the messages offered by those affected by media investment in China, corporations create their own narratives about industrial growth. In the examination of dominant discourses of both government and industrial players, industrial paratexts bring to light both the upsides and the downsides of these industrial activities.[35] Corporate disclosures and policy documents are therefore invaluable as meaning-making tools for both industry and government.[36] Publicly disclosed (albeit not always publicized) documents explain the development of Sino-US branded media real estate collaborations from the perspective of corporate stakeholders.

Figure 5. Homes being demolished during construction for the Shanghai Disney Resort. (Photo by Aynne Kokas, Shanghai, PRC, July 2013)

Figure 6. Farmer's home slated for demolition to prepare for the Shanghai Disney Resort, with a sign challenging Premier Wen (Jiabao) to protect farmers' homesteads. (Photo by Aynne Kokas, Shanghai, PRC, July 2013)

Figure 7. Sign marking Shanghai International Tourism and Resorts Zone Construction Command Center adjacent to the Shanghai Disney Resort construction site. (Photo by Aynne Kokas, Shanghai, PRC, July 2013)

Accounting researcher Jane Davison's notion of the "literary turn" in annual reports asserts that the descriptive language in such reports constitutes another useful paratext for the examination of real estate collaborations, as well as other industrial processes.[37] In the case of Disney in China, annual reports describe stakeholders who are in the process of generating new joint brandscapes. Publicly disclosed financial documents tend to be most readily available from US media conglomerates because of the financial reporting requirements imposed on companies that have raised money via US stock markets—though more and more PRC-based media companies are also raising money in global capital markets.[38] In addition to showing how organizations understand collaborative ventures from an operational perspective, publicly released institutional documents brand shared corporate and government accomplishments.

One helpful way to understand Sino-US media investment is by looking at how corporate discourse differs with respect to global and domestic investments, particularly the language that companies use when addressing their boards and shareholders. Corporations often report their annual results by business unit—digital, production, theme parks and resorts, and so on. Corporate communication related to the development of international media infrastructure often differs from business unit–based reporting about the domestic market.

Disney, one of the major Hollywood media investors in China, has one leader for all of its international businesses, indicating a clear separation of international and domestic. The company's website stated the following on October 9, 2016: "As chairman, Walt Disney International, Andy Bird is responsible for Disney's businesses outside of the United States. Reporting to Disney Chairman and CEO Bob Iger, Mr. Bird and his global team develop and implement strategies to increase Disney brand affinity and awareness in key international markets, introduce new customers and guests to Disney's unique storytelling legacy and iconic characters, and invest in and maximize opportunities in emerging markets." Walt Disney International's chairman therefore has a mandate to address broad-based infrastructure development across production and consumer sectors, not just within a specific business unit. Walt Disney International's businesses are vertically and horizontally integrated and linked throughout product life cycles under the leadership of one individual, who then reports on all international businesses to the company's CEO. The consolidation of corporate reporting for international investments across business units demonstrates that the company views its China investments as media investments across an entire brandscape.

Images of Mickey Mouse and Donald Duck appeared across the PRC in the 1980s as part of a landmark deal to internationalize Chinese television.[39] Disney's initial infrastructure investments in China, however, were not related to production. The company's first brick-and-mortar investment in China actually involved a more unexpected income stream: schools, which it began opening in the PRC in 2005. Media and communication scholar Ulrike Rohn outlines how China forbade foreign companies from investing in Chinese television stations through 2004, only loosening up on restriction on production (but not ownership) after that time.[40] Restrictions on the amount of foreign content allowed on Chinese streaming sites have further constrained Hollywood studios' access to distributing content to Chinese markets.[41] But the characteristics that have hindered the company's Chinese market development have paradoxically led children into participating in the company's brand in a different way.

The Chinese government's ambivalence about foreign expansion into China's market does not extend equally across industrial sectors. After the PRC's 2001 accession to the WTO, the central government demonstrated a renewed interest in expanding English-language education but faced a dearth of well-trained instructors and teaching materials.[42] Throughout this book, the term "policy" most often refers to media policy. In the case of Disney English language schools, the relationship between regulators and industry leaders occurs in the context of PRC education policy and how it facilitates the continued expansion of US media brands in China. In order to expand its presence in the Chinese market, Disney invested in English schools in Chinese urban centers, teaching language lessons with assistance from the Disney canon.

By expanding into this market, Disney contributed to the success of the policy to enhance the PRC's English-language instruction to build China's long-term economic might. However, the schools also offered the company an unparalleled opportunity to reach young people after regulators blocked its prior market-entry strategy—television station ownership. Disney English schools become de facto screening spaces, taking the place of theaters and television screens to distributed Disney media products. Disney's extension of corporate branding activities into the educational sector demonstrates how shared development of the China-Hollywood brandscape meets both PRC policy and US corporate expansion priorities, but often in a way that is suboptimal for both groups.

The proliferation of English-language education operates on multiple levels with regard to the Sino-US brandscape. In addition to creating a larger number of English speakers interested in consuming English-language content, the more complex, underlying impact of Chinese education policy is that Disney's English-language schools deputize Chinese youth to promote the brand. On my visit to Disney's English-language school in Shanghai's Xujiahui neighborhood in July 2013, I observed a small clubhouse area in which children and their parents could relax, a "parents' board" with pictures of parents and children, and a kid-sized Mickey Mouse statue outside the building's main doorway. (See figure 8.) The role of children as brand evangelists via their activities in these schools means that they simultaneously mimic fan activity and the behavior of Disney employees; in the schools, children role-play as Disney

Figure 8. Disney English school entrance. (Photo by Aynne Kokas, Shanghai, PRC, July 12, 2013)

characters, acting in much the same way as paid Disney employees do when embodying these characters in the company's theme parks.

Inside the classroom, Disney's English-language schools also imitate other forms of commercial media distribution. The classroom spaces are set up as stages, with heavy velvet curtains framing a movie theater–like screen, on which children can watch Disney content. The hallways are studded with images of different Disney characters. Disney toys are available for young children aged two or three who are in their first English class. Even the bathrooms are covered with Mickey Mouse ears. Every aspect of the Disney experience that could be participatory and branded is treated as such. This brand-driven play notably takes place outside the confines of traditional contexts of media production and distribution, yet Disney's English-language schools function as a central component of the company's brand development in China. Many scholars have written about the need for critical media literacy in the classroom.[43] Disney's

English-language schools turn that idea on its head, and instead offer brand-driven, media-based education that teaches children to be media consumers. The question of what happens when students are consumers first is rife with complexity but is beyond the scope of this book. For the purposes of this chapter, it is most important to think about how, in Disney's eagerness to invest in the PRC, it built Hollywood's brandscape in China through the country's private English-language education system.

Children and parents are not the only ones who act as brand ambassadors in Disney's English-language schools, however. The Walt Disney Corporation hires both foreign and local teachers to foster the cultural-exchange process; the company's hiring website boasts, "At Disney English, you'll be able to experience a new culture through the eyes of its children."[44] The branding process therefore relies on multiple stages of cultural interaction between the corporation, its foreign guest workers in the PRC, and Chinese families. The Walt Disney Corporation promises on its hiring site to act as a broker of an intimate cultural experience, claiming in English, "No one speaks the language of children better than Disney."[45] On its Chinese-language website, Disney English promotes the ways in which using Disney characters and stories makes studying English easier for students. The relationship between students, teachers, and the corporation represents a new form of cultural bond grounded in the commercial interests of Disney shareholders, extending the marketing utility of the company's educational investments. (See figures 9 and 10.) These schools reveal the ambivalence with which the PRC balances the competing goals of accessing foreign expertise and controlling the distribution of foreign content to its young people.

Disney is not alone in its interest in marshaling language-education resources to build a brand. The Chinese government has actively advocated for Chinese-language education outside China. Around the world, the PRC has ignited a not-small amount of controversy through its investment in Confucius Institutes, which provide Chinese-language and cultural education to foreign students at the primary, secondary, and tertiary levels.[46] The Confucius Institute curricula incorporate not only materials generated by instructors but also PRC government policy, and they attempt to promote awareness of China's changing place in the world.[47] Media and communications scholars Terry Flew and Falk Hartig argue that the network effect of Confucius Institutes, combined with these schools' educational mission

Figure 9. Disney English–branded luggage for cosmopolitan
students. (Photo by Aynne Kokas, Shanghai, PRC, July 12, 2013)

and ability to engage local stakeholders, enhance the effort's cultural soft
power.[48] Disney English operates a network of schools in six cities across
China, and Chinese regulators are clearly aware of the branding advantage
this approach offers, because the Chinese government employs a similar
model.[49] The English-language learning provided by the Walt Disney
Corporation is similar to the brand evangelism through language teaching

Figure 10. Navy blue Shanghai Disneyland "dream passport"
(*mengxiang huzhao*) documents visits to different park attractions.
(Photo by Aynne Kokas, Shanghai, PRC, June 20, 2016)

engaged in by the Confucius Institutes. Just as the Confucius Institutes
disperse information about Chinese culture through the language-
teaching process, Disney English drives brand awareness for Shanghai
Disney Resort, a joint venture targeted at the same youth demographic as
the Disney English language schools.

The leveraging of Disney's English-language school network to build
brand awareness for Shanghai Disney Resort highlights one of the myriad
ways in which Hollywood is staking a physical claim in the PRC. The

Disney schools extend corporate activity during a period of relative restriction, whereas the company's theme parks involve more traditional Disney fandom. Rather than being exclusively driven by content, children consume images and language while participating in educational activities. Students learn Mickey Mouse's native language while learning about Mickey. What more formative experience could a brand share in the life of a child than language acquisition?

Although Disney's English-language schools pale in comparison to other global Disney-branded experiences (e.g., the entire Disney-branded city of Celebration, Florida), the rise in popularity of these schools and related brandscapes suggests a new, complex order at the vanguard of the relationship between consumers, policymakers, and media corporations. The Walt Disney Company has enticed the city's youth with images of the Magic Kingdom, products bearing the images of Mickey and Minnie Mouse, and even English-language classes, and these young people are ready to be amused.

Disney received official state approval for its Shanghai Disney Resort Project Application Report in November 2009, which allowed the company to move forward with the park.[50] Before this point, Disney's investments in the PRC were low-infrastructure endeavors focused on partnership with local clients. Examples include local video game production branded by Disney and local film productions (e.g., 2007's *The Secret of the Magic Gourd* and a co-production of 2010's *Disney High School Musical: China*). Until that first government agreement was reached on Shanghai Disney Resort, Disney's only other substantial Chinese brandscape was its English-language schools. After Disney received official central government approval for Shanghai Disney Resort, other infrastructure investments became much more feasible, as deeper government relationships subsequently developed.[51] From that point on, the company began to build its physical infrastructure in the PRC.

SHANGHAI DISNEY RESORT

Shanghai Disney Resort exports an iconic Hollywood brand image, with the new park following in the tradition of the company's earlier parks in

Paris, Tokyo, and Hong Kong. The presence of a new Disneyland can evoke multiple critiques, including those of cultural imperialism, Western neoliberal expansion, and rampant consumerism.[52] Yet to understand Shanghai Disney Resort, we can look to earlier discussions of the complex role Shanghai plays as a site of negotiation between China and external global cultural influences. Chinese cultural critic Zhang Xudong argues that Shanghai is "neither a reified, reduced and twisted version of the modern or of the Chinese nor a muddy, undifferentiated mix of the two. Rather, the existence of Shanghai urban culture lies in a deterritorialization and reterritorialization."[53] Shanghai Disney Resort fits within the larger context of the city's urban culture, which currently and historically has balanced both foreign and domestic influences.

The increasing number of spaces in China branded with the names of Hollywood media conglomerates presents a complex picture. As communications scholar Wendy Su has argued, Hollywood's buildup in China is part of the PRC's strategy to increase the variety of films and media infrastructure available in its market.[54] In a lecture at UCLA on April 14, 2010, Ben Schwegler, chief scientist with Walt Disney Imagineering, stressed that developing a theme park—which, in the case of Disney's resort, took place in cooperation with Shanghai's municipal government—was a cultural process as well as an economic one, and that Disney had to understand the tools necessary for other forms of collaboration beyond theme park development.[55]

Chinese newspapers and Disney officials alike have attempted to distance themselves from the notion that Shanghai Disney Resort would be an extension of Western commercial culture in China. Walt Disney Company chairman Robert Iger was quoted as saying that the venture would be "authentically Disney and distinctively Chinese."[56] Although Iger's words may indicate a shift in strategy, they also reveal an anxiety about how to blend an iconic brand with the Chinese government's demands for increased soft power. After all, the park is called Shanghai Disney Resort, with the brand emblazoned throughout the resort property, and an iconic Disney castle, called the Enchanted Storybook Castle, towering over the park's skyline. Spaces such as Shanghai Disney Resort become beacons of a moment in which the PRC and the United States are negotiating the terms of a new global media order.

Disney's cultural negotiations in theme parks in Asia began before its investments in Shanghai. On the topic of Tokyo Disneyland, organizational theorist John Van Maanen notes differing consumption patterns by attendees at the park.[57] In the case of Hong Kong Disneyland, despite a relatively unprofitable beginning, the park began to see an increase in popularity after better incorporating local tastes, including changing menus to offer Chinese banquet food, integrating *feng shui* design principles, and improving locations for guest amateur photographers.[58] These "soft" cultural collaborations, which occur at the level of the lived experience of the park or of the corporation's marketing strategies, are also visible in the plans for Shanghai Disney Resort. For example, the Shanghai resort's "Garden of the Twelve Friends" features Disney and Pixar characters representing each of the twelve figures in the Chinese zodiac. The corporate-run *Disney Parks Blog* reported on February 19, 2015, that the feature "blends Disney storytelling with traditional Chinese culture, while honoring the role the Chinese zodiac plays in local daily life and offering some terrific photo opportunities." Disney's public relations language self-consciously references the Chinese elements of the company's Shanghai resort and underscores the complex power dynamic that exists between the media conglomerate and its Chinese partners in both the public and the private sector.

When speaking at the University of Southern California as part of the UCLA International Institute's Media and Culture in Contemporary China conference on October 22, 2011, Thomas E. McLain, one of the US leaders of the multiyear Tokyo Disneyland negotiations, discussed the contractual difficulties inherent in the globalization of the theme park industry. Shanghai Disney Resort is a similarly lengthy project. The park's evolution helped to render some of the challenges involved visible; for example, "Main Street, USA" was replaced with "Mickey Avenue," as the *Disney Parks Blog* reported on July 16, 2015. The park thereby recasts a US-themed street in the formerly partly American-occupied Shanghai with additional Disney corporate branding.

When grounded in history, PRC-based and Hollywood-branded projects such as Shanghai Disney Resort and Oriental DreamWorks occupy a difficult political position. To talk about massive capital investment on Chinese soil by American media companies without addressing the historical relationship between Shanghai and Hollywood ignores the historical realities evoked by the Shanghai international settlements, the extraterritorial foreign settlements located in Shanghai from the end of the First Opium War in 1842 until 1943.[59] Hollywood films were a prominent US cultural export to Shanghai even during the Japanese occupation.[60] Chinese reluctance about the collaborative development of brandscapes could reasonably also stem from past American incursions onto Chinese soil. Granted, the balance of power is different now: the Chinese government can force foreign investors to exit the market. China and Hollywood compete to share their narrative with the world, but, in the process, jointly build new projects driven by a thirst for soft power growth and market expansion. Nowhere is this symbiosis more visible than in a new branded fortification located in Shanghai.

The challenge of creating a Hollywood-branded yet uniquely Chinese Disney park emerges most clearly in the park's most prominent feature: the Enchanted Storybook Castle. The Walt Disney Company models its castles on European edifices built in the Middle Ages.[61] Despite its European architectural antecedents, the image of the castle is emblematic of the Disney brand. Cultural studies scholar Ilan Mitchell-Smith describes the Disney castles as "contemporary America writ medieval by the fantasy of Disneyland."[62] Walt Disney World in Orlando and Tokyo Disney Resort both feature Cinderella's Castle. Sleeping Beauty's Castle is the centerpiece of Anaheim's Disneyland, Disneyland Paris, and Hong Kong Disneyland. To minimize the significance of the Shanghai Disney Resort castle's cultural origins, the edifice's name—the Enchanted Storybook Castle—evades classification in any specific national or regional category.

For many Americans, the image of the Disney castle logo evokes an almost inescapable childhood memory of advertisements singing the siren song of Walt Disney World in Florida or Disneyland in California. The Shanghai Disney Resort website billed the Shanghai Disneyland Park as part of a "Magic Kingdom-style Disney theme park featuring classic Disney characters and stories blended with brand new attractions and experiences specifically designed for the people of China."[63] The resort's publicity information explains that the park's infrastructure is a physical manifestation of the blending of US corporate media culture with Chinese domestic values. The complexity of explaining how classic Disney characters can meld with fresh, China-specific experiences comes at the expense of snappy marketing language.

To explain the insertion of a large Western architectural centerpiece in Shanghai Disneyland Park, Disney marketing materials describe the Enchanted Storybook Castle as "the largest and most immersive castle at any Disney park around the world and . . . the first of our castles not dedicated to a specific princess because it represents all of them," which both asserts China's relative importance in the Disney corporate hierarchy and obfuscates the cultural lineage of the other castles around the world.[64] The website tempers the significance of a Western architectural feature in the Shanghai park of a California-based, multinational brand by asserting that the Chinese castle is superior in size and scope to all other Disney castles outside China. In addition to invoking the castle's global superiority, the language describing the Enchanted Storybook Castle at Shanghai Disneyland as the "largest and most immersive castle" echoes the marketing language used to promote Shanghai's Pudong District, the home of not only Shanghai Disney Resort but also one of the world's most dramatic urban skyscapes.[65] (See figure 11.)

The financial ownership structure of Shanghai Disney Resort further underscores the complex politics at work with regard to the ownership of the brandscape. Although Disney's Enchanted Storybook Castle lords fantastically over the park, Chinese partners own more than half of the site. The Enchanted Storybook Castle exemplifies a tentative partnership between overlapping interests with potentially conflicting long-term goals. The paradox of a dominant Hollywood-designed brandscape sitting on land whose majority stakeholder is Chinese manifests the complex relationship between the Hollywood dream factory and the Chinese Dream.

Disney located earlier theme parks in international media capitals that were already hubs of major national and regional film production, including Paris, Japan, and Hong Kong. With the rise of Shanghai Disneyland Park, Shanghai takes its place alongside these other locations as a place of strategic priority for Disney's brand development. Theme parks offer an important means of building and capitalizing on audiences. However, to increase the number of Disney films available in China, production facilities are also significant because of foreign film import quotas in the PRC.

Figure 11. Image from Shanghai Disneyland grand opening souvenir bag depicting the Enchanted Storybook Castle towering over architectural landmarks on the city's skyline. (Photo by Aynne Kokas, Shanghai, PRC, June 20, 2016)

After the 2008 global financial crisis, Chinese television stations and film studios offered a unique source of funding for enterprising Hollywood producers. Chinese firms—including search engine Baidu, e-commerce giant Alibaba, and commercial property and cinema chain Wanda Group—started their own funds to support international and Chinese productions.[66] Although the result appears to indicate a rapid rise in Chinese film investment, it is important to know that, like Hollywood studios, two of these firms—Alibaba and Baidu—are now publicly traded entities on global capital markets. International investors underwrite the growth of many of these firms.[67] As a result, new Chinese capital investment in Hollywood projects is a collaborative endeavor that requires the markets, talents, and financial resources of both countries.

As this book discusses in other chapters, official film co-productions circumvent China's film quotas to get more high-profile foreign films into Chinese theaters. Like theme parks, co-productions are a form of capital investment for the development of China's media industries. Unlike theme parks, which rely primarily on tickets, concessions, and licensed merchandise to maintain profitability, production studios offer a more tantalizing value proposition within the context of the PRC's incentives for the media industries, specifically for the generation of original content in China. Production studios co-branded with US media conglomerates are an important source of this type of work. But creativity is unpredictable. Although foreign-backed, China-based production studios offer a potential increase in high-quality, locally produced content in China, they also face the ever-present challenge of regulation on boundary-pushing content. Disney's real estate investment in Shanghai Disney offers a test case for the capital risks involved in building more Hollywood production spaces in China.

CONCLUSION

As Disney's various brandscape-building efforts in China reveal, viewing branded real estate investment as separate from production ventures in the analysis of media industries ignores the complexity of Hollywood's involvement in China, and vice versa. The need for additional analysis of the relationship between content and brands is particularly true in developing media economies such as China's, where new marketing, branding, and production capacities are evolving simultaneously.

The concurrent development of media markets, branding, and production capabilities meets key policy priorities for the PRC government. Developing global brandscapes in China can diminish the government's perceived "cultural trade deficit"—its unfavorable balance of cultural exports. At the same time, branded real estate investments such as theme parks provide media conglomerates with an important opportunity to enter into long-term capital investments and capitalize on their intellectual property in the Chinese market. This is possible by establishing financially binding ties with key partners in media investment, production, and distribution. In many ways, media brandscapes in China demonstrate how Hollywood is literally stamping its brand on Chinese land. Yet, as the analysis in this chapter has shown, the bigger picture is much more complex. The rise of Hollywood's brandscapes in China has occurred almost entirely under the auspices of Chinese policy focused on growing China's global competitiveness.

Hollywood's China is also China's Hollywood: huge, long-term capital investments that are beholden to continued relationships with Chinese regulators and that can exist only with the continued favor of local hosts. Although it may be tempting to view Disney's China investments as a revisiting of America's semicolonial occupation of Shanghai, Hollywood's China in the twenty-first century involves a much more tentative relationship. Rather than having extraterritorial rights like those accorded to Shanghai's foreign occupants during the city's occupation, the occupants of Hollywood's China operate under a radically different power paradigm, one in which losing access to media brandscapes in China would deal a dangerous blow to transnational media corporations interested in accessing the world's largest audience.[68] Companies such as Google and Facebook have already discovered the market-access limitations that come from being unwilling to comply with local regulations on doing business in the media and technology industries.[69] Therefore, when we think of Hollywood's growth in China, it is a concept inflected heavily with aspiration and tempered by uncertainty.

3 Soft Power Plays

HOW CHINESE FILM POLICY
INFLUENCES HOLLYWOOD

In a world in which Chinese regulations can treat a movie from the *Iron Man* series as a domestic film, we must move beyond questions of what constitutes "Chinese cinema" or a "Hollywood blockbuster" and instead focus on what being a product of China or Hollywood means. Chinese film policy reveals the tension between culture and industry, the ties between the United States and the PRC, and the interplay between media cultures of production. This chapter examines the structure of Sino-US film production deals to trace how PRC media policy shapes the interactions between Hollywood and China.

Sino-US film deals are easy neither to make nor to execute. Significant anxieties about the collaboration process exist within Chinese studios and policymaking bodies, as well as among American filmmakers, policymakers, and film workers. At industry gatherings such as the Shanghai International Film Festival's SIFFORUM, the topic of film co-production in the Chinese film industry has provoked heated debates among state-owned film conglomerate leaders, private film group CEOs, and international trade association representatives. Sino-US film collaboration is a highly contested practice with respect to the "preservation" of the Chinese film industry in the face of foreign box-office competition, and also with respect to China's influence on Hollywood.

The questions brought forth about collaboration each year at key media forums reveal a significant cultural divide between American filmmakers seeking to shoot films in the Chinese market without experience in China and Chinese bureaucrats in charge of managing Chinese shooting and distribution permissions.[1] While addressing the US-China Film Summit in Los Angeles in 2013, then president of the China Film Co-Production Corporation Zhang Xun emphasized the differences in language and lifestyle that impeded film deal negotiations.[2] Emphasizing her point, Zhang noted that, while she was told her lunchtime presentation slot at the summit was a position of honor, she perceived it as a terrible time to speak because of all of the activity in the room, much to the chagrin of the event's planner, who was seated next to her.[3] But Zhang went on to emphasize the importance of partnering with Hollywood because of its track record of commercial filmmaking, which far exceeds China's.[4] Zhang's speech underscores the ambivalence behind Sino-US production deals. On one hand, they can lead to uncomfortable situations. On the other hand, they present new opportunities for both sides.

Sino-US collaborations are not the only option for Chinese companies seeking to develop their products with assistance from foreign firms. Film scholar Chris Berry discusses de-Westernizing the blockbuster in China, or efforts to develop East Asian production brands without the assistance of Hollywood.[5] But both the strategy to de-Westernize Chinese blockbusters and the strategy to partner with Hollywood media conglomerates reflect the reality of commercial filmmaking in the PRC—that filmmakers are under pressure from regulators to produce global Chinese hits. As noted in the *China Daily* on June 28, 2014, the runaway Chinese box-office success of *Transformers 4* drew the following suggestion from Zhang Hongsen, director of the film bureau under the SAPPRFT: "Have faith in domestic movies! How can we repeat the mistake on 'Lost in Thailand' [a Chinese-made film] in 2012 when we thought it would only reach 200 million yuan and finally found it was a 1.2 billion yuan movie?" The political pressure to advance local films also underscores the reality that, if Chinese movies become more appealing to international audiences, Hollywood productions may become less relevant on a global scale, because some filmmakers and policymakers in the Chinese film market seek to limit collaboration with foreign partners.

Hollywood's success in China is by no means certain. American studios' anxieties about failure in the Chinese market are grounded in the financial missteps that characterized Hollywood investment in China in the first decade of the twenty-first century. For example, Warner Bros. Entertainment entered the DVD market in China in 2004, distributing DVDs at prices that were competitive with pirated DVDs, but the company exited the market in 2008 because of a lack of financial success.[6] At the time of its departure from the DVD market, Warner Bros. Entertainment was also distributing films in the Chinese market for other Hollywood studios, including Universal Studios and Paramount Pictures.[7] The Weinstein Company received, and then lost, approval from the PRC to shoot in Shanghai for its 2010 film *Shanghai;* the company subsequently relocated the shoot to Thailand.[8] SARFT only reinstated approval for the film's PRC release immediately before the film's red-carpet opening at the 2010 SIFF. In *Disney High School Musical: China* (dir. Chen Shi-Zheng 2010), disagreements about marketing strategy between the one American and two Chinese companies involved in the production ultimately led to a much smaller release than planned.[9] When major players such as Warner Bros. Entertainment, the Weinstein Company, and Disney face impediments to production and distribution in the PRC, the broad anxiety about the market becomes infectious.

Yet the impulse for collaboration between Chinese and US companies continues, grounded in Hollywood's pursuit of the Chinese market and China's pursuit of global cultural power. The combination of policy tools that expand Chinese influence in the global media industries and Hollywood's thirst for industrial expansion into China have increased collaboration between Chinese and US media industries after the PRC's 2001 accession to the WTO.[10] In addition to policy tools, technology, the flow of media capital, the growth of global Hollywood markets, movie studios, production labor (see chapters 5 and 6), and media industry events (see chapter 4) all play an important role in structuring collaboration between China and Hollywood.[11] However, the film deals that occur as a result of official policy frameworks reveal the symbiotic development of Chinese and Hollywood media brands.

Table 1 Forms of Sino-US Film Production Collaboration

Chinese Domestic			International		
Domestic production (mainland Chinese talent and resources, or talent based in mainland China; must undergo Chinese domestic film approval process)	Local production (Chinese talent and infrastructure but outside funding; may be sold to/branded by foreign corporation)	Film collaboration options • Faux-production • Technical collaboration • Talent exchange • Foreign-branded local productions	Film co-production (official PRC-approved, jointly made film production)	Assisted production (SAPPRFT approval to shoot but not to distribute the film in China)	Foreign production (film made outside of China)

Film deals between Hollywood and China exist on a continuum of relative degrees of influence. Domestic Chinese film productions are films that exclusively use mainland Chinese talent and resources, or talent based in mainland China. On the other end of the spectrum, film co-production in the Sino-US context refers to projects that adhere to PRC government–approved production agreements for sharing resources. In the gray area between these two approaches are foreign-branded local productions, which are either films made almost entirely with Chinese talent and infrastructure but funded by an outside entity (such as Disney), or Chinese-funded films that involve prominent American talent. Table 1 provides a continuum of Sino-US collaboration styles. The following pages examine these different approaches in detail.

To ground my exploration of Sino-US film collaborations, this chapter first focuses on one of the most publicly visible modes of collaboration: Sino-US film co-production. A topic often written about, film co-production is the subject of numerous policy handbooks and how-to guides for the industry professional.[12] What constitutes "co-production" is often contested. Outside the Chinese context, the meaning of the term varies from market to market and from production to production, and is based largely on state policy and funding sources.

Understanding the general definition of film co-production outside the Sino-US context helps to explain why Sino-US co-production is so distinctive. Film and media scholar Doris Baltruschat asserts that Euro-American film co-productions are projects that are "governed by official treaties or [that] consist of co-venture type arrangements between producers for the duration of film or television production and distribution."[13] The distinction between official, treaty-based co-productions and co-venture-type arrangements does not exist within the official Chinese context. Co-productions in the PRC are policy agreements administered by the CFCC on behalf of the SAPPRFT, which is the PRC's main broadcast regulator.

The PRC requires official approval for any legal production activity in the country. According to sociologist Seio Nakajima, the vast majority of illegally shot films can never be legally distributed in the PRC.[14] As a result, collaborative production under the oversight of Chinese regulators is the most direct route to market entry for foreign producers seeking to make films for the Chinese market.

Chinese regulators treat official film co-productions as "local" films for the purposes of distribution, allowing the projects to circumvent the PRC's film import quota.[15] Film co-production is therefore a market-access tool for foreign filmmakers seeking to distribute their films in the Chinese market. Foreign producers also receive a higher percentage of domestic Chinese distribution revenue from co-produced films than from imported films.[16] The SAPPRFT and the CFCC do not recognize financial co-ventures as co-productions if they have not received official co-production approval. Lower production labor costs made possible by the lack of production unionization in China further increase the financial incentive, particularly for films with huge period sets and large numbers of extras. The market-driven focus of Chinese co-productions makes examining their long-term cultural implications particularly important, especially in the field of Sino-US co-production, in which American filmmakers are motivated more often by profit than by culture.[17]

RECENT HISTORY OF SINO-US FILM CO-PRODUCTION

Film co-production is a relatively recent phenomenon in the PRC's history, despite playing an important role early in the cinematic history of semicolonial Shanghai.[18] Before 1984, the Chinese film industry operated as part of a state-controlled monopoly, and by the early 1990s, co-productions constituted one-third of the films produced in the PRC.[19] However, after a screening of the Sino-Japanese co-production *The Blue Kite* (dir. Tian Zhuangzhuang) in Japan in 1994 without the permission of the Chinese government, the SARFT (now part of the SAPPRFT) introduced more stringent film industry regulations that allowed only ten foreign "megaproductions" each year.[20]

After its WTO accession, the PRC increased its annual quota of foreign films from ten to twenty.[21] The Chinese government then revised its import distribution policy in 2012, after five years of WTO negotiations between China and the United States, to guarantee 25 percent of the country's gross box-office receipts to foreign films admitted into the market.[22] These revenue-sharing practices drew criticism from US trade partners for not going far enough.[23] The import quota elicited competition from producers around the world who hoped to screen their films in the Chinese market.

The United States' WTO complaint and subsequent negotiations led to another increase in the foreign film profit-sharing import quota in February 2012, from twenty to thirty-four, with the stipulation that the additional fourteen imported films be in the "special format" category, such as IMAX or 3-D.[24] The limit on opportunities to access the Chinese market encouraged producers who wanted to distribute their films on the mainland to consider applying for co-production permission so their movies would be treated as local films in the market.

Theatrical distribution capacity in the PRC is expanding, creating an increasingly attractive market that totaled USD 6.8 billion in 2015.[25] But unpredictable distribution practices, even for foreign films included in the quota, create uncertainty in the market. Films imported into the PRC under the profit-sharing film import quota remain in a much more vulnerable position with regard to distribution permissions than do films that regulators consider "local." James Cameron's *Avatar* was removed from 2-D screens in the PRC to make way for director Hu Mei's 2010 Chinese New Year film *Confucius*.[26] Regulators removed Quentin Tarantino's *Django Unchained* (2012) from theaters less than twelve hours after its PRC release on April 11, 2013.[27] When *Django* was re-released on May 12, after regulators changed their minds about the film's suitability for the Chinese box office at the last minute, the film's box office was a mere USD 2.65 million—a dramatic contrast to its USD 423 million take in the rest of the world.[28] The SAPPRFT is involved in the entire filmmaking process for co-productions via its production arm, the CFCC. CFCC approval procedures for co-produced films fall into three categories. The first stage is the application for project establishment. The second stage is production. The final stage is the review and approval of the completed film. The SAPPRFT is much less invested in the production process for imported films, which makes those films easier to pull from theaters. And because imported films are not "local," there are financial incentives to set their release dates to coincide so that the movies cannibalize each other's box offices. On July 27, 2012, the animated films *The Lorax* (dir. Chris Reynaud and Kyle Balda) and *Ice Age: Continental Drift* (dir. Steve Martino and Michael Thurmeier) opened opposite each other and were thereby forced to compete directly for the same opening weekend audience.[29] Similarly, Christopher Nolan's *The Dark Night Rises*, Ridley Scott's *Prometheus*, and Marc Webb's *The Amazing Spider-Man* opened in the same week.[30] Hollywood film exports to China have continued to face similarly competitive release dates. Unpredictable distribution for films imported into the country presents a strong financial incentive for increased media collaboration between China and Hollywood.

Co-Production, Chinese Style

In terms of the letter of the law, film co-production in the PRC appears to be a transparent, almost linear process. The CFCC is a quasi-government agency that was founded in 1979, and it is authorized to oversee the administration and coordination of mainland film co-productions.[31] According to the CFCC, all foreign production entities seeking to legally make films in the PRC must operate under its auspices. All co-productions involve contractual arrangements between a foreign party and a Chinese party and are agreed on with the consent of the CFCC. Chinese co-production law requires Chinese talent and financing at levels stated in production contracts, subject to final approval by SAPPRFT.[32]

But official policies obscure the inherent subjectivity of the process. In her speech to the Asia Society US-China Film Summit in 2013, Zhang Xun, then president of the China Film Co-Production Corporation, outlined some types of content that filmmakers in Sino-US co-productions should avoid—including sex and violence, but also religious issues, complex political issues involving other nations, and "ugly" representations of China that do not fully reflect the country's economic growth over the past thirty years.[33] Zhang also expressed skepticism about Hollywood's attempts to pander to Chinese regulators by adding only small amounts of Chinese content into their projects, stating the often superficial changes made by Hollywood studios to access the Chinese market: "If I raised the bridge of my nose and made my eyes larger, would I be Chinese or American?" Zhang Xun ended her tenure as head of the CFCC in May 2014, but she helmed the organization for seven years of transformative growth, and her words presage many of the challenges faced by Hollywood filmmakers making films in China.[34]

Despite a subjective content-approval process, there is an important simplicity in the process of co-producing films in China: all roads lead through the CFCC. Without a CFCC-sanctioned partnership, film co-production cannot legally commence in the PRC.[35] A film initially approved for co-production during the preproduction process, as is required, must be vetted again before receiving final approval in the form of a "Film Public Exhibition Permit," which allows legal distribution. Without screening at the preproduction stage, imported films run a higher risk of being completely rejected due to unsanctioned content.[36] Thus, the practice of co-production takes on an important role in terms of managing censorship risk. Films with greater local political buy-in during the production stages have a better chance of reaching theatrical audiences, because they are more likely to meet censorship requirements.[37] Censorship begins at an early stage for co-produced films, which both allows greater predictability and also has a potentially chilling effect on content. In the co-production process, Chinese film bureaucrats and American film producers co-create global films for Chinese viewers. Thus, film co-production in China, while primarily a policy- or finance-based choice, also informs a new cultural landscape of filmmaking.

Co-Production, Hollywood Style

By contrast, in Hollywood, general co-ventures and official co-productions both fit within the rubric of what constitutes a co-production for American studios. No centralized US federal government definition of film co-production exists. US companies therefore understand co-production differently than their Chinese counterparts do.

Filmmaking in Hollywood presents producers with a broader range of legal structures for a co-production deal. If, metaphorically, in China, all (legal) avenues to film co-production are through the CFCC, then in Hollywood, everyone uses the surface streets to avoid unnecessary traffic—that is, the routes to financing a film and gaining approval are substantially more flexible. US government oversight of motion picture production and co-production is limited to the tax and financial laws applied to all corporations and to agreement with the MPAA with regard to ratings and other trade issues. As a result, Hollywood producers often have difficulty navigating the policy-driven Chinese model. A fundamental cultural disconnect therefore exists with regard to the best way to manage the co-production process. Experienced US film co-production professionals are quintessential masters at identifying multiple ways of getting a film made using funds from overseas. However, in China, not dealing appropriately with the central government's film authorities can mean anything from a failed initial deal to a film not being allowed to play on mainland screens.

Sino-US film co-production takes place at all budget levels of the filmmaking process, though blockbusters receive the bulk of coverage in the trade press. Independent filmmakers were actually among the first to maneuver successfully through the world of Sino-US film co-production. Smaller-budget films are unique in that the cost-savings and production incentives derived from shooting in mainland China allow for the production of films that would have otherwise been difficult to make. It should be noted that, as production in China becomes more expensive, this type of film will become more difficult to make, but independent co-productions will always remain a formative part of Sino-US film co-production culture.

The Sino-US film co-production process provides a way for independent filmmakers to produce lower-budget films that more actively bridge cultural gaps both in narrative and production style.[38] Indeed, co-production policy uniquely supports films that profile global citizens because of the way in which their lives accommodate narratives that speak to both foreign and domestic Chinese audiences. Co-productions are the ideal venue for representing urban cosmopolitan populations. As a comparison, film workers on US-Japanese co-productions have described the richer interactions between film workers that occur within smaller-budget or independent films.[39] Global media scholar Yoshiharu Tezuka argues that the "banal cosmopolitanism" of global cities such as Tokyo (or, in this case, Shanghai) offers a population of "actually existing cosmopolitans" from which to create narratives that fit within the culture of that city.[40] Examples of Sino-US independent film co-productions in this category include Oscar L. Costo's *Shanghai Red* (2006), David Ren and Kern Konwiser's *Shanghai Kiss* (2007), and Daniel Hsia's *Shanghai Calling* (2012). The phenomenon of independent titles invoking the site of transnational film co-production extends beyond American filmmakers.

Europeans Berengar Pfahl and David Verbeek directed *Shanghai Baby* (2007) and *Shanghai Trance* (2008), respectively, and Chinese director Zhang Yibai directed the 2007 Sino-Japanese co-production *The Longest Night in Shanghai*. These films, which depict globally mobile city dwellers, demonstrate the phenomenon of independent film co-productions that feature stories about urbanites in a cosmopolitan city.

Although not necessary for films such as *Iron Man 3* and *Transformers 4*, with their oversized productions and need for CGI, this banal cosmopolitanism offers global reach for independent films with constrained budgets. Daniel Hsia's low-budget, independent movie *Shanghai Calling* leveraged preexisting cosmopolitan communities within the city to build its narrative. Hsia had lived and worked in Shanghai before making this feature film there. The co-produced film, which had its only large-scale theatrical release as a local movie in the PRC, had box-office receipts of slightly more than USD 10,000 in the United States from its one-week run, according to the trade website Box Office Mojo. The film's main characters are Amanda Wilson (played by Eliza Coupe), a Caucasian American relocation consultant who speaks fluent Mandarin, and Sam Chao (played by Daniel Henney), a New York–based Chinese American lawyer who is reassigned to his firm's Shanghai office despite his nonexistent Mandarin skills. The "fish out of water" romantic comedy follows Sam's exploration of corrupt Sino-US manufacturing joint ventures, as well as his gradual understanding of the cultural life of Shanghai and its residents. In interviews about the screenwriting process, Hsia referenced specific archetypes in the city on which he had based his characters, like Donald Cafferty, a longstanding expatriate resident of the city (played by US actor Bill Pullman).[41] The film's model differs dramatically from that of superhero films, which leverage globally branded narratives in a Chinese setting but have nonetheless also been influenced by Sino-US co-production policy.

Independent film co-productions, by definition, lack the sweeping distribution scope of the big-budget studio films covered in this study. In its entire theatrical run, *Shanghai Red* took in a total of USD 30,353, according to Box Office Mojo. The film's theatrical release in the PRC, at the 2007 SIFF, was sparsely attended. The movie also had limited mainland DVD distribution. *Shanghai Kiss* was a direct-to-DVD release. *Shanghai Calling* had a theatrical release in only four theaters in the United States, despite wider distribution in China. Although studio-financed films such as *Transformers 4*, Rob Cohen's *The Mummy 3* (2008), and even Ang Lee's *Lust, Caution* (2007) have substantially greater influence on global screen culture, small-budget, independent co-productions have an outsized influence on the culture of China-Hollywood collaborations.

When film co-production was a relatively new phenomenon after the PRC's accession to the WTO, independent filmmakers were in a unique position as leaders in the process. Partially because of her role in producing the film *Shanghai Red* (dir. Oscar L. Costo 2006), Vivian Wu sat at the head table at the 2009 SIFF industry forum luncheon, alongside such key co-production players as Tong Gang (the deputy director general of the SAPPRFT), Ren Zhonglun (the president of Shanghai Film Group), and Zhang Xun (then general manager of the CFCC). *Shanghai Kiss* director David Ren wrote a testimonial entitled "A Love Letter to Shanghai," which was published on the CFCC's website in 2008; in it, he detailed both the benefits and the drawbacks of shooting a film in the city, as well as his plans to film a follow-up movie there. Like Ren, Wu described her experience shooting in Shanghai on the CFCC's website in 2008. These testimonials were available on the site through 2014. The prominence of such testimonials from low-budget filmmakers bears witness to the path that Sino-US film co-productions have traveled—from small, independent features, to major China-Hollywood blockbusters such as *The Mummy 3* or *Forbidden Kingdom,* to major art films like *Lust, Caution* and faux-productions like *Iron Man 3* and *Transformers 4*.

Beyond official co-productions, other types of films may not complete the co-production process but nonetheless contribute to the creation of new collaborative industrial practices. These include films that are collaborations between Chinese and US partners on some level that are not released as official co-productions. These movies demonstrate the complex ways in which policy, commerce, and art intersect in the creation of Sino-US media.

Faux-Productions

Marshaling a co-production from start to finish is a complicated process. Not all films make it through every stage of approval. However, all movies that attempt to gain film *co-production* approval in the PRC at the preproduction stage have the bureaucratic imprint of Chinese regulators. *Faux-productions* are films that have co-production status through at least part of their production process but are not distributed in the PRC as "local" films. Faux-productions can be part of the co-production process as early as the preproduction phase and remain a co-production even into postproduction. This category largely comprises films that begin as co-productions but are ultimately released within the PRC's revenue-sharing import quota system due to reasons related to partnerships, financing, or percentage of Chinese content.

Sino-US faux-productions allow Hollywood studios to collaborate with the CFCC on film production sans final-cut approval, unless the film is later exported to China and reviewed by regulators at the import stage. Faux-productions such as *Iron Man 3* and *Looper* unsuccessfully tested the Chinese content restrictions for co-productions in China. As noted by Yu Yan in the *Beijing Review* on September 23, 2013, after both films' initial co-production processes and eventual release within the PRC's revenue-sharing quota, the SAPPRFT released multiple public statements regarding the types of Chinese content that film co-productions must include to receive distribution approval. The SAPPRFT refined the parameters of what constitutes co-production activity after the release of these faux-productions, thereby shaping the nature of Sino-US media through Chinese policy intervention.

Faux-productions offer Hollywood filmmakers an opportunity to assess the Chinese market and experiment with the feasibility of collaborations with Chinese partners. They can also indicate failure to successfully collaborate with Chinese partners. Director Oliver Stone's controversial comments at the 2014 Beijing International Film Festival (BJIFF) that co-productions "don't work" reflected his three failed attempts to complete official co-productions.[42] In contrast to laudatory statements about big-budget co-productions made by MPAA chairman and CEO Christopher Dodd in his BJIFF keynote address in the same year, Stone emphasized the limitations in the types of stories that could be told in the Chinese market, zeroing in on rosy portrayals of Mao Zedong as the type of films he thought might get produced.[43] Indeed, media scholar Jing Meng has documented the complexity of contemporary Chinese historical representation in media, particularly with regard to the Cultural Revolution.[44] Via faux-productions, US filmmakers can test the limits Chinese regulators present and critically examine what those limits mean with regard to their creative freedom in the filmmaking process. High-profile faux-productions, whose ups and downs in the approval process the trade media rabidly cover, are in many ways more helpful in educating filmmakers than successful co-productions because they show the commercial and creative limitations of Sino-US film collaboration.

Finally, the existence of faux-productions attests to the enmeshment of Hollywood studios in the Chinese media industry, even before the Chinese conglomerate Wanda Group purchased American studio Legendary Pictures in 2016. Even if films do not end up as co-productions, they may still rely on financial relationships with Chinese companies. When films start as co-productions, even if they are not released as co-productions, they remain subject to Chinese regulatory guidance at any stage of production where the production has the status. Faux-productions are a testament to the growing influence of Chinese regulators, even in the inception of "Hollywood" blockbusters.

Assisted Productions

Faux-productions test the boundaries of official co-productions. Assisted productions, known as *xiepai dianying* in Mandarin, permit production in the PRC with fewer content constraints but more distribution restrictions. The term refers to movies that are shot in the PRC with the assistance of local film studio facilities but without official government approval for Chinese distribution, and often without Chinese financial support. Assisted productions must still be approved by the SAPPRFT and CFCC but have substantially more flexibility with regard to the final product. At the first stage of approval, referred to as "Application for Project Establishment," assisted productions—unlike official co-productions—do not need to notify the CFCC of the film's intended creative contributors, nor do they require an English-language title application.[45] During the second stage, known as "Production," assisted productions do not require an application letter to hire "overseas major creative contributors," as in the case of official co-productions.[46] Chinese film workers and spaces are part of the film but are not preconditions for the filmmaking process.

Assisted productions use Chinese locations, though these settings are often not portrayed as "China," such as in Michael Winterbottom's *Code 46* (2003), Kurt Wimmer's *Ultraviolet* (2006), and Spike Jonze's *Her* (2013). Unlike co-produced films that directly represent China as itself, the three films use Shanghai to generically represent life in the near future. Although these movies enjoyed varying levels of box-office success in the United States, ranging from USD 285,585 for Winterbottom's *Code 46* to more than USD 25 million for Jonze's *Her,* none had a mainland China theatrical release.

To be released in the Chinese market, assisted productions must receive both production approval and import approval from SAPPRFT. Gaining approval for multiple administrative processes from the same agency can present challenges in the collaboration process, particularly if the first approval process goes poorly. For example, in the case of J. J. Abrams's *Mission: Impossible III,* problems with permits during the shoot complicated the relationship between SARFT (now SAPPRFT) and the production.[47] Then, at the distribution stage, SARFT delayed the film's release before censoring certain content, including a scene of elderly Shanghainese playing mah jong; a scene of the main character, Ethan Hunt, distracting two Chinese henchmen and killing one; and, finally, a scene of tattered underwear hanging outside a building.[48] Because of the availability of pirated copies of the film after its international release, the distribution delay for *Mission: Impossible III* reduced demand for the movie when it was finally released in theaters in the PRC. Similar challenges befell Sam Mendes's *Skyfall* (2012), a James Bond film with contemporary Shanghai as a backdrop. Because of a scene in which James Bond, played by Daniel Craig, kills a security guard in Shanghai, as well as a scene of prostitution in Macau, regulators delayed the film's release in the PRC by two months, once again creating a significant gap between the international release date and the Chinese one.[49] Like that of *Mission: Impossible III,* the case of *Skyfall* demonstrates the financial penalty paid for airing China's dirty laundry—both literally and figuratively—on screen. With a far more precarious status than official co-productions, assisted productions have no guarantee of being distributed to mainland screens at all.[50] Like faux-productions, assisted productions reveal not only successes but also the pitfalls of Sino-US collaboration.

Talent Exchanges

Talent exchanges are Chinese films that use foreign on-screen media labor and Hollywood films that feature Chinese on-screen media labor as part of the production. Using global acting talent is a common practice, but it is important to note here because such cross-pollination between talent exchanges and co-productions shapes Sino-US film collaboration more broadly. The presence of a famous non-Chinese actor in a film can suggest that the work is a co-production when it is merely a high-budget, outward-looking Chinese film. For example, Beijing-based Chinese American director Dayyan Eng's *Inseparable* (2012), starring well-known American actor Kevin Spacey, was a Chinese-financed local production with prominent US talent. Donald Sutherland appeared in Feng Xiaogang's *Big Shot's Funeral* (2001), a dark comedy with a very narrow release in the United States. In 2012, Feng, a star mainland director whose works have never achieved significant critical or financial success outside the PRC, released *Back to 1942* with Hollywood stars Adrien Brody and Tim Robbins acting beside Chinese counterparts. The film took in less than USD 313,000 in the United States, according to Box Office Mojo. Brody later also appeared in the 2015 Chinese action film *Dragon Blade* with Jackie Chan and John Cusack. A 1980s and 1990s American heartthrob, Cusack made his China debut in the 2010 co-production *Shanghai* before appearing in *Dragon Blade*. It might be tempting to think of Chinese productions with Hollywood talent as venues for actors past their prime put out to pasture for large paydays in foreign markets—in the tradition of Bill Murray's character Bob Harris in *Lost in Translation* (dir. Sofia Coppola 2003)— but high-profile actors have increasingly accepted roles in projects shot in China. Matt Damon, Oscar winner and the tentpole star of the *Bourne* film series, starred in *The Great Wall* (dir. Zhang Yimou 2016) after his turn in *The Martian* (dir. Ridley Scott 2015), a film with such favorable treatment of China that it was pilloried on late-night TV for demonstrating naked pandering to the PRC market.[51] The casting of Damon as the lead for *The Great Wall* was widely criticized in the United States because, as the lead of the China-based historical film, Damon took an opportunity away from an Asian or Asian American actor. At the same time, casting a Caucasian American lead actor is a strategic move, one that has been long employed by Chinese directors trying to break into a conservative American theatrical distribution market that has long limited headline opportunities for people of color.

Despite this, Asian American actors play a invaluable role in bringing Hollywood and China together. *The Pavilion of Women*, a Chinese film starring American actor Willem Dafoe, was one of the first feature film roles for Korean American actor John Cho. Cho rose to fame in the pioneering buddy comedy *Harold and Kumar Go to White Castle* (dir. Danny Leiner 2004), and later, playing the character of Sulu in the *Star Trek* film series. Working in China's developing film industry offered an early feature-film opportunity for Cho. By choosing to work in China, Cho expanded his role options beyond those available in Southern California, a necessary strategy given Hollywood's resistance to casting Asian American men, while also building formative connections between China and Hollywood.[52] Leehom Wang, a Chinese American singer and actor who has made his career in Asia, has served as a cultural ambassador on multiple films. Following his star turn in the Sino-US film co-production *Lust, Caution* (dir. Ang Lee 2007), Wang headlined the 2013 local Chinese film *My Lucky Star* and assisted the movie's non-Chinese-speaking director American Dennie Gordon in navigating the language and cultural complexities of the production process.[53] Global film production in China's rising film market provides new types of opportunities for Asian American talent to play an instrumental role in the global film industry.

Talent exchanges are instrumental in advancing China-Hollywood collaborations. This idea is apparent in films such as *Hollywood Adventures* (dir. Timothy Kendall 2015), a film starring Chinese actors shot in Southern California and produced by Taiwanese American director Justin Lin. Lin is best known for his work in the global blockbuster *Fast and Furious* series, which has had significant box-office success in China. Official co-productions such as *Lust, Caution* and *Kung Fu Panda 3* also pioneered other types of talent exchange practices, such as shared script writing and translating.[54]

Similarly, Hollywood films with Chinese talent, many of which were not legally distributed in China, have also had a substantial impact on the shape of collaboration between China and Hollywood. *Rush Hour* (dir. Brett Ratner 1998), starring Jackie Chan, was one of the actor's first significant mainstream box-office successes in the US market. *Rush Hour 2* (dir. Brett Ratner 2001) was the English-language film debut for Chinese star Zhang Ziyi, after her success in Ang Lee's Chinese-language, Academy Award–winning film *Crouching Tiger, Hidden Dragon* (dir. Ang Lee 2000). Chinese actress Li Bingbing starred in both *Resident Evil: Retribution* (dir. Paul W. S. Anderson 2012) and *Transformers 4* (dir. Michael Bay 2014) after her role in the Sino-US co-production *The Forbidden Kingdom* (dir. Rob Minkoff 2008). Leading PRC star Fan Bingbing played the role of Blink in the blockbuster *X-Men: Days of Future Past* (dir. Bryan Singer 2014). Fan later played the role of Samantha Bai in the Sino-US co-production *Skiptrace* (dir. Renny Harlin 2016), as well as the role of the mermaid in *The King's Daughter* (dir. Sean McNamara 2017), a film financed by both Chinese and American sources. Placing Chinese stars in Hollywood films marks the importance of Chinese audiences in the global box office and is easier to execute than potentially more lucrative PRC revenue-sharing deals. The practice, though often financially driven, has the potential to further diversify representation in Hollywood.

Commissioned Productions

Another alternative model that presents less risk for foreign investors seeking to become involved with the Chinese film market is the commissioned production. Commissioned productions are films that are made by a Chinese firm, for the Chinese market, but are sold as the product of an international brand. This model draws from other modes of industrial production used by American corporations in the PRC. For example, a popular dish at McDonald's in mainland China is taro pie—a dessert product whose shell is like the crust of the company's apple pie but whose interior is filled with cooked taro root, rather than cooked apples. Though fundamentally a McDonald's product, the pie uses an Asian dessert ingredient to make the menu item better suit the tastes of the local market. Disney has released films made using local talent and subsidiaries with the "shell" of the Disney brand: a corporate structure that is as "glocal" as taro pie. Examples of such commissioned productions include Frankie Chung's 2007 *The Secret of the Magic Gourd* and Zhong Yu's 2009 *Trail of the Panda*, released in China by Disney. Commissioned productions demonstrate the ways in which brands drive industrial collaboration between China and Hollywood.

Disney's local productions will soon be joined by DreamWorks's entries into the local Chinese market. After DreamWorks agreed in 2012 to establish the Oriental DreamWorks production studio, it released plans to produce films for both the global and domestic Chinese markets.[55] DreamWorks' first major release, *Kung Fu Panda 3*, was a Sino-US co-production, but the firm also has expressed interest in making local productions with the Oriental DreamWorks brand. Labeling studio-branded local productions as co-productions is tempting. However, by the Chinese government's official standards, the films are local productions because of the corporate status the production companies have in the Chinese market. This distinction is important. By making local films for the local market, these firms are pioneering a new form of hybrid "local" film—a McDonald's taro pie–like fusion.

Buyout Films

Buyout films (*jinkou maiduan pian* in Mandarin) constitute another category of foreign films distributed in mainland China. Technically not collaborative productions, they are worth mentioning briefly as a category of Sino-US film collaboration to clarify the other categories already discussed. Unlike films imported under the PRC's revenue-sharing import quota, buyout films are films (usually B-level or lower) that Chinese companies purchase for a fixed fee to distribute within the Chinese market. The film's Chinese distributor then receives all the proceeds from each film's distribution, though producers can negotiate for a portion of the back-end distribution profits.[56] In 2011, thirty-eight of the seventy-eight foreign films screened in the Chinese market were buyouts.[57] One example of a rather prominent buyout film is Kimble Rendall's 2012 *Bait (3D)*, an Australian shark movie presented by Enlight Pictures that grossed USD 20 million in the Chinese market. Other examples include the first two films in the series *The Expendables*, distributed by LeVision Pictures.[58] Buyouts offer potentially less lucrative financial terms for American producers, but they transfer the risks related to a film's Chinese distribution process back to the local PRC firms.

Film co-productions between Chinese and US companies draw on macro-level cultural practices established via China's relationships with other foreign co-production partners. Sino-US film co-productions therefore clearly benefit from other forms of co-production filmmaking. The following section considers China's co-production practices established in conjunction with other non–East Asian economies outside of Hollywood. These practices are particularly valuable in understanding Sino-US co-productions because of the shared challenges in production. Unlike filmmakers from Korea, Japan, or Hong Kong, filmmakers from outside East Asia must overcome issues ranging from additional travel and jet lag to total unfamiliarity with Chinese characters and radically different foundational literary texts.

EUROPEAN CO-PRODUCTIONS

Understanding the European model of film co-production is useful in discerning how the cultural dynamics between European and Chinese co-productions inform Sino-US relationships. In addition to providing an example of an alternative approach, the European model acts as a useful foil for understanding the nuances of the film co-production policies, practices, and cultures that exist between Hollywood and China. Co-productions with European countries shape Chinese film co-production culture in two key ways. First, European filmmakers pioneered film co-production practices earlier than other international filmmakers did because of more permeable economic boundaries among European countries. Their approaches, therefore, serve as theoretical models for many other countries engaging in similar co-productions. Second, European producers were among the first to participate in the inchoate world of contemporary Chinese film co-production. Therefore, on a pragmatic level, they brought with them their approaches to film co-production, which in turn shaped mainland co-production practices.

The Council of Europe's European Cinema Support Fund began financing European film co-production before the establishment of the European Union.[59] As an organization devoted in part to the promotion of European cultural identity, the Council of Europe had much to gain in implementing clear regulations for co-productions between European signatories. The preamble of the European Convention on Cinematographic Co-Production states that regulators designed the accord with the consideration that "cinematographic co-production, an instrument of creation and expression of cultural diversity on a European scale, should be reinforced."[60] Film co-production, at least from the perspective of the Council of Europe, is a matter of crucial importance for building and disseminating the pluralistic cultural identity implicit in a "European" production. The charter of the European Convention establishes one of the foundational documents on the practice of multilateral co-production. Differing from the more fluid Hollywood model, European co-productions must be accepted into the Council of Europe approval process. However, the European model offers substantially greater transparency for multilateral co-production collaboration than does the Chinese model.

The European model provides important insights to better understand how governments can assess and guide the co-production process. For a Chinese co-production to be considered an official film co-production, 30 percent of its main talent must be Chinese, a policy that supports the local industry.[61] There must also be equal proportions of Chinese and foreign creative crew.[62] Yet the official ruling on the number of Chinese above-the-line and below-the-line workers who must be part of the shoot is at the discretion of the CFCC. In contrast, the European model offers a more discrete way of determining the cultural ownership of a film. Although both approaches have strengths and weaknesses, the European model is instructive in that it reveals how one multinational governing body conceives of the question of cultural ownership of a media work. To be considered a European co-production, a film must have at least fifteen of nineteen possible points, as illustrated in table 2, or receive special dispensation. The privileging of above-the-line labor in determining a film's eligibility for preferential treatment is immediately evident in the European co-production chart. We see a similar practice within the context of film co-production in the PRC, where films must involve a certain percentage of Chinese starring roles and appropriate "cultural content." However, the intriguing difference between the Chinese and the European models lies in the greater emphasis on crew labor in the Chinese context. The privileging of above-the-line roles in European co-production agreements provides useful insight into the reasons behind film co-production regulation.

Table 2   European Convention on Cinematic Co-Productions

European Element	Weighting Points	Totals
Creative group		
Director	3	
Scriptwriter	3	
Composer	1	7
Performing group[a]		
First role	3	
Second role	2	
Third role	1	6
Technical craft group		
Cameraman	1	
Sound recordist	1	
Editor	1	
Art director	1	
Studio or shooting location	1	
Post-production location	1	6

SOURCE: European Convention on Cinematographic Co-Production, by the Council of Europe, 1992, Appendix II, conventions.coe.int/Treaty/en/Treaties/Html/147.htm.

NOTE: So far as article 8 (of the European Convention on Cinematographic Co-production) is concerned, "artistic" refers to the creative and performing groups, and "technical" refers to the technical and craft group.

[a] First, second, and third roles are determined by the number of days worked.

It reveals the policy's focus on building and disseminating the accomplishments of high-level domestic creative workers, rather than on creating the greatest number of jobs or training the most below-the-line workers, as is suggested by China's policy.

European co-production policy measures the monetary and above-the-line factors, not the domestic labor considerations of below-the-line work. Above-the-line workers, particularly those who contribute to co-productions, most often have blended national and linguistic identities, to say nothing of the convoluted international path of funding sources. Significantly, France, Belgium, Italy, Spain, and the United Kingdom have all also signed individual co-production treaties with China, signaling the continued importance of bilateral co-production in conjunction with larger European efforts.[63]

AUSTRALIAN CO-PRODUCTIONS

Australia has a special co-production relationship with mainland China and is one of a small but increasing number of countries that have legislated an official co-production treaty with the PRC.[64] The combination of stream-lined co-production regulations and a population of comparatively flexible film workers makes Australian co-productions with Chinese companies a useful foil for understanding Sino-US film co-production practice. In principle, Australia's co-production program offers few limitations to producers from countries with which it has joint treaties or memoranda of understanding. Films that can bypass the "significant Australian content" standard are considered "Australian content" for broadcast purposes, and they are eligible to receive investments from Australian government screen agencies, including Screen Australia.[65] However, all relevant government officials in charge of co-production in each country must agree on the terms.[66] In both mainland China and Australia, the practice of film co-production involves public diplomacy at the highest levels throughout the film approval process.

Also significant within the Australian model is the importance of co-production participation for Australian partners. For official co-productions with China, both countries must make a minimum financial contribution of 20 percent.[67] But in exchange for this financial investment, each co-producer must apply for co-production status in their own country of origin.[68] This provision is particularly lucrative for Australian producers because of the increasing importance of the Chinese market to the Australian media industries.[69] The way in which Australia's co-production treaty structures efforts to navigate co-production policy as part of a shared financial commitment innovatively addresses the complexity of Chinese market entry while enhancing Australian growth.

In Sino-US filmmaking the work of Australians as cultural translators is still an understudied phenomenon, largely because most Australians in the industry hold below-the-line positions. A notable exception is Australian filmmaker Christopher Doyle, best known as the main cinematographer for

Hong Kong–based director Wong Kar-wai. While Doyle is a boundary breaker in terms of Australians working on films from the Greater China region, co-production activity has created a highly skilled group of intermediaries working in mainland China (for more on this topic, see chapter 6). Holding such difficult jobs as stunt performer and logistics manager on Sino-US co-productions, these workers mediate between American and Chinese production practices by providing an important cultural link between the highly codified filmmaking practices typical of American big-budget productions and the more "rough-and-tumble" approach popular in mainland filmmaking circles. Both Australian film labor and Australian film co-production practices underscore the culture of collaborative media production that supports the global expansion of China as a media brand.

THE SIGNIFICANCE AND COMPLEXITY OF SINO-US FILM COLLABORATIONS

As the discussion of Chinese film policy in this chapter attests, official film co-production policies influence the practical aspects of Sino-US media brand collaborations. Film collaboration offers a productive, though not infallible, base from which Hollywood can expand its market share and China can increase its influence in the global cultural industries. In short, both industries can feed into a system of media collaboration that, at least in part, advances their particular interests. Ultimately, these practices play an important role in informing the pragmatic details of Sino-US production collaborations. Although co-production is the most explicit form of collaboration, it exists within a much larger context of collaborative media production practice.

The overlapping interests of Chinese and US partners in the co-production process can shift the nature of the relationship from active collaboration to suspicion to antagonism and back to actual collaboration, all in the course of one project, as the phenomenon of the faux-production so vividly illustrates. Yet because film collaborations offer unprecedented access to the Chinese market for American investors, as well as technology and talent transfer for Chinese film groups, both sides have an incentive to learn how to navigate this contentious process. Through analysis of collaborative film deal structures, both the advantages and disadvantages of the Sino-US industrial relationship become visible.

Understanding film collaboration is crucial for appreciating how China and Hollywood are both expanding their global reach. Unlike examining domestic film production, studying Sino-US film collaborations reveals the interactions among government-run Chinese film groups, private companies operating in the PRC, and privately held entertainment conglomerates in the United States. First, these connections are becoming an increasingly important aspect of film production practice in mainland China. Second, the private-public nature of these interactions is emblematic of other types of industrial interactions between the PRC and the United States, offering important lessons for related industrial sectors. Finally, Sino-US collaborations involve powerful negotiations over the ownership of representation. The nature of the production of visual images is such that it allows us to understand both how we see others and how we see ourselves. Thus, their importance is not just as industrial products, but also as a means of understanding how Chinese and US cultural interests coalesce and contradict each other on a macro scale. Film collaborations must be understood as part of a larger cultural and technological intersection of American and Chinese media production, and, by extension, of a radical shift in global media industrial culture.

CONCLUSION

Sino-US film collaboration is both a clearly defined and wholly changeable phenomenon. The paradoxical coexistence of fixed rules and malleable practices makes the study of this particular mode of cultural production particularly illuminating. Analysis of Sino-US film collaborations reveals the complexity not only of the changing cultural relationship between China and Hollywood but also of the dynamic mediascape of an increasingly globalized China. These models reveal the specific production strategies that balance what constitutes a "Chinese" film and what making a movie in the "Hollywood" style means.

The regulatory structure of Sino-US film collaborations underscores the precariousness of Hollywood's film investments in China. Imported films, co-produced films, assisted productions, buyout films, and local productions are all subject to variable regulatory scrutiny by the SAPPRFT and the CFCC. Though currently offering a vehicle for foreign corporations who seek to access Chinese audiences, co-productions could change over time to be less accommodating to foreign capital investment. Increasing regulation of assisted productions, buyout films, and local productions could further constrain foreign capital investment in the Chinese theatrical exhibition industry, as well as indicate future limitations in other forms of media exhibition in China.

The domestic Chinese film market's regulatory and financial development will determine how important the phenomenon of Hollywood film co-production will be in the long term. With successful mainland Chinese commercial films such as *Lost in Thailand* (dir. Xu Zheng 2012) and *Finding Mr. Right* (dir. Xue Xiaolu 2013) and the prevalence of China–Hong Kong blockbusters such as *The Monkey King* (dir. Cheang Pou-soi 2014) and *The Mermaid* (dir. Stephen Chow 2016), China's need to accommodate Hollywood capital investment to advance its film industry and the Chinese Dream may diminish over time as the country expands its global production capacity for large-scale film releases and related multiplatform media brands. However, the exploration of the role of media policy in production collaborations following China's accession to the WTO forms the foundation for the future of global Chinese media, as well as of global Hollywood.

China-Hollywood co-productions have expanded the capacity for filmmaking in the PRC and injected dynamic China-focused story lines into American popular media. Yet what we discover by analyzing these film collaborations is that, even though Hollywood studio films challenge Chinese state-owned film groups and American investors have difficulty navigating less transparent filmmaking and distribution regulations, the industries have already become entwined. Protectionists on both sides of the Pacific may be right to be concerned. Considerations of the "Chinese film industry" versus the "Hollywood film industry" must take into account the fact that, for years, China and Hollywood have intimately overlapped in financing, production, and distribution and are poised to become only more intertwined, dramatically changing commercial filmmaking as we know it.

4 Whispers in the Gallery

HOW INDUSTRY FORUMS BUILD SINO-US
MEDIA COLLABORATION

On November 5, 2013, Chinese and US policymakers and media industry leaders met in downtown Los Angeles to talk about making movies across the Pacific. They were not at a film festival or a film market but at the Asia Society Southern California's US-China Film Summit. Although the summit lacked a flash-filled red carpet and promised no immediate film deal, Christopher Dodd, chairman and CEO of the MPAA, and Li Bingbing, star of *Transformers 4*, gathered for the event's gala dinner at the Millennium Biltmore Hotel. Over 150 attendees filled the hotel ballroom. Among the participants were power players in law, finance, and entertainment.[1] Free streaming videos of the day's speakers were available on the Asia Society website, further expanding the forum's scope. At the time of China's accession to the WTO in 2001, or even a decade later, an event of this scale would have been unimaginable.[2] When the PRC joined the WTO, many of the Chinese companies represented at the forum did not yet exist. In 2013, Hollywood studios were sending C-suite executives to be speakers, an occurrence that would have been unlikely even three years prior. The visible presence of leading media and entertainment figures from both countries brought significant global entertainment clout to the 2013 event and, by extension, attention to the importance of talks between China and Hollywood.[3]

Instances of public self-definition like the US-China Film Summit become critical during moments in which media industries are reshaping themselves. The US-China Film Summit is one of the largest annual events focused on facilitating collaboration between Chinese and US partners in media production. Yet this summit is not the only event of this nature. At the time of its creation, it was just one in an expanding array of events brokering the changing relationship between Hollywood and China. Media industry forums like the US-China Film Summit bring industry stakeholders together to discuss media production in China at a time of transition.

The PRC's theatrical market has already begun to surpass Hollywood in size during the month of the Chinese New Year period, and it is poised to become the largest market in the world.[4] To advance their global market share, Hollywood studios have new incentives to aggressively pursue fresh collaborative ventures to take advantage of China's growth. China's policy priorities for increased global cultural influence partly dovetail with Hollywood's efforts. This chapter elucidates how film industry players are branding the power transition from Hollywood to China using strategic narratives: instructive stories about how to understand China's rising role in the media industries. First developed by international relations scholars Andreas Antoniades, Alister Miskimmon, and Ben O'Loughlin in 2010, the idea of strategic narratives explains the rise of industry forums largely comprising individuals sharing their stories of collaboration (or, at times, discord) in Chinese and US media relations. They write: "Strategic narratives are representations of a sequence of events and identities, a communicative tool through which political elites attempt to give meaning to a past, present and future in order to achieve political objectives. Examples include the justification of policy objectives or policy responses to economic or security crises, the formation of international alliances or the rallying of domestic opinion."[5] Scholarship on Sino-US media industries can draw much from international relations research. Many of the issues surrounding the changing relationship between China and Hollywood parallel the shifting political balance of power between the PRC and the United States.

Governments deploy strategic narratives to "account for the transition process toward new forms of international order," suggesting that "great powers attempt to determine that [order] by using strategic narratives."[6] Political scientist Ronald Tammen argues that *"socializing* a challenger into the international system with rules and norms defined by the domi- nant state might play a crucial role in whether the emerging state will challenge the status quo."[7] The strategic narratives generated by Sino-US media industry forums prepare both Hollywood- and China-based players for the challenges of a new market. Industry forums and related events train workers and institutions from China's rising media industry to work in the existing Hollywood system in part by socializing partners.

The forums help film workers who operate primarily or exclusively in one film production context to better understand which assumptions and prac- tices may impede their success in collaborations with international part- ners. Forums broaden discussions about media industry collaboration—the events provide a more expansive perspective than project-based discus- sions. The emergence of joint film-industry forums around the world sug- gests that the messaging is multidirectional and occurs in both China and Hollywood, as well as in other markets.

This chapter draws on insights from industry forums that, for the most part, were designed for commercial practitioners in the media industries. Therefore, clearly outlining the conditions of my access is important both from a methodological perspective and in order to understand the politics of access to these industry-building events. First, some of the forums, par- ticularly those directed toward city branding in relation to the growth of the entertainment industry, were free and open to the public. Others, such as the festival-adjacent forums, were open to the public for a fee. In other cases, I was able to request access to the forums because of my position as an academic writing about Chinese media. In almost all of the forums, a gatekeeping function was in place, particularly for the festival-sponsored, festival-adjacent, and production-sponsored forums. However, the forums rarely employed the types of access barriers common to other types of industry events, such as film openings and award shows.

In addition, online digital media distribution has changed the barriers to entry in the context of fee-based forums, or forums for which one must prove some type of industry affiliation. The practice of live streaming or uploading video expands access to any casual industry observer with an Internet connection. The access considerations for Chinese participants are slightly different, because some event videos are available only on YouTube, which is blocked in China without a virtual private network or proxy server.[8] The online distribution of videos that document what would previously have been private industry events also mark co-evolving definitions of privacy and publicity. As digital media scholar Patricia G. Lange argues, videos "launch connections that did not exist prior to the mediated event."[9] Lange's work demonstrates how strategic narratives distributed online both reinforce the importance of the messages at live events and expand networks across the Pacific.

Online viewing often has limitations, but interested individuals unable to watch the event live must often wait for its sponsors to upload videos to their platform of choice. The forums themselves are typically located in major production centers. As a result, whereas access was previously the keystone of industry privilege, in the context of Sino-US media industrial reflexivity, timeliness of access now characterizes industrial privilege.

Similarly, direct access to key players is a significant feature that the digital forum fails to provide. Being physically present at the forum and shaking hands, going for coffee, and exchanging contact information with other attendees are all essential elements of the industry-building process. Though one can witness and critique the content of the forum, it is still nearly impossible as an outsider to comment on the private conversations that happen during the coffee breaks between sessions or in whispers among participants during a particular session. This chapter therefore asserts the importance of both the public content of the forums themselves and the whispers in the gallery.

Industry forums are one segment in a larger landscape of events of self-definition. As scholars have noted, festivals play an essential role in the growth of transnational media industrial circuits.[10] Festivals indirectly promote transnational film production by showcasing particular international movies and bringing film workers together, and they also do so directly, by promoting individual films.[11] Festivals connect film workers on a systematic basis, offering physical meetings that give life to the broader Sino-US media ecosystem. Film festivals such as the landmark event in Cannes, France, each May shine with glamour and gowns, and offer opportunities for industry insiders from Hollywood, China, France, and beyond to connect with one another. Concurrent with the Cannes

Film Festival, with its Palme d'Or awards for artistic excellence, is Le Marché du Film, a competitive market at which businesspeople try to sell movies for global distribution. While deals are being transacted, practitioners are developing standard operating procedures for how these deals are to be carried out. The festival-market combination presents a powerful venue through which to promote new films while also facilitating production and distribution deals.[12] But festivals promote individual films and film markets facilitate distribution deals. Industry forums offer a broader perspective on macro-level changes across the industry.

Thus, the glitz of the red carpet and the dealmaking of the film market have recently seen the addition of film-industry forums that are held either during or immediately before international film festivals in spaces that are clearly separate but located nearby. These forums offer real-time commentary on the larger industrial framework within which other, more narrowly targeted deals and promotion occur. From a spatial and temporal perspective, the proximity of the forums to these festival-market combinations in major cities facilitates attendance by both out-of-town guests, who may already be in the vicinity for business, and local rainmakers, who can participate without extensive travel. Forums tend to be located near, but slightly removed from, more public-facing events like festival red carpets. For example, a film market may be in the same hotel as a festival but in a different wing, or in the same city but at a different hotel. The combined impact of film festivals and film markets as sites where large numbers of industry professionals gather together amplifies the impact of media industry forums.

Times of tumultuous transition warrant more formalized discussions about the very nature of the industry. Examining media industry forums revises existing scholarship on film festivals by tracking a different type of industry commitment that cultivates global production practices driven by critical industrial discourse. Sino-US media industry forums have developed over the past decade—first in Shanghai, then in Los Angeles, and most recently in Beijing. According to its website, the Shanghai International Film Festival began its Jin Jue International Film Forum (later changed to the SIFFORUM) in 2004. The Asia Society web page notes that the group's US-China Film Summit began in 2010. The timing of the US-China Film Summit is linked to the American Film Market, a major global film marketplace, and the American Film Institute Festival.

Karen Chu from *The Hollywood Reporter* wrote about the first Beijing Film Market and co-production forums in parallel with the Beijing International Film Festival on April 24, 2012. Forums promote dialogue by providing directors, producers, agents, and policymakers with a space in which to discuss the rapidly evolving structure of the industry. Media industry forums have as much in common with industry forums related to other disruptive business trends as they have with a decadent, bejeweled red carpet. Though filmmakers and producers around the world are experts at putting on a show, at Sino-US events, they also engage in important discussions about industry-level production practices that do not occur in a formalized way at festivals.

Both China and the United States have a substantial stake in developing collaboration standards. The Chinese government actively promotes China's place in the world through media production, and private-sector media firms are flourishing. In the United States, media conglomerates are paying more attention to the ways in which one can access the Chinese media market. Industry forums proffer norms of collaboration between China and Hollywood through the repetition of strategic narratives about the growth of Sino-US media collaborations. At each forum, participants are essentially rewriting a story about two global behemoths—Hollywood and the growing Chinese media market. Rather than relying on informal discussions of deals at Le Marché du Film or at galas such as those at the Cannes Film Festival, the players in these events meet with one another as part of structured master classes designed to set global standards for new players.

Events like the US-China Film Summit allow Chinese and US industry insiders to come together to discuss opportunities presented by China's rapidly growing media industries. The event is one way that the Chinese and US film industries have started to internally navigate the challenging process of industrial convergence. This is particularly salient in the era of the PRC's global economic ascendancy. As the Hollywood and Chinese film industries connect and converge, we are witnessing a meeting of two very different entities—the Chinese industry, emerging from a long tradition of state media, and Hollywood, long reliant on private corporations and increasingly driven by quarterly earnings expectations.

Media industry forums circulate narratives describing the growth of the Sino-US media brandscape, a quintessentially "Hollywood" tactic that weaves a new reality from the dreams of untold riches (this time coming from the Chinese media distribution market). However, rather than reifying the myths of a tightly knit Hollywood culture of production, as production studies scholar John Caldwell describes in his exploration of pitch events, Sino-US media industry forums are constructing new norms of dispersed global production.[13] Star-studded film festival events are the gold leaf–encrusted icing embellishing pragmatic, vanilla-flavored forums for financiers, lawyers, and government officials, outlining the specific processes through which individual projects produce revenue.

Forums reward speakers who contribute to larger strategic narratives. Those divulging their tales from the front lines have the opportunity to sell themselves as experts in a new, growing field. But good advice does not come free, especially in the film industry. As with the Hollywood "genesis myths" Caldwell describes, above-the-line actors, producers, directors, and agents with experience working in the Chinese market offer insights gleaned from their failures and successes while promoting their films and production capabilities.[14]

Transnational industry forums test out new power relationships. This negotiation of the terms of engagement shows the efforts of film producers pushing for greater market share and of government policymakers driving for soft power influence by both supporting and troubleshooting these markets' growth. Major industry players make a point of meeting to share knowledge.[15] Government officials also avail themselves to industry stakeholders. But what do these forums look like, and how do they shape industrial engagement? The following pages examine in detail two industry forums, one in Hollywood and one in China, while profiling the other types of semipublic industry events that have emerged in concert with the rapid international growth of China's media industries and Hollywood's increasing financial interest in the PRC's entertainment market.

US-CHINA FILM SUMMIT

Formal industry forums in Los Angeles that focus on the growth of China's film industry began after those in China. The US-China Film Summit was first incarnated as the US-China Film Co-Production Summit hosted by the US-China Institute at the University of Southern California in 2010. Shanghai, by contrast, already had a series of industry forums about global film production with Chinese companies in 2004. However, Los Angeles's location at the nexus of the global film industry meant that the forums there highlighted the growing significance of the Chinese media in the very heart of Hollywood. The US-China Film Summit is a day of panel events in which industry leaders (as determined by the Asia Society Southern California's Entertainment/Media Asia Group) present their experiences as part of Sino-US industrial collaborations. The speakers at the 2016 US-China Film Summit included leaders from major global media companies. At the summit, organizers separated participants into discrete groups, emphasizing an awareness of how convergence happens. Through the repeating pattern of industry events, the way the industry self-identifies became evident in how Chinese and US media industries came together. At the Asia Society summit, the groups of forum speakers are based on employment function in the industry. Like film-school departments or divisions on a movie set, the groupings are of business-people, creative people, journalists, scholars, and regulators, with film producers brokering dialogue among all groups. Individuals with a broad array of work experiences in both China and Hollywood attend the forums—mainland directors, bicultural producers working on co-productions, American executives negotiating a film deal with Chinese government regulators, and so on. The forums reinforce the multiple dimensions of international experience required to build products between the two countries.

At its core, the US-China Film Summit reinscribes industrial identities for workers displaced by pressures to collaborate across cultures. Within the US-China Film Summit, workers fully inhabit the role of cultural bridge that they play in these productions, a role that is subsumed by the demands of production schedules outside the summit. By grouping pro-ducers with other producers, journalists with journalists, and directors with directors, the summit creates a semipublic place where leaders of Chinese and US industrial collaboration can perform their role in a Sino-US context, both to test it and to establish a template for audience members interested in attending the summit to learn more about this changing industrial practice.

Pairings between Chinese and US leaders are not always congruent. For example, in 2013, then CFCC general manager Zhang Xun spoke on the organization's behalf as the lunchtime keynote speaker. Despite the US government's relatively hands-off approach to the film production process, former US senator and chairman/CEO of the MPAA Christopher Dodd delivered the dinnertime keynote speech. The presence of a former US senator in many ways underscored the complexity of matching Chinese and US industry culture. Zhang Xun was a PRC government employee at the time, working in a state-run corporation, the CFCC. Dodd, by contrast, is a lobbyist, leveraging previous political connections to move a private US industry's interests forward within the US government system. That being said, US government officials' involvement in the summit is only increasing. In 2014, Charles Rivkin, the assistant secretary of state for economic and business affairs and former CEO of the Jim Henson Company, spoke at the forum.[16] Conversely, state-run film groups in China are privatizing. Events such as the Asia Society's US-China Film Summit demonstrate the ways in which these not-quite-matching figures come together to structure the strategic narratives of the changing balance of power between Hollywood and China.

International Chinese film industry forums offer industry insiders the chance to learn about new industrial practices as they are happening, but that is not the only way the forums encourage the growth of Sino-US media collaboration. They have also acted (and in some cases, still act) as a way of promoting Chinese sites as locations for global media production. Specifically, the city of Shanghai has leveraged events surrounding the SIFF as a way to draw heavy hitters into the region for production deals, technology transfer, and other capital investment.

The US-China Film Summit was not necessary to establish Los Angeles as an esteemed site to produce movies; this was a fait accompli. However, despite its golden past in filmmaking, the city of Shanghai lost most of its international media significance in the 1930s before reviving its role on the international stage in the late 1990s. But events like forums have helped reestablish the city as a destination for global filmmaking. Marketing and management scholar Mihalis Kavaratzis argues that city behavior helps create an urban brand.[17] Shanghai media events assert the city's role in the internationalization of the greater Chinese media production network.

Through this process, Shanghai recreates the regional and international film industry prominence it once enjoyed, staking a new, stronger position vis-à-vis Hong Kong, which for much of the past half century has been the leading producer of Sinophone film, and Hollywood, the world's global leader in media production.

Shanghai has industry forums similar to the Asia Society US-China Film Summit that are designed to further enhance international collaboration and technology transfer. These forums offer at least a partial answer to the question of how film workers in China and Hollywood broker collaborations between divergent industry traditions in different countries. Founded in 1997, the SIFF is Shanghai's foremost brand-building event in the field of international film production. In addition to its international competition component, the SIFF sponsors the SIFFORUM, which focuses on facilitating global Chinese productions.[18]

The industry forums related to the SIFF demonstrate the broad range of industry-building activities that Chinese partners have organized to support collaborative media production in the Chinese theatrical market. The growing number of Chinese-US collaborations represents a landmark change in the global media industries, or, as Dan Mintz, the American CEO of Beijing-based media company DMG Entertainment, was quoted as saying on Forbes.com on January 2, 2014: "Things have moved rather quickly for such a big traditional established industry like Hollywood. Things haven't changed much in the last 75 years, and then comes China." Mintz's words underscore the uncertainty that the industry forums affiliated with the SIFF have sought to manage.

The SIFFORUM, which was initially called the Jin Jue International Forum, is the premiere industry forum in Shanghai. (See figures 12 and 13.) The forum was the first of its kind in China, beginning three years after the PRC's accession to the WTO. The event has become a fixture of the SIFF. SIFFORUM meetings and panels offer an annual point of contact for global filmmakers interested in Chinese deals.

The level of detail in the topics of the individual panels at the SIFFORUM has increased substantially over the years, demonstrating the growing level of sophistication in Sino-US media production deals. For example, in 2004, SIFF titled the one panel on international cooperation with Chinese filmmakers "Diversified Cooperation of Chinese Film Industry and Global

Figure 12. Michael Ellis, managing director of the Asia-Pacific Region for the Motion Picture Association, speaking at the SIFFORUM. (Photo by Aynne Kokas, Shanghai, PRC, June 16, 2013)

Development."[19] Rather than addressing general principles of "global development," as in 2004, the panels in 2014 covered more nuanced areas of concern for industry leaders, as well as future collaborations in production, financing, and distribution. Specific panel topics included "The Future of Co-Production," "Finance Films with Domestic and International Resources," "Selling Chinese Films Internationally and Innovatively," and "China Films, World Opportunities."[20] Although the forum's organization placed the Chinese media industries in dialogue with foreign partners, the SIFFORUM panel entitled "Chinese Stories VS Hollywood" also suggested the tensions in the growth of transnational industrial collaboration.[21]

By 2016, multiple industry forums were operating under the SIFF, dwarfing the lone panel offered in 2004. Beginning in 2013, entertainment

Figure 13. Speakers from Australia, China, Singapore, and the United States at the SIFFORUM. (Photo by Aynne Kokas, Shanghai, PRC, June 16, 2013)

finance conference production firm Winston Baker partnered with the SIFF to host a separate industry forum on the challenges and opportunities involved in financing Chinese films.[22] The first stand-alone film finance forum that operated in conjunction with the full 2013 SIFFORUM had global co-executive hosts that included representatives from multiple international entertainment law firms and the Motion Picture Association.[23] As a result, the forum served as a rapid way for potential co-production partners to meet and negotiate new deals. Such forums therefore offer an early-stage intersection of potential industry partners in the genesis of new Sino-US media collaborations. Both forums take a much more granular approach to industrial collaboration between Chinese and US filmmakers than was seen in earlier years by, for example, including whole sessions catering to specific industry developments, such as Chinese investment in Hollywood films and Hollywood-produced films in the PRC.[24]

The SIFFORUM and related events offer industry observers a way to monitor the changing transnational Sino-US production culture. Examining the history of forums helps clarify who the key players have been in the genesis of Sino-US filmmaking. Although the forums' exact outcomes are typically opaque, participant rosters offer valuable insight into which people have been shaping the strategic narratives of Sino-US media collaboration. The history of the forums reveals how Sino-US collaboration has changed between 2004, when China's growth as a global media market was largely hypothetical, and the present day, when the Chinese market is a major global powerhouse.

The SIFFORUM, US-China Film Summit, and other Sino-US industry events offer a vantage point from which to examine the growth of the transnational Chinese media industries because they bring stakeholders together to learn about and discuss every significant aspect of the collaboration process, from development, to production, to distribution, to journalism and research. Operating in tandem with generalized industry forums is a series of more narrowly focused film-pitch forums, where individual filmmakers look for film financing while promoting themselves as global filmmakers in China. Though there is less discussion of the growth of the industry as a whole in more specialized pitch forums, the genesis myths of industrial collaboration come together through discussions of the process of making specific films.

FILM PITCH AND CATCH FORUMS

The China Film Pitch and Catch (CFPC) forum—the first of its kind in China—introduced Chinese filmmakers to the practice of Western pitch sessions in a formalized film-industry environment. The forum, quite literally, relies on mini-narratives—otherwise known as "pitches"—about how a film might succeed in the Chinese market. Filmmakers deliver the pitches to financiers in order to secure funding. This type of practical intervention results in a forum that socializes Chinese and Western filmmakers to interact with one another in direct, project-based contexts. By extension, these interactions shape the practices of China's global collaborations with foreign film workers.

Whereas the industry figures at the SIFFORUM narrate Sino-US media collaboration writ large, participants in the CFPC forum pitch potential film projects to investors. Hosting a pitch forum in Hollywood is an attempt to define industry standards.[25] By hosting a pitch forum in Shanghai, the SIFF defined standards, even though pitch forums are an imported type of event.

Cindy Mi Lin, a film producer and the CEO of Beijing-based film production, import, and export company Infotainment China, started the CFPC forum as a way to connect new domestic projects—including her own—with foreign investors.[26] Lin offered pitch training sessions for Chinese filmmakers and investors during the first CFPC in 2006.[27] As the pitch coach, or the person who teaches others how to tell their story, Lin became an arbiter between China and Hollywood while also gathering insights from both groups.

Scholars have expressed an understandable skepticism about how truly international pitch forums such as the CFPC really are.[28] But what is significant about the international pitch sessions—and, in particular, Lin's trainings—is the way the international pitches, while drawing from Western practices, still take place at a Chinese state-run film festival. Thus, regardless of the outcome of an individual pitch forum, having a Chinese coach at the Shanghai International Film Festival guide the international deals represents a significant change in the PRC's aspirations to influence global media. Despite the difficulty in measuring the CFPC's role in the growth of cultural exchange through filmmaking, it is clearly tied to an increase in the marketing of China as a global destination for film production.

The CFPC forum produced enough funded projects for Lin that she transfered responsibility for the event over to the SIFF in 2007. SIFF added the Co-Production Film Pitch Forum (Co-FPC) the same year. Both forums were then integrated into a larger pitch forum called SIFF Project in 2011. The language and practice of a pitch forum—previously absent from even Chinese film co-production development—made its way into the bureaucracy of a state-owned enterprise—in this case, the SIFF, a subsidiary of the Shanghai Media and Entertainment Group. International pitch forums circulate the inchoate narratives of film co-production. Such forums exist as part of festivals all over the globe, but the the growth of international pitch forums in China shows that small steps can lead to major shifts in the branding of a country as a production site.

CHINESE INDUSTRY FORUMS AROUND THE WORLD

Chinese industry forums have become more prevalent as China's film market has grown. While the SIFFORUM and the US-China Film Summit welcome some of the biggest global power players as participants, the process of "soft" standardization of industrial practices extends into

European and East Asian markets as well. Unlike events hosted in the PRC or the United States, industry forums in Europe and other parts of East Asia operate as neutral meeting grounds, where neither China- nor United States–based producers act as hosts. The forums also connect with major international film festivals where collaborators can meet in person, and the everyday demands of production are more limited.

In Europe, Germany's Berlin International Film Festival (International Filmfestspiele Berlin) hosts a co-production market for filmmakers. The festival offers speed-matching events as well as tables hosted by representatives from individual countries. After her success with the CFPC in Shanghai, Cindy Lin created a similar event for Chinese filmmakers at the Berlin International Film Festival in 2009, and Berlin continues to be heavily involved with Chinese filmmakers.[29] The China Film Group Corporation also hosts an annual Chinese Film Week in the city of Berlin, expanding awareness of the global reach of Chinese cinema in Germany outside the festival circuit.[30] Though the intersection of China and Hollywood may be the most financially lucrative, other global markets are paying close attention to how they build their own filmmaking brands in relation to that of China—often in conjunction with Chinese state-branding enterprises.

In East Asia, both the Busan International Film Festival (BIFF) in Korea and ScreenSingapore have begun incorporating China-focused events into their industry forums.[31] These events circulate strategic narratives about the growing global profile of the Chinese film industry in Asia. The forum at the Busan International Film Festival, in particular, demonstrates how PRC government sources support the rising profile of the Chinese film industry globally.

Busan is a small seaside town known primarily for its *huit chip* (raw seafood restaurants), but each October, it hosts the BIFF, which is the premier film festival for developing East Asian screen talent within East Asia and a major Asian film festival destination for global filmmakers interested in Asian cinema.[32] As the BIFF has grown, Korea has become a major source of talent and financing for global Chinese productions, supporting the growing Chinese industry via both talent and technology.[33] In 2013, the BIFF held a three-day forum adjacent to the festival, half of which dealt directly with the Chinese film industry. The China-focused panels covered seemingly noncommercial topics such as "The

Secret History of Chinese Independent Cinema" and the theoretical-sounding "Chinese Film and Humanism Spectrum." However, the opening session of the forum belied the public diplomacy mission of some parts of the event; the Confucius Institute at Busan's Dongseo University was the sponsor. Global Confucius Institutes are Chinese government–funded entities with specific content mandates from the Chinese Communist Party.[34] The Confucius Institute's sponsorship links the BIFF forum closely with larger-scale cultural-diplomacy policy efforts in the PRC's public sector, as well as with the strong emphasis on growing China's global media industries in contemporary Chinese cultural policy. Whereas the Asia Society's forums primarily feature industry representation, with one panel devoted to academic and nongovernmental organization perspectives, the BIFF forum reveals the role research and the public sector play in facilitating new global Chinese collaborations at industry forums outside both China and Hollywood.

Far away from the lights of Hollywood, Shanghai, Berlin, and Busan, smaller festivals and events both draw from and contribute to the growing cultural practices of film promotion in East Asia. In the cold reaches of the northern Baltic, a seemingly unlikely place to publicize Asian film collaborations, Estonia's Tallinn Black Nights Film Festival lacks the international luster of Cannes. However, by documenting its industry forums and posting the videos on YouTube, the festival offers additional resources for filmmakers clamoring to expand their reach into East Asia but unsure how to proceed.[35] The videos reveal that attendance at the forums is limited and funding opportunities are smaller in range and budget than those at the US-China Film Summit. But the Tallinn event extends the scope of this global industrial phenomenon while contributing to the larger corpus of stories the industry tells itself about what the growth of global Asian media production looks like.[36]

Festivals such as the Tallinn Black Nights Film Festival may not have the same physical audiences as larger festivals. However, they can still influence the process by raising the topic of industry collaborations and documenting and circulating archives in which filmmakers and policymakers share their film-production experiences. These smaller festivals thereby contribute to the strategic narratives guiding international production with Chinese companies. Media industry forums located outside the United States and the PRC reveal additional nuances in the strategic narratives about global media production in China.

INDIVIDUAL FILM-PROMOTION EVENTS

Although the annual nature of industry forums offers continuity, filmmakers also strategically disclose parts of their Sino-US production process at other publicly visible, industry-focused occasions. Whereas industry forums focus entirely on the "behind-the-scenes" perspective of production, other types of production events—namely, those surrounding individual film releases—are much more public facing. Film-release events for transnational films demonstrate how the Sino-US collaboration process forms the foundation for future joint ventures.

At the event celebrating the relationship between Beijing-based DMG Entertainment and the Walt Disney Company for the film *Iron Man 3*, DMG CEO Dan Mintz publicly lauded his Chinese partners while repeatedly referencing his desire to work with them again.[37] Industry insiders populated the event, which, based on videos released, appeared to host fewer than one hundred people.[38] The reason for the celebration was corporate—a production agreement between two studios. However, even this event was outward facing. The event video, despite being hosted on the film and media industry site Aipai.com, used footage from the major Chinese entertainment website Sina.com.[39] The publicly available video not only showed the business partners appearing together in public but also had the hallmarks of a celebrity gossip show, with extended close-ups on jewelry and nail art, as well as images of celebrities gossiping with one another in the audience. It publicized deal making between the Beijing-based company and Disney as a business move, while offering juicy images of the entertainment industry for consumption by viewers. In this sense, the individual film-based media events facilitate the creation of strategic narratives by and for decision makers (or future decision makers), while reinforcing a transnational celebrity system in which Chinese stars can achieve fame within a global context.

Like individual film events, red-carpet photo calls also identify Sino-US collaboration through publicly visible, industry-oriented events. Red-carpet events, while not explicitly industry forums, bring high-level figures from the Chinese media industries into dialogue with others in the global media industries. Chinese stars now walk the famous red carpets at Cannes and in Venice, Italy, thereby solidifying their positions as global brands.[40] The visibility of Chinese stars at international red carpets is only part of the role that these events play in circulating strategic narratives about the relationship between China and Hollywood. For example, at the 2006 SIFF, Academy Award winning–director Ang Lee both walked the red carpet and was invited by the state-run Shanghai Media and Entertainment Group to shoot his next film (which became the erotic spy thriller *Lust, Caution*) at the Shanghai Film Studios. Red-carpet events publicize relationships between Hollywood players and Chinese production groups through these moments of co-branding.

Lee is not the only above-the-line talent to have walked the red carpet at SIFF in relation to a production deal. American actor John Cusack did so with his Chinese costar Gong Li at the thirteenth annual SIFF in 2010, after the reinstatement of co-production and distribution approval for their film *Shanghai* (dir. Mikael Håfström 2010), produced by the Weinstein Company.[41] Significantly, for both *Lust, Caution* and *Shanghai,* the presence of these transnational media stars on the red carpet was linked to domestic regulatory approval. While red-carpet events promote individual films, in the case of the SIFF, they also present a façade of seamless collaboration between partners based in China and Hollywood, whether or not this is actually the case.

The red carpet in Shanghai is not merely a star-studded celebrity showcase but also a space in which firms and regulators visually manifest Sino-US production practice. In the case of the SIFF red carpet, John Cusack and Ang Lee physically represented production deals, either already completed or about to begin. Like individual film-deal events that are recorded for distribution online, the production process is on display for consumers and industry watchers eager to understand what the growth of the Chinese film industry means for Hollywood, and vice versa.

While industry forums and film-release events speak directly to film-industry professionals and fans who are interested in learning more about how to make movies in China, municipal governments in China also circulate strategic narratives as a way to attract FDI. Shanghai's municipal government has actively promoted the city as a media destination through urban media-branding events like the 2010 World Expo.[42] Municipal government officials are actively engaged in building strategic narratives as part of their work promoting the city. For example, on June 6, 2013, when I interviewed Ren Xiaowen, the director of the Shanghai City Government News and Public Affairs Research Bureau, he asked me what strategies I, as a foreign researcher, would recommend for drawing media-production investment to Shanghai to increase representation of the city to foreign media markets. As part of our meeting, he outlined the strategies the Shanghai city government was using to expand awareness of Shanghai as a global destination for the media industries. These projects included the growth of Oriental DreamWorks and of the Shanghai Disney Resort (both discussed at length in other chapters of this book). When I asked about the propaganda (*xuanchuan*) function of the office that had been described to me by my colleagues at the Shanghai Institutes for International Studies, Ren Xiaowen politely told me that they had changed the focus of the office from propaganda to public relations (*gonggong guanxi*) in 2011.[43] The public affairs department even renamed its mission in order to align with global-branding norms, demonstrating a keen awareness of the importance of presentation in attracting FDI. The city of Shanghai stands as a particularly interesting case, in that co-production-promotion activities overlap with general trade-promotion activities there. Media branding increases the city's international profile as a place to conduct business— and, by extension, to produce more international media content. These robust citywide branding practices promote strategic narratives about global media collaboration in China.

CONCLUSION

Forums and related activities are creating and circulating new strategic narratives, guided by Hollywood shareholders' demand for increasing global market share, the Chinese government's policies, and the influx of private capital in the Chinese media industries. What has emerged are strategic narratives circulated at events in which above-the-line media workers—along with regulators, lobbyists, academics, journalists, and

Table 3 Industry Forums

Forum Type	Industrial Sectors Speaking	Additional Industrial Sectors in Live Audience	Project vs. Industry Orientation	Participant Mix
Festival adjacent	C-level executives, lawyers, private equity investors, directors, production managers, agents, producers, executive producers, online distribution partners, distribution partners, journalists, academics, regulators, lobbyists	Talent, journalists, academics	Industry orientation	Global
Festival sponsored	C-level executives, lawyers, private equity investors, directors, production managers, agents, producers, executive producers, online distribution partners, distribution partners, journalists, public affairs bureaucrats, regulators	Journalists, academics	Industry orientation	Global
Global production sponsored	Executive producers	Talent	Project orientation	Local
Pitch forum	Producers, directors, agents, private equity	Jury, festival selection of industry figures	Project orientation	Global
Red carpet	Talent, producers	Fans	Project orientation	Global
City sponsored	Representatives from city promotion bureau, Ministry of Public Affairs	Consumers	Industry orientation	Local

professionals in private equity and law—come together to assess the changing nature of China's global media production relationship with Hollywood. Table 3 provides a taxonomy of the types of forums outlined in this chapter that focus on generating Sino-US industrial connections. The table also outlines whether the event in question is oriented toward building a broader industry or focuses instead on a specific project. Finally, the table shows that industry-building events have either a primarily global or primarily local participant mix. Industry forums are proliferating, and these events present a dynamic area of inquiry as the strategic narratives of Sino-US collaboration evolve.

The expansion of the Sino-US media industries entails a concerted effort across multiple time zones and a broad range of iterative events designed to advance both the Hollywood dream factory and the Chinese Dream. Industry forum activities reinforce China's maturation as a site of global media production. Through structured industry dialogue between private production companies, policymakers, and state-owned production groups, forums simultaneously create and institutionalize the language and practice of Sino-US media production in the PRC. Industry development events have a long-term effect on China's growth as a global film-making brand in relation to Hollywood.

With their built-in population of industry executives, forums offer a crucial avenue through which Sino-US media industries can grow. Forums host a large number of high-level film workers and eager industry spectators poised to examine new income-opportunity trends in the industry. The promotion of norms of collaboration both establishes industry standards and sets the tone for future collaborations.

Industry forums and related public events of self-definition create and circulate strategic narratives used to negotiate the terms of the global media industries. And, indeed, much like the construction of theme parks in China, strategic narratives circulated at forums are a type of branding. Thus, both the process and the product of Hollywood-China collaboration are beholden to a Sisyphean cycle of public relations and self-definition. To witness this dramatic industrial coming-of-age story, consumers of media should shift their attention away from the red carpet, toward the conference rooms and catered lunches, in order to witness a global media industry in transition.

5 Compradors

HOW ABOVE-THE-LINE WORKERS BRAND
SINO-US FILM PRODUCTION

While forums offer a way to see industry-wide changes in China-Hollywood relations, above-the-line workers on Sino-US film co-productions reveal the complex cultural, economic, and geographic structure of Hollywood's changing relationship with China through their work promoting individual productions. Above-the-line players—a film's director, producers, writers, and lead actors—complicate the idea of a spatial or national understanding of the media industries. They need only be connected to the process and their peers—not a particular location, nation, or even source of capital. Media collaborations rely on these individuals to negotiate between international stakeholders in joint productions. The complex demands placed on above-the-line workers who navigate between Chinese and American cultures of industrial production help us better appreciate the importance of their cultural labor in terms of the growth of the Chinese film industry and Hollywood. This chapter explores how above-the-line workers frame Sino-US film collaboration for other media practitioners, members of the press, and global audiences using the case of Ang Lee's seminal 2007 co-production *Lust, Caution,* a pioneering Sino-US co-production.

According to sociologist Pierre Bourdieu, occupations involving presentation and representation—particularly those involving high cultural capital—constitute the work of the cultural intermediary.[1] Scholars have characterized cultural intermediaries as individuals who, beyond producing goods and services, convey values ascribed to particular products through the process of distribution.[2] Sociologist Mike Featherstone, and media scholars Sean Nixon and Joanne Entwistle, among others, have extended Bourdieu's work to a broad range of culture industries.[3] The term "cultural intermediary" most frequently refers to brokers of taste or of an aesthetic, usually within a specific national context.[4]

But the term has its limitations. Media studies scholar David Hesmondhalgh suggests that the concept of a "cultural intermediary," although useful, can be excessively general, overwriting the nuances of different types of cultural production activity.[5] This is very much the case when considering the differences between Sino-US co-ventures and other, more common international collaborations with Hollywood studios. Cultural intermediaries working between the United States and Canada must navigate the differences between the communities of film workers in Vancouver and Los Angeles, among others, as well as geographic borders and public-private media partnerships, even though they may be located on the same coast and speak the same language.[6] The cultural, linguistic, regulatory, and geographic challenges involved in Sino-US collaborations are substantially greater. Collaboration with privately owned US production companies can create a cultural challenge for both Chinese film producers, many of whom were trained in the state-run system, and US filmmakers unaccustomed to working with government partners. But the role of the cultural intermediary expands in Sino-US collaborations because of the particularly relationship-dependent nature of media production in the PRC. Issues of language and the complexity of arranging Chinese visas for American workers and US visas for Chinese workers further complicate the process. To that end, this chapter asserts the need for a specific set of terms addressing the role of above-the-line workers in the media production process between the United States and China.

THE LATTER-DAY COMPRADOR

As a way of deepening the discussion of the cultural intermediary in Sino-US film collaboration, this chapter proposes a reinscription of the late Qing-period term "comprador" (*maiban*), a term for economic intermediaries referring to the Portuguese traders who settled in Macau.[7] The term's origins within the Sino-international trade arena make it uniquely suited to a discussion of film collaboration between the PRC and the United States. US Commercial Attaché to China Julean Arnold wrote about the term in the introduction to the 1920 edition of the United States Bureau of Foreign and Domestic Commerce's *Commercial Handbook of China*.[8] I would like to resurrect this usage of the term in reference to Sino-foreign engagement with indebtedness to work by media critic and sociologist Herbert Schiller and communications scholar Dallas Smythe on the political economy of media. Schiller's characterization of comprador activity underscores the unidirectional cultural imperialism of American media systems.[9] Smythe's characterization of the comprador refers to "that sector (or fraction) of capital within the colony that prefers policies within the colony that favor foreign capital over the interests of population and resources within the colony."[10] By contrast, Chinese compradors of the late Qing period formed the foundation for "a golden age in an emerging metropolitan landscape of treaty ports and coastal cities."[11] In other words, as in the present day, late Qing Chinese compradors were cosmopolitan power brokers in their own right.

The term "comprador" has already developed traction in discussions of economic activity in contemporary China by thinkers of the New Left as a way to critique the growing influence of commercial activity on culture. Renowned leftist scholar Dai Jinhua describes how more contemporary compradors enhance class divisions in the PRC.[12] After all, the term has been central to debates regarding capitalism and economic growth in contemporary Chinese commercial life. Combining the late Qing usage and the contemporary usage of the term yields a meaning that encompasses economically driven class distinctions and cross-cultural collaborations. Present-day film compradors are perpetually suspended between financial motivations and the creation of new channels for cultural dialogue, and these two contexts exist concurrently. The tension between economic gain and cultural cooperation is what makes this categorization so essential to understand.

Contemporary compradors in the Chinese film industry leverage capital for gains in China, as well as for the interests of Hollywood media conglomerates. Government pressures to expand China's brand appear in everything from the advancement of the culture industries in the twelfth five-year plan to the rebranding of city propaganda (*xuanchuan*) bureaus as public relations (*gonggong guanxi*) bureaus, to Xi Jinping's Chinese Dream, which supports Chinese domestic media development policies.[13] A reinscription of the historical meaning of "comprador" suggests the value of the role for not just foreign partners but also the home country. Compradors reduce the enormous gap between these two differing worlds of film production, and, in the process, they connect the large and fragmented industrial cultures on either side of the Pacific. Compradors facilitate not just the transnational development of cultures of visual media production, but also the process of cultivating a broader understanding among audiences of transnational media-production practice. While brokering deals, they bridge cultural differences. This chapter focuses on compradors who have visible roles in the film-collaboration process—a film's producers, stars, director, and other key production players—to reveal ways in which such above-the-line workers act as brokers and translators of culture.

THE COMPRADOR: OVERARCHING CHALLENGES

Compradors translate the cultural-linguistic differences between Chinese and American production contexts at the highest levels—language being the most obvious. English speakers must contend with the differences between Hong Kong's British linguistic influence, as well as among American, Australian, New Zealand, and Singaporean English. Within the PRC, Hong Kongers are often native speakers of Cantonese, Beijingers prefer *putonghua* (standard Mandarin), and Shanghainese often opt to speak the Shanghai dialect—and these are just the main dialects spoken in Chinese media capitals. Although above-the-line compradors are less involved with daily interactions among crew members, they must be aware of and sensitive to cultural and linguistic distinctions to nurture a cohesive culture of production on set. Psychologist Sara Rubenfeld and colleagues demonstrate that individuals who are able to work across multiple linguistic contexts are more effective at supporting antidiscrimination efforts between groups.[14] Thus, knowing how to navigate issues of language preference among speakers of Mandarin, Cantonese, Shanghainese, and other dialects is a particularly helpful trait for above-the-line workers in the production process.

In addition to meeting the linguistic challenges posed by polyglot crews, the comprador must be able to navigate the different cultural expectations for the film-collaboration process—expectations grounded in the unique filmmaking cultures of Hollywood and China. For example, Chinese film crew members report that most American film crew members expect much more time between takes and more lavish craft services.[15] American film crew members report that Chinese crew members are comfortable taking greater physical risks during filmmaking, such as not wearing protective gear during demanding physical tasks.[16] These perceptions support competing expectations that may become apparent only in the midst of the filmmaking process. Such differences have the potential to affect the economic calculus of film collaboration. The disparate industrial cultures of filmmaking in China and Hollywood require the comprador to broker relationships among multiple distinct industrial cultures inflected by dissimilarities in language, local cultural norms, and economic systems.

The expectations of deal making in the Sino-US production context force negotiation between different industrial cultures to negotiate to produce a film. Compradors in Sino-US film collaborations manage not only the expectations film workers have based on their own experiences, but also their expectations of what the *other* group of workers will demand. One example of a cultural conflict that can arise from divergent expectations is grounded in the economics of film collaboration. American production companies often seek film-collaboration opportunities in the PRC because of the financial advantages of shooting there—an advantage that exists in part because of lower (but rising) labor costs.[17] China's film industry does not have the same type of union protections that the United States does, which keeps labor costs comparatively low.[18] For their part, film workers with the major Chinese film groups are both highly aware of and ambivalent about the cost advantage film collaborations offer foreign filmmakers.[19] Thus, successful negotiations demand sensitivity to the economic expectations of trading partners throughout the production process.

WHY *LUST, CAUTION?*

Lust, Caution was one of the first post-WTO Sino-US film co-productions to move through the process from preproduction through distribution. The film combined a Taiwan-born, US-trained director, Chinese- and English-language screenwriters, and a team of producers from the United States and Hong Kong, as well as Chinese government production partners. The film's diverse range of leadership offers an excellent case for demonstrating the role of above-the-line compradors in creating Sino-US media. The Ang Lee vehicle is one of few Sino-US film collaborations created by individuals that have worked consistently and successfully both in the Greater China region and in the United States. Audiences in both places were already familiar with director Ang Lee's work prior to the film's release. As a result, his team had less work to do in terms of building awareness of the film's director and could instead focus on bridging cross-cultural gaps in understanding related to the film's narrative and production process.

In addition to Lee, all key parties involved in the production of *Lust, Caution* had extensive experience navigating between Asian and American cultural contexts. The late author of the film's narrative source material, iconic Chinese American figure Eileen Chang (Zhang Ailing), moved between the Chinese mainland, Hong Kong, and the United States throughout her life.[20] James Schamus, an American producer with significant Asia experience prior to *Lust, Caution*, produced and adapted the story for the screen. Schamus and his longtime writing partner, Taiwanese screenwriter Wang Hui-ling, collaborated on the writing process. Together, Schamus and Wang worked to structure a new narrative that attended to both US and Chinese cultural sensibilities. Thus, the script's development was a practice of transnational negotiation. In producing, directing, and screenwriting, the team behind *Lust, Caution* had a deep sensitivity to the cross-cultural issues involved in the creation and distribution of a Sino-US co-production. The following sections break down the roles played by key above-the-line figures in advancing Sino-US media trade as part of their work with *Lust, Caution*.

ANG LEE: DIRECTOR AS COMPRADOR

Directors in Sino-US collaborations influence media co-ventures between China and the United States. Beyond their creative role in the production process, one key activity is negotiating with public-sector stakeholders in film production. Ang Lee participated in the SIFF while conducting negotiations between Ren Zhonglun, the president of the state-run Shanghai Film Group, and Lee's production company for *Lust, Caution*.[21] The close relationship between the director and Ren, a high-level player not just in the Chinese film industry but also in the Chinese government, reveals the importance for compradors of working with private-sector and government stakeholders in the film-collaboration process. Lee also established an industrial precedent with regard to collaboration between Chinese government and American private-sector media funding.

The work of directors as compradors extends beyond how they interact with major figures in the film-collaboration process to how news of those interactions circulates. Information about the meetings between Ren and Lee emerged as part of the "making-of" text about *Lust, Caution*, a book bringing together the work of James Schamus, Wang Hui-ling, and Eileen Chang to promote the Sino-US collaboration.[22] *Lust, Caution: The Story, the Screenplay, and the Making of the Film* not only describes Ren's meeting with Lee, but also guides readers through the experience of film production in China.[23] Ultimately, it articulates how Lee negotiated the terms of his presence at a public industry event with Ren (though negotiations did not take place *in* public), and this story was transmitted to American audiences through texts authored by the production team. Thus, the mediation between cultures took place on three levels: between Lee and the Chinese public at the SIFF, between Lee and Ren, and via the portrayal to the American public of Lee and Ren's relationship in this behind-the-scenes text.

Interviews with directors like Lee also helped shape the discourse of collaboration. In an interview during his publicity tour for *Lust, Caution,* Ang
Lee asserted a framework for collaboration between Hollywood and Asia.
Of the future role of Sino-US collaboration, the director argued, "Hollywood
is not just made for America. It's foreign. Like the whole Hong Kong film
industry is meant to be seen by Taiwan and Southeast Asia, not just locally
by Hong Kong. . . . I'm trying to pull the audience Eastbound. . . . But only
the big directors can do that. Some are more successful, some are not. I
cannot say this is an entirely good model, but it's a move forward because
the film industry needs to be big and China has the potential of a big market."[24] Beyond marketing his own film, Lee asserted a vision of Hollywood's
"foreign" essence, paying particular attention to what this means for the
importance of China in Hollywood. Thus, the work of compradors in
Sino-US film collaboration extends beyond marketing just the *film* to spectators to marketing the *process of making the film* to spectators.

In addition to the filmmaking process, Lee also played an important
role in "translating" the importance of the film's Chinese stars for foreign
audiences. A barrier to Lee's work—cross-cultural recognition of stardom—is visible in marketing materials such as the film's publicity documents. For example, the *Lust, Caution* press kit re-created an Asian "star
system"—what creative industries scholar Paul McDonald terms "the
mechanisms for the production of popular identities."[25] Three actors
stand out in the press kit: female protagonist and then newcomer Tang
Wei, Asian movie star Tony Leung, and crossover music industry star
Wang Leehom. The press kit identified the pedigree of each of these individuals within the Chinese star system and translated that pedigree into a
corresponding archetype of Hollywood fame: Tang is a "rising star," Leung
is an "icon," and Wang is a "pop music idol."[26] The interview with Tang
included in the press kit is titled simply "Who Is Tang Wei?," underscoring
her ingénue status. By contrast, as part of the production's publicity
efforts, the biography of Shanghai-born actress Joan Chen—already
known in the United States for her roles on the American television series
Twin Peaks and in Oliver Stone's film *Heaven and Earth* (1993), among
others—lists only her filmography and does not articulate a Hollywood
archetype for her. Translating the star status of Asian actors thus became

part of the filmmakers' English-language marketing discourse in anticipation of ignorant or indifferent press reception for these stars.

Rather than introducing the actors on their own terms as part of the film, Lee translated preexisting models of stardom into the American context to counteract perceived ignorance about Chinese "stars" in American media. In interviews, the director reconstructed the mechanisms of stardom surrounding newcomer Tang and icon Leung. Lee repeatedly informed interviewers that he considered ten thousand candidates before choosing Tang because he felt that she had a special "old-fashioned Chinese look."[27] Of Leung, Lee said that he had "never seen anyone play a traitor so well in Chinese film history."[28] In later interviews for the British market, Lee further explained Tang and Leung's stardom. Of ingénue Tang, he stated, "It feels like fate brought us together," but he said that he "went after [Leung] because he's [Chinese cinema's] best actor."[29] Marketing *Lust, Caution* required Lee to translate standards of stardom across cultural contexts. Yet disseminating information about the Greater China region's star system also required articulating ideals of stardom itself. Thus, the process not only transmits ideals of stardom, but also often constricts the identity of highly versatile actors in the service of foreign spectators. While the director's role in framing his cast has the potential to expand each actor's global name recognition, the process also artificially narrows their perceived range.

When internationally renowned directors like Ang Lee speak about their production work, they have an impact. Their experience allows them to speak as authorities. Lee can publicize industrial practices, encourage new standards of collaboration, and introduce foreign talent to international audiences in his role as a comprador. But just as these industrial processes are often broken down for the public into small sound bites or publicity materials, so can much of the complexity of Sino-US industrial relations be lost in translation.

DAVID LEE: PRODUCER AS COMPRADOR

Like Ang Lee, *Lust, Caution* producer David Lee shaped Sino-US media trade through his involvement with the film. David Lee's commentary on the film-collaboration process structures the discourse about collaboration and the compradors' place within it. In an essay in *Lust, Caution: The Story, the Screenplay, and the Making of the Film,* David Lee discusses the process through which the then head of the Shanghai Media and Entertainment Group offered the full support of Shanghai Film Studios, including doubling or tripling the studio's official workforce, after Ang Lee accepted his invitation to attend the SIFF.[30] David Lee's revelation in his essay of Ang Lee's particular relationship with the SIFF expanded public understanding of the co-production process. Ang Lee's actions as a director established an important precedent, but David Lee's essay promoted the event to the public. Like the Sino-US industry forums, David Lee's essay on co-production in China was a marketing tool. David Lee's role as a facilitator of Sino-US co-production deals positioned him as a storyteller both within the filmmaking process and about the filmmaking process.

JAMES SCHAMUS: SCREENWRITER AS COMPRADOR

James Schamus, executive producer and screenwriter of *Lust, Caution,* acted as a comprador in the co-production process. Although Schamus was also the film's executive producer, this chapter explores his role in the writing and translation of the movie's script in conjunction with his work promoting the film. Screenwriters of co-produced films are in a unique position to broker the cultural demands of two markets. Schamus began his work as a screenwriter on *Lust, Caution* after Ang Lee and Wang Hui-ling had reached an impasse in the development of the film's screenplay, which had been in the works for several years. When Schamus came on board, the two were struggling with the adaptation process. Schamus agreed to sign on as a screenwriter with the caveat that he must be allowed to freely make adjustments to the text. One of the challenges the co-production team faced in the transnational adaptation process was the cultural importance of the works of Eileen Chang in contemporary Chinese literature. Whereas Ang Lee and Wang Hui-ling had been brought up in Chinese-language contexts that viewed Chang's work with a cult-like affinity, Schamus came to the material with fresh eyes. By approaching the script of *Lust, Caution* from a different cultural view-point, Schamus was able to infuse a fresh international perspective into the work of a canonized Chinese-language author, thereby shaping a new generation's perspective on the original novella. Schamus emphasized the development of the internal psychology of the main character, Wang Jiazhi, beyond what was present in Chang's novella, and he adjusted the script to provide more of a three-act structure. These changes to the narrative incorporated Euro-American storytelling traditions while also making the film a more saleable cultural product for global markets.[31]

Schamus's role in managing the combined economic and cultural aspects of the film also extended to language translation, highlighting how the use of language shapes the relative "foreignness" of a film.[32] Schamus took an active role in the film's English-language subtitling and also supervised translation of the French subtitles.[33] While Schamus's ability to oversee the film's subtitles was due to his aptitude as a writer, his rationale for spending time on them reflects the perspective of a producer: by providing highly edited subtitles in two Western languages, he maximized access to the Chinese-language film in non-Chinese-speaking markets. With both English and French subtitles available from the production team, groups distributing the film into markets for other languages had the resources to triangulate their subtitle translations, thereby making them more accurate for audiences. However, the fact that the film's executive producer was involved in overseeing the film's subtitles draws attention to the complex cross-cultural translation activity demanded by the Sino-US filmmaking process.

Schamus's translation contributions also underscore the financial imperative connected to the practice of cultural exchange in the film-collaboration process. In describing his linguistic labor for the production of *Lust, Caution*, Schamus noted how paying special attention to details, such as adapting a narrative and translating subtitles, can help expand the reach of film collaborations.[34] Schamus was at the forefront of the practice of film collaboration in terms of his sensitivity to the cultural implications of the film co-production process. His work offers a template for collaboration as Sino-US co-ventures become more widespread.

BILL KONG: DEALMAKER AS COMPRADOR

Much of the work of the compradors on *Lust, Caution* involved bridging the cultural gaps between economic cultures. The ability to navigate multiple cultural contexts to get a film green-lighted is essential in the film-collaboration process. An excellent example of the cultural understanding transmitted through the deal-making process can be seen in the role played by *Lust, Caution*'s producer Bill Kong. A key player in the film-collaboration process for the Ang Lee blockbuster *Crouching Tiger, Hidden Dragon*, Kong was also instrumental in securing shooting privileges for *Lust, Caution* on the ground in Shanghai.[35]

Kong's role as a comprador in the Sino-US co-production process relied on his ability to navigate cultural, financial, and policy challenges to facilitate the film's production. Permission to shoot *Lust, Caution* in Shanghai was by no means guaranteed.[36] In fact, because of tensions between the PRC and Japan in 2006 and 2007, the material about Sino-Japanese relations in the film's narrative was particularly sensitive. However, Kong combined his understanding of the filmmaking process with his awareness of the cast and crew's multiple culturo-linguistic contexts—American, mainland Chinese, Hong Kong—to help make the film's production and distribution on mainland Chinese screens possible. In addition to being involved with the financial aspects of the production, Kong helped open up important new frontiers within the larger context of filmmaking in China. The introduction of co-produced content tested the boundaries of the representation of twentieth-century Chinese history on mainland screens in a way that probably would not have otherwise occurred on a domestic film production. New renovations to the Nanjing West Road set at the Shanghai Film Studios for *Lust, Caution* were part of attempts to court international investment in the Chinese filmmaking process.[37] (See figures 16–21 in chapter 6 for images of the Shanghai Film Studios.) Kong repaid the support by endorsing China as a filmmaking destination. The Focus Features publicity kit quoted Kong praising the Chinese government's "openness" and "dedication" to the project: "Over the past several years, China has become more friendly to filmmakers and more open to the world than it once was." Kong facilitated the film's production in mainland China while simultaneously asserting China's value as an international production space for Hollywood at a time of industrial transition.

ZHANG XUN: REGULATOR AS COMPRADOR

Although the notion of Chinese government regulators may seem irreconcilable with that of capitalist compradors, this chapter argues that state-owned corporations charged with both regulation and investment promotion play a vital role in Sino-US film collaborations. Zhang Xun, former general manager of the CFCC, was one regulator who played the role of regulator as comprador. The CFCC is a state-owned enterprise charged with the facilitation of film collaborations in the PRC. During the production of *Lust, Caution,* Zhang guided Chinese government funds into specific projects and was involved in the content regulation of film collaborations. Thus, her role was a peculiar combination of promoting international investment and regulating international content.

Zhang's work as a regulator positioned her as an arbiter of collaborative creative production between China and Hollywood. Her duties encompassed three major functions. First, she identified potential projects for co-production based on requests from foreign producers. As part of this process, she assessed whether a film would be feasible as a co-production based on broad strokes of genre. For example, family films offer promising possibilities because of their inherently wholesome content. The internationally popular horror genre, in contrast, encompasses a broad range of content potentially objectionable to SAPPRFT regulators, ranging from violence to supernatural themes. Second, she assessed the particulars of a given film. The CFCC requires film producers to submit everything from script drafts to story synopses before co-production approval is granted. At any point during this content assessment, the CFCC can ask filmmakers to change the film to meet content requirements. Third, Zhang maintained regulatory authority over the filmmaking process throughout the production of the film. Filmmakers in co-productions must be willing to update the CFCC throughout the filmmaking process about any changes in content. This continuous dialogue gave Zhang significant power in regulating the type of cross-cultural products that could be produced between

Hollywood and China. Zhang eventually shifted from the public sector to the private sector as a broker between China and Hollywood. She moved from the CFCC in 2014 to become president of the state-owned Yunnan Film Group and then became chairman of the board of Chinese distributor Max Screen Distribution.[38] Zhang's career as a regulator and later as a private-sector leader in Sino-US film collaboration demonstrates the overlapping roles of policymakers and media executives in post-WTO China.

The CFCC regulates the content of the films it co-produces, but it is also a corporation, and the CFCC's president manages its economic output. The president's twin duties of enhancing co-production activity in the PRC and serving as a cultural gatekeeper mirror the roles of above-the-line compradors working on the investment side. Just as compradors in the private sector must consider a film's potential in the commercial market, the CFCC president must balance financial and cultural constraints in his or her advocacy of projects. The CFCC president's role demonstrates that navigating the co-production process requires leaders who are sensitive to the economic, policy, and cultural demands of producing a collaborative product.

Notably, the CFCC president's job as gatekeeper has the potential for broad-reaching global impact because of its relation to content restrictions on global blockbusters. Filmmakers who would like to access the Chinese market via a co-production must meet the CFCC's requirements. For example, some representations of Republican-era China in Rob Cohen's *The Mummy 3* had to be altered.[39] Earlier chapters of this book describe changes made to other films that targeted the Chinese market, such as *Shanghai, Iron Man 3, and Doctor Strange.* The power of the SAPPRFT and the CFCC suggests that just as Hollywood money has the potential to shape the landscape of contemporary Chinese cinema, the influence of Chinese regulators can shape Sino-US media brand collaborations in the long term.

TWENTY-FIRST-CENTURY COMPRADORS AND MEDIA CO-PRODUCTIONS

In many ways, compradors' most visible work occurs in the public sphere, where they sell the idea of the production to the public. *Lust, Caution,* for which Ang Lee won the Golden Lion prize at the Venice Film Festival in 2007, is a particularly rich case study for examining the role of compradors in Sino-US film collaboration because of the publicity the movie generated as part of its its distribution in both the Chinese and American markets. Despite its NC-17 rating in the United States, *Lust, Caution* received broader distribution than comparable Chinese-language dramas from Chinese directors whose work was distributed in the United States.[40] The film was Ang Lee's first effort since his Oscar-winning film *Brokeback Mountain* (2005). *Lust, Caution* garnered additional media attention because it was Lee's first Chinese-language film since his landmark martial arts blockbuster *Crouching Tiger, Hidden Dragon.*[41]

The following section examines how compradors framed *Lust, Caution* within media discourse to bridge the gap between Hollywood and China. This section argues that the strategic placement of the film at the crossroads between China and Hollywood was a key factor in its public relations discourse, which included consideration of China as a shooting and co-production location, as well as of the film's "Chinese-ness" (as related to its historical and narrative accessibility). As compradors marketed *Lust, Caution*, making it more accessible to global audiences, they also created a bridge between American and Chinese film communities. Examining a broad selection of publicly disclosed materials designed to market the film reveals how compradors on this Sino-US film collaboration built understanding between different filmmaking cultures at a formative stage in China-Hollywood collaboration.

Lust, Caution's publicity kit, an industrial text designed to explain the film to journalists, further reveals the role of compradors in the film-collaboration process. The publicity kit suggests that demystifying the process of film production in China was a critical part of making the film accessible to the press. Approximately one-third of the quotes presented in the kit are from members of the filmmaking team regarding the experience of shooting in China. Even though the crew spent a month in Hong Kong and several days in Malaysia, discussions of the shoot focus on Shanghai. The Shanghai emphasis is noteworthy both because of the complexity of shooting in mainland China and because of the city's position as a site of contemporary international industrial collaboration between Hollywood and China. Schamus complimented the "extraordinary craftsmanship" of the Chinese set builders. In a similar vein, the movie's cine-matographer, Rodrigo Prieto, stated, "I've worked well with foreign crews before, but ours on *Lust, Caution* was really top-notch. We tend to think, 'Well, if it's not Hollywood crews . . .' but there is a big industry in China and there are many quality workers."[42] Taken alongside similarly laudatory comments from others on the film-production team, Kong's and Prieto's statements suggest that marketing the transnational co-production in part required overcoming popular reluctance about cultural production in China.

Concerns about the accessibility of spectatorship arise in many of the publicly disclosed texts surrounding the film. These issues consist of two main types: language and content. On a linguistic level, compradors engage in multiple acts of translation to make the film's cultural back-ground more accessible to Western spectators. Random House, the pub-lishing company, produced two volumes of translation through its Pantheon and Anchor Books divisions that coincided with the film's release. One volume, Julia Lovell's 2007 translation of Chang's novella, makes the original Chinese-language story available for Western audi-ences. Translating the story into English in time for the film's US release was an attempt to teach Western audiences about one of the major writers of twentieth-century China. On one level, the translated novella was an obvious product choice for Random House. The success of Ang Lee's *Brokeback Mountain* dramatically increased sales of the Annie Proulx short story on which the film was based. The publisher's choice to trans-late Chang's text assumed no American market for the novella in Chinese. In other words, the English-language text was intended at least in part for the film's non-Chinese-reading audience. While the choice of English over Chinese may seem to have been intended to increase market share, the film's distribution strategy actively considered the location of Chinese-speaking communities in the United States, leading to distribution of the film to commercial cinemas in Los Angeles's heavily Chinese San Gabriel Valley.

Similarly, the Random House omnibus *Lust, Caution: The Story, the Screenplay, and the Making of the Film*, mentioned earlier, provided both the translated short story and the film's script, in addition to essays by cast and crew members detailing the cultural process of film collaboration.[43]

The English-language script of the Chinese-language film distributed in the US market operates as a form of mobile "subtitle," offering an additional layer of explanation for spectators uncomfortable with the Chinese dialogue track. Cues throughout the script and presented in the book suggest the tome's additional function as a handbook of linguistic accessibility. The extended script offered a linguistic translation of the movie, expanded the market for the film, and was a commercial product in its own right. In the case of *Lust, Caution*, the editors at Random House took a more erudite strategy for branding the film than would be appropriate for most co-productions. Nonetheless, the companion texts for *Lust, Caution* expanded the film's market by situating the work in a new cultural context.

The annotations of the script mark this cultural function even more explicitly. Footnotes define key romanized terms throughout the text. For example, the Chinese *tai-tai* (wife) is footnoted as "a married woman with a certain social status; and *Ma Tai-tai* means something like 'Madame Ma.'"[44] This explanation offers both a linguistic translation and insight into the class and cultural context presented in the film and novella. The ancillary text thus also provides a cultural framework for the reader through which to better understand the film's content. By educating global audiences, the texts also help to economically sustain less globally accessible collaborations like *Lust, Caution*. Beyond their educational function, ancillary texts also leverage the intellectual property generated by a Sino-US film collaboration for an additional income stream.

A film's cultural promotion may not succeed simultaneously with its economic promotion. Although *Lust, Caution*'s box-office numbers in the US market failed to reach even the USD 5 million mark in a release on 143 screens over 119 days, the film's cultural impact on the media industry took root. *Lust, Caution*'s public relations discourse may have been far more successful as a means of building cultural awareness of Chinese cinema than as an income-generating strategy. In an interview with Jennifer Rice of the *Columbia Spectator* on October 4, 2007, Schamus identified the key differences in the film's cultural status as it traveled from country to country: "It's pretty much the biggest cultural moment in Chinese culture in maybe years, or a long, long time," Schamus said, though his expectations for American audiences were comparatively modest. "The film opens here to a number of obstacles: a foreign language, the NC-17 rating and an altogether slower pace to which Americans aren't accustomed." The loci of accessibility (or inaccessibility), as repeatedly articulated by interviewers and interviewees alike, explained some of the major barriers to entry in the American market for Chinese-language Sino-US co-productions, both as perceived by filmmakers and marketers and as articulated by critics. Notably, *Lust, Caution*'s ancillary texts addressed many of these potential weaknesses.

Dealing with the relative "inaccessibility" of the film's historical romance narrative for American viewers was a central issue in building the market for *Lust, Caution*. However, *Crouching Tiger, Hidden Dragon*, a film grounded in the Chinese literary trope of the *wuxia* (knight-errant), was the highest-grossing foreign-language film of all time at the US box office.[45] Some audiences perceived *Lust, Caution* less accessible than films based on Chinese *wuxia* stories, despite the film's modern subject matter—namely, the Japanese occupation of Shanghai during World War II.

The filmmakers' responses to media critiques of "inaccessibility" reveal important perceived biases on the part of American audiences while fore-grounding the work of the filmmakers as interpreters of the film for viewers from different cultural backgrounds. In an interview with film and TV writer Orlando Parfitt at the time of the film's release in the United Kingdom, Schamus detailed the cultural issues involved in the film's American release in contrast to its popular reception in the Chinese market: "But in the context of the States we've had to treat it as an art film for the elite, and that's okay. . . . But we do have these cultural headways—the kind of hypocrisy, the rating—that kind of crap. We know there's a kind of head-wind that's pushing against us and all we can do is fight it."[46] More tellingly, a statement Schamus made at the film's Los Angeles premiere that was picked up by the culture magazine *Asia Pacific Arts* calls attention to the filmmaker's strong perceptions that the media's cultural biases shaped the film's treatment in the American media: "If you don't like our movie, that's perfectly fine, that's your job. Sometimes, however, I have to object against a certain amount of ignorance, that, when accompanied by smugness and an unwillingness to see what you're trying to do, I have to object to. . . . When somebody is too lazy to even go back and see who Eileen Chang was and what was really going on in Shanghai and how the politics and sexuality of it figure into Chinese culture, then I feel like, 'Well, maybe you should get another job.'"[47]

Schamus's critique of Western media pinpoints a significant perceived gap in American media awareness of Chinese literary and political history. The *Lust, Caution* producer's statement also demonstrates the way American media producers can leverage their influence to help advance the global impact of China as a filmmaking brand. The film's compradors attempted, with various levels of transparency, to contend with the cultural barriers to strong media coverage, promoting both the film's Hollywood studio and its Chinese story. Thus, Schamus's critique of Western critical discourse about the film can be seen as an expression of his role as an intermediary in the co-production process.

Taking Schamus's criticism of American media into consideration raises the question of what responsibility the filmmaker of a historical genre co-production has in providing a historical context for spectators. In the Chinese context, *Lust, Caution* was hailed as opening a superb window onto twentieth-century Chinese history, but a review by *Screen Daily* writer Dan Fainaru on August 30, 2007, in Venice—where, as mentioned earlier, the film took home the Venice Film Festival's major prize—argued as follows: "Had Lee accepted that his film is about the conflict between duty and desire, and worked smoothly on this premise, this could have been a far more focused and precise film. . . . But by wishing to expand the story into a vast period portrait, first of Hong Kong, and then of Shanghai, Lee opens up avenues that he never has time to follow up."[48] Fainaru's critique of the film speaks directly to Schamus's dismissal of the movie's critics. Viewing Schamus's responses to the reviews of *Lust, Caution* in concert with the reviews themselves suggests a tension in the perceived role of the American media, raising the question of whether critics should be cultural arbiters—particularly in the context of film collaborations, for which critics often must work harder to fully assess the cultural implications. Amid the dialogue between Schamus and the critics of *Lust, Caution* is a debate about the relevance of modern and contemporary Chinese culture to the American media—a rather shocking revelation, given the United States' tremendous financial dependence on the PRC.

The public discourse surrounding *Lust, Caution* reveals that compradors offer an important service when they attempt to quell Sino-US cultural misapprehension as part of the business of filmmaking. The rise of a variety of types of compradors appears to be part of a larger trend in marketing films made in China—namely, the practice of educating the Western media about the viability of Chinese film in the American market. As tempting as it may be to judge the cultural narrowness of the United States, observing the efforts to introduce a challenging cultural work such as *Lust, Caution* proves far more productive. Beyond translations and "making-of" texts, the production of *Lust, Caution* led to events such as Asia Society panels based on the film.[49] Co-production publicity efforts in the American market further emphasized the gaps in American media coverage of Sino-US collaboration—and, more important, formed a foundation for improved future understanding. The work of compradors as promoters of industrial collaboration suggests not only that a movie's cultural context and economics are intertwined, but also that American critics and audiences expect filmmakers to cater to their cultural tastes to gain their economic support. Creating films between China and Hollywood requires a sophisticated understanding of market conditions, audience desires, and the nuances of both national and international storytelling practices.

In the case of *Lust, Caution*, compradors negotiated the place of Chinese history in the American media while situating film collaboration in China within the context of global production. Examining public relations materials produced to support the film's release reveals a distinct move to sell the American market on the idea of a co-produced film shot in the PRC. Interviews with filmmakers and other paratextual materials address film production in China on varying levels, depending on the intended audience (industrial, spectatorial, or a combination thereof). Whereas industry materials discuss attempts to localize filmmaking, compradors describe the practice of shooting in China as a way of bringing the film's "foreignness" home, explaining why one makes a Hollywood film in China.

CONCLUSION

The case of *Lust, Caution* illuminates the role of compradors in filmmaking by demonstrating how the film-collaboration process connects the cross-cultural and economic work of filmmakers. Through the deft strategies of compradors in the film's production and marketing, *Lust, Caution* helped shape the filmmaking brands of both China and Hollywood. On the level of language, screenwriters play an important role in communicating not just language itself but also the narrative arcs of distinct literary traditions. On the level of film direction, stories drawn from a co-production challenge regulators and rejuvenate spaces of production. In the financial context, producers who finance Sino-US co-productions gather production funding from a wider range of public and private sources. The process of shaping and brokering a film across distinct production cultures is essential to the growth of joint media systems. As China and Hollywood become increasingly intertwined, the ability to navigate between the two becomes all the more important for above-the-line workers, not just in Sino-US co-productions, but in all content that will be distributed in both China and the United States.

Compradors in the film-collaboration process form the very foundation of transnational filmmaking. Without the cross-cultural intelligence of James Schamus, Ang Lee, Bill Kong, and others, *Lust, Caution* could not have come together in the industrial context of contemporary China. The cultural work of selling the film to the public was crucial for the creation of an audience for the movie, especially in the United States. An examination of *Lust, Caution* in particular offers extensive examples of the multiple layers of complexity that compradors address. Within the Sino-US production context writ large, compradors face the same types of challenges. In the Sino-US context, much is at stake because of the cultural distance between China and Hollywood. Different structures of language and culture play a major role in the work required of compradors to manage the film-collaboration process. As box-office demands increasingly require cross-cultural work—in the inception of films as well as in their marketing and distribution—paying attention to the cultural labor of film compradors is essential. The next chapter explores another integral part of the cultural-translation process for Hollywood in China: below-the-line work.

6 Farm Labor, Film Labor

HOW BELOW-THE-LINE WORKERS
SHAPE SINO-US FILM PRODUCTION

The *Lunyu,* or *Analects of Confucius,* provides guidelines to ensure fairness in communual dining rituals.[1] Writers have used Confucius's words as postmortem commentary on many modern phenomena. It is nonetheless surprising that the sage prefigured the challenges of Sino-US film co-production. Dining practices on set that crew members perceived as unfair reduced morale for interviewees. During the production of Rob Minkoff's *The Forbidden Kingdom,* the first Sino-US co-production to take the number-one box-office position in both the Chinese and the US market on the same weekend, the movie's Chinese and American cast and crew ate together. But during filming for Rob Cohen's *The Mummy 3,* shot at the same Chinese studio and in the same year as *The Forbidden Kingdom,* the cast and crew had separate dining areas, with Hollywood-style craft services for the foreign workers and the ubiquitous *he fan,* or box lunch, for the Chinese workers. (See figure 14.) Such production dining practices echo the much-maligned segregation of Westerners and Chinese during Shanghai's semicolonial period, when foreign powers occupied parts of the city. To crew members, the different dining options on *The Mummy 3* reflected inequality among production personnel from different countries. Much of this book focuses on the way policymakers,

Figure 14. Catering lunchbox (*he fan*) during the production of *The Forbidden Kingdom*. (Photo by Jason Siu, Hengdian, PRC, May 18, 2007)

businesspeople, and journalists brand Hollywood and China, but film crews have an equal or greater impact on how Hollywood and China view each other. This chapter claims no proof of direct causality between dining practices and production outcomes (though Confucius might). However, it is worth noting that, according to the trade website Box Office Mojo, despite an estimated budget of nearly USD 100 million more, *The Mummy 3* took in USD 10 million less than *The Forbidden Kingdom* in its PRC release. Ultimately, examining the role of below-the-line workers in Sino-US collaborations demonstrates how labor practices shape the relationship between China and Hollywood.

Power—often grounded in the relationship between citizenship, mobility, and language—influences the development of the media-labor networks between China and Hollywood. While similar hierarchies exist on Canadian-US, European-US, and Australian-US productions, the culturally and often nationally inflected power dynamics in the production process are emblematic of the industrial culture of Sino-US co-productions.

Figure 15. Multinational crew of *The Forbidden Kingdom* walking together on set, Cangyang Shan, September 7, 2007. (Photo by Jason Siu, Cangyang Shan, PRC September 7, 2007)

As with issues of power and labor in other international manufacturing contexts in the PRC, the role of labor in international film co-productions is often both misunderstood and underappreciated. Examining media production as a labor network–driven, studio-based system, or production ecosystem, asserts the complexities of film-labor collaborations.

Production ecosystems require a specific combination of people, practice, and place to facilitate the continued development of the relationships that foster Sino-US media collaborations. Below-the-line cultural intermediaries (to borrow from Pierre Bourdieu) hold the production ecosystem together.[2] (See figure 15.) The temptation to examine only the power brokers in Sino-US media culture is strong. People such as director Ang Lee and producers Bill Kong and James Schamus, as well as government officials in both countries, have had an indelible impact on how the culture of Sino-US media production operates.

Communities of industrial media workers who co-evolve with their environment—communities that develop their own practices of relating and surviving in the context of globalizing Chinese media industries—are equally important to the growth of Sino-US media cultures of production. Scholars have examined how increasingly flexible work processes have led to the development of communities in the film production process, but little work has been done to examine the development of those communities in the context of Sino-US collaboration.[3] This chapter offers a framework for understanding the labor relationships that form the foundation of China-Hollywood collaboration and competition.

Scholarly research in media studies tends to focus on above-the-line players, from auteurs to producers, but the effect that below-the-line film workers have on cultures of film production is equal, if not greater. International below-the-line media work trains new talent for future below-the-line work in local crews and, in fact, substantially affects the development of the national film industry. It also draws attention to a blind spot in our understanding of transnational film production, which I seek to remedy in this book. In the context of film co-production between China and Hollywood, in which the question of labor plays a role in production decisions, examining the role of below-the-line workers becomes particularly salient.

Media studies scholars have previously analyzed the role of groups of national and international labor in relation to media production. Doris Baltruschat posed the notion of global media ecologies as the "networks of media and cultural agents," particularly in the context of co-productions between Canada, Britain, Europe, and Australia, while communication scholars Ben Goldsmith and Tom O'Regan examined the role that film studios play in creating production ecologies—local, regional, national, and international production communities.[4] Both the spatial focus of Goldsmith and O'Regan's work and the human-network focus of Baltruschat's work are valuable for examining the communities of production that form in connection with contemporary Sino-US film collaboration. Together, the notions of production and media ecologies demonstrate the deeply interconnected nature of international film co-productions, in terms of both people and spaces.

Models such as Baltruschat's media ecologies and Goldsmith and O'Regan's production ecology focus on production relationships between Western countries. However, in China these models must extend further to incorporate the power differentials that can exist in this type of collaboration. The PRC's media-labor market, despite radically changing by the day, still does not have the same types of union protections for workers that exist for some craft workers in the United States. Moreover, the media and production-ecology models do not deal directly with issues of Orientalism or with the neocolonialist investment practices that can influence production cultures that emerge in the relationship between China and Hollywood.

By defining what China is for outsiders, Chinese workers reshape the global brand of media production in China. Equally important to note is that the Chinese workers on Sino-US collaborations contribute to the development of a robust domestic industry with highly trained media professionals. That the precise dynamic of Sino-US production relationships is in flux cannot be overstated, yet a more capacious model is needed that factors in the challenging racial, ethnic, linguistic, and economic considerations of labor collaborations between the two countries. As in the natural world, networks exist on multiple, interconnected levels. Networks driven by policy, state-level actors, and CEOs inform but also differ from the networks shaped by the work of production labor, both local and transnational.

Addressing the potent implications of power involved in the use of locally hired labor in international networks of production requires a conceptual rubric to explain the intertwining of Chinese and US media industries. The idea of the production ecosystem emerges from the combination of network- and studio-based ecologies as proposed by Ben Goldsmith and Tom O'Regan and by Doris Baltruschat,[5] in combination with the notion of the "business ecosystem" defined by business strategist James Moore as "an economic community supported by a foundation of interacting organizations and individuals. . . . The member organizations also include suppliers, lead producers, competitors, and other stakeholders. Over time, they co-evolve their capabilities and roles, and tend to align themselves with the directions set by one or more central companies. Those companies holding leadership roles may change over time, but the function of ecosystem leader is valued by the community because it enables members to move toward shared visions to align their investments and to find mutually supportive roles."[6]

Moore's ecosystem model, which has become a standard for analysis of the high-tech industry, acknowledges the role of industrial hierarchy in the development of systems of production. Uniting the work of Moore with that of Goldsmith and O'Regan and of Baltruschat, this chapter asserts that the production ecosystem is a place-based network of media labor and capital, structured by hierarchies of industrial power and influenced by ethnicity, language, culture, and citizenship.

SPOKEN LANGUAGE AND THE PRODUCTION ECOSYSTEM

The cross-cultural complexities of craft services in Sino-US film collaborations, while particularly evocative, are hardly the only labor challenge that film workers face. Language and dialect also present obstacles to the growth of production-labor networks. While above-the-line workers on Sino-US film co-productions engage in translation work related to script development and production negotiations, below-the-line workers must navigate multiple spoken dialects of Chinese and English on a daily basis. The use or misuse of a particular language or dialect by film crews can—like dining practices—encourage or discourage collaboration between different groups on a particular film shoot.

How and when crews speak a particular dialect or language depends on both the power dynamic of the production ecosystem and the cultural norms of the production. Crew members from Beijing, Shanghai, Hong Kong, and the United States may all speak some Mandarin, but the politics of using Mandarin on set are tied to the structure of the production ecosystem. As scholars have written and film workers have confirmed in interviews, speaking in a Beijing dialect marks workers as being from China's capital, or as using professional language from outside their home dialect group.[7] If crew members from Shanghai choose to speak in Shanghainese, a choice that limits communication primarily to Shanghai natives, this reinforces stereotypes about the insularity of Shanghainese culture.[8] The hierarchy of language usage in the film co-production process is one reason analysis focused on production labor is helpful in understanding the nuances of transnational production cultures.

The use of Cantonese can also mark hierarchies in the production ecosystem. An excellent example of the linguistic dynamic in the co-production context can be seen in the production world of Teddy Chan's Hong Kong historical action film *Bodyguards and Assassins* (2009). Although it was a mainland China–Hong Kong co-production rather than a Sino-US co-production, the film's production process dealt with a blend of linguistic challenges, with crews based in Beijing, Shanghai, and Hong Kong. Producer Peter Chan, one of the main figures of cinematic collaboration between Hong Kong and mainland China, emphasized the importance of understanding crew members' cultural and linguistic backgrounds before disciplining them to prevent cultural disruptions on set.[9] Chan pointed out that when Cantonese-speaking crew members on mainland shoots needed to be reprimanded, he had to make sure that the Hong Kong–based crew used Mandarin rather than Cantonese. The Hong Kong crew members likewise had to be careful in exercising authority over mainland workers, lest they create ill will on set.[10] Chan's concerns as a producer underscored what has been called "language ideology," or "the perceptions held by people about a specific language or language in general, what language can do, and how language should be used."[11] Chan's articulation of the language ideology of production indicates how, even in the context of Chinese dialects, careful use of language is an essential part of a production's social formation. Proper use of linguistic nuance is just as—if not more—important in teamwork-focused, below-the-line work, such as executing stunts, as it is in high-level production negotiations. This level of complexity only increases when Anglophone workers from Hollywood enter into production agreements with Chinese partners. As a result, below-the-line workers form the foundational power relationships that structure the production ecosystem.

THE LANGUAGE OF MONEY

Beyond language issues, below-the-line workers must navigate complex cultural negotiations within productions. Nowhere is this challenge more significant than in the area of production spending. Although establishing prices for services may seem like a largely financial consideration, the mode of interaction between foreign and Chinese below-the-line workers greatly affects the development of the production ecosystem, as workers deploy different types of negotiation practices across cultures.

Financial transactions shape the power relationships within a production ecosystem. In my interviews, Chinese film workers expressed displeasure that American above-the-line workers accused them of price gouging, even though the accusation originated from the parties' first major financial interaction, when the parties had not yet formed the *guanxi* (relationships) necessary to secure preferential pricing deals.[12] This lack of understanding caused Chinese service purveyors not only to reflect on their own pricing system but also to critique the "other" for misunderstanding how that system works.[13] In cases where American above-the-line workers paid full price for a service, the financial costs may have been slightly higher, but the long-term social costs were decidedly lower than if they had demanded a discount before establishing their relationship. Considerations of status in the production ecosystem as related to culturally inflected "deal making" are integral to understanding the cultural structures of the crew labor in this ecosystem.

ACTS OF TRANSLATION: THE BELOW-THE-LINE LABOR OF FILM CO-PRODUCTION

Co-productions require a new class of media-production ambassadors on the production team. Addressing one such new ambassador, chapter 5 examined the role of compradors—the individuals involved in setting the conditions that can bring a production ecosystem into existence—in above-the-line film production roles. Below-the-line cultural intermediaries—crew members other than the director, writers, producers, and lead actors—act as liaisons, directly facilitating cross-cultural production activities on set. Bicultural crew members create vital connections. Examining the role of these workers can reveal what type of cross-cultural translation facilitates collaboration, as well as the ways in which hierarchies of culture, nationality, and gender bring Chinese and US crews together or drive them apart.

This chapter divides the labor of translation in the Sino-US production ecosystem into several categories. The taxonomy includes those who manage language (interpreters), space (location managers and set builders), and logistics (production managers, assistant directors, and production assistants). These individuals smooth interactions between workers from China and Hollywood within the crew on individual film sets. Many then use their experiences in future productions. Analyzing each role reveals how film co-productions produce not only visual culture but also fluid relationships among media communities over time.

LANGUAGE

The most obvious cultural-translation role of below-the-line cultural workers in the Sino-US production ecosystem is that of interpreter. Theoretical explorations of the role of a translator in literature recall the Italian adage "*traduttore, traditore*" (translator, traitor), suggesting that even translators who seek to be faithful to the text are, by definition, still disloyal in their representation of it. As for interpreters in the film-production ecosystem, workers can be placed in ambivalently "traitorous" positions by virtue of their need to navigate between Chinese and Hollywood crews. A Chinese translator on a Sino-US co-production may have the privilege and status of a foreign worker but the identity of a local worker.

Wang Fang, a master's degree student at the School of Film and TV Art and Technology at Shanghai University, took a part-time job on the set of the co-production *The Mummy 3* as a way to earn money, but in the process, she became a key player holding the production together.[14] As a graduate student in film studies, she had a more advanced knowledge of English than most of the low-paid workers on the film's crew, as well as some knowledge of the filmmaking process, though largely on a theoretical level. During *The Mummy 3* shoot in Shanghai, Wang worked as an interpreter for Western background actors. As such, Wang bridged two different worlds and, as mentioned earlier, two different dining experiences. Wang would move back and forth between the craft services tent for local Chinese workers, who were sometimes served unidentifiable porridge, and the Hollywood-style craft services tent for foreign workers.[15] Her status as a culture worker in training within the local Shanghai context made her uniquely capable as an intermediary between the different parts of the crew.

Her role in the production process demonstrates the fluidity of the position of workers with bicultural adaptability within individual films. Although Wang started working on *The Mummy 3* as an interpreter, she eventually shifted roles and became a stand-in for actress Liang Luoshi because of her "look" and her English-language abilities. She moved from working with foreign background actors to working with Chinese "stars," but throughout the process, she bridged the gap between different groups on set.[16]

Wang is just one of many below-the-line film workers who translate for above-the-line workers in the film co-production process. By facilitating the work of both non-Chinese and Chinese above-the-line workers, interpreters such as Wang are simultaneously essential to and invisible within the filmmaking process. This is precisely why discussions of power in the production ecosystem—particularly for transnational co-productions— are essential.

Media studies scholar Mark Deuze suggests that a shift toward mobile employment practices, such as those in the international film co-production context, is breaking down the boundaries between work and private life.[17] By building on his argument, one can examine how mobile employment practices in industrial contexts such as film co-production can break down geographic and cultural boundaries as well. Sino-US film co-production demands groups of workers who are capable of shifting between different cultural and geographic worlds.

SPACE

In addition to cultural workers who focus on language, such as interpreters, a core group of crew members manages the physical environment on and in support of production sets to keep the Sino-US production ecosystem operational. These workers do everything from arranging accommodations and travel logistics to organizing the physical spaces of production. Four types of workers operate in this category: production managers, production logistics facilitators, location managers, and set builders. By overseeing and controlling the Chinese spaces of Sino-US co-productions, this relatively small group of workers (often literally) builds China-Hollywood collaboration in the PRC.

One of the major modes of cultural translation on a co-production shoot is the translation of places—the conversion of sites in mainland China for Euro-American production crews. Whereas film workers such as Wang interpret language between Chinese and foreign crews, these individuals translate spaces across cultures. Translating space requires a deep knowledge of the expectations of all nationalities of film workers in terms of how they view and use space. The idea that Chinese film workers in the PRC would have to "translate" Chinese spaces for an international shoot meant to represent China may seem counterintuitive at first. However, location managers on Sino-US film co-productions with Hollywood leadership facilitate a world in which both the image and use of spaces in China conform to the expectations of American filmmakers.

External location management and scouting are excellent examples of the type of cultural-translation work that film crews do in the Sino-US film co-production process. Location managers, who are responsible for finding and securing production sites, play an often underappreciated role in shaping a film's "look." Following Goldsmith and O'Regan's film-studio model, the production logistics work of managing spaces reformulates those spaces according to cultural expectations.[18] This process has long-term implications for the representation of China in global commercial media.

When a film director is unfamiliar with local spaces, as is often the case with big-budget US co-productions shot in the PRC, the location manager plays a key role in the representation of the space of China. Location manager Chen Fenglei planned the shooting locations of several major film co-productions in the early 2000s: Stephen Chow's *Kung Fu Hustle* (2005), Peter Chan's *Perhaps Love* (2005), Rob Cohen's *The Mummy 3*, and Ang Lee's *Lust, Caution*. Chen said, "The foreigners I have worked with view China as a new *ticai* [material] so the people interested in looking for locations are quite numerous."[19] He exhibited a deep awareness of the role he has played in the cultural context of the filmmaking process. Chen's work in the capacity of location manager puts him in the position of providing cultural "material" for a co-production. (See figures 16–20.) The use of the

Figure 16. Location scouting images for re-creation of Shanghai street Nanjing West Road in the 1940s for *The Mummy 3*. (Photo by Chen Fenglei, Shanghai Film Studios, Shanghai, PRC, summer/fall 2007)

Figure 17. Location shoot for re-creation of Shanghai street Nanjing West Road in the 1940s for *The Mummy 3.* (Photo by Chen Fenglei, Shanghai Film Studios, Shanghai, summer/fall 2007)

word *ticai* evokes a commodity designed to materially augment the preexisting narrative without fundamentally changing it. Chen's characterization of the process speaks to the assumptions made about film co-production in the PRC—assumptions based on the notion that China is a place where Hollywood filmmaking can be "applied" rather than operate in sync within local media production communities. But production workers like Chen demonstrate the creative role of below-the-line workers in shaping these productions. As the Chinese film industry develops and local workers gain more experience, the impact of Chinese below-the-line creative talent on Hollywood films can be expected to become more profound. Chen later became the China unit production manager for assisted production *Skyfall* (dir. Sam Mendes 2012), among other films. He then parlayed his expertise to become a production consultant and Sino-US media collaboration expert for FilmFinances, a Sino-US media investment firm based in both

Figure 18. Location scouting image for re-creation of Shanghai street Nanjing West Road in the 1940s for *The Mummy 3*. (Photo by Chen Fenglei, Shanghai Film Studios, Shanghai, summer/fall 2007)

Shanghai and Southern California. Chen's success underscores the importance of cross-cultural skills in the production process, particularly with increased amounts of Chinese media capital flowing to Hollywood.

Location managers curate the types of domestic Chinese spaces that are represented on screen, while set builders on foreign co-productions create sets representing Chinese interiors, facilitating cultural exchange by physically constructing the production ecosystem. The practice of building Chinese set spaces in the PRC—sets created by Chinese film workers at the behest of a foreign production company—is an act of cultural co-creation, one in which film workers can be charged with re-creating a version of their own culture for consumption by global audiences. The re-creation of Chinese spaces by Chinese film workers for American co-productions underscores the political, economic, and cultural significance of production collaboration.

Figure 19. Location shoot for re-creation of Shanghai street Nanjing West Road in the 1940s for *The Mummy 3*. (Photo by Chen Fenglei, Shanghai Film Studios, Shanghai, PRC, summer/fall 2007)

Figure 20. Location scouting image for re-creation of Shanghai street Nanjing West Road in the 1940s for *The Mummy 3*. (Photo by Chen Fenglei, Shanghai Film Studios, Shanghai, PRC, summer/fall 2007)

Figure 21. Interior photos of a 1940s Shanghai nightclub set on Shanghai Film Studio's Nanjing West Road for *Mummy 3*. (Photos by Lü Jiansheng, Shanghai Film Studios, Shanghai, PRC, April 16, 2007)

One particularly fascinating example of cultural co-creation in the set-building process is the career of Lü Jiansheng, the lead set builder for Shanghai Film Studios. On *The Mummy 3*, Lü was responsible for procuring all the necessary wood, metal, glass, and synthetic materials needed to create sets, such as the 1940s Shanghai lounge space that served as a major site for the production. (See figure 21.) *The Mummy 3* was one of Lü's first major international film productions, though he had previously transformed the Shanghai Film Studios' lot into a New York City facsimile for a Coca-Cola commercial. When we spoke, Lü was in his fifties and at the top of his craft, working as a set-building team leader for international films and commercial productions. He received his initial training during the Chinese Cultural Revolution at a small institute in Shanghai that trained people to make *yangban xi* (revolutionary-themed model operas that came to prominence during the Chinese Cultural Revolution). Thus, Lü, who trained as a filmmaker under Mao Zedong's propaganda regime, is part of the process of synthesizing international and Chinese filmmaking cultures. As a result of the rapid economic liberalization of film production in the PRC, many people who began their careers within the state-controlled filmmaking system now work on foreign, privately funded projects. Lü's work underscores the way in which workers act as a bridge between differing traditions of filmmaking in China and Hollywood, as well as between different eras of filmmaking in China.

LOGISTICS MANAGERS

While builders such as Lü construct co-production sets that translate space within a film shoot, logistics managers translate the space used to physically accommodate the cast and crew. Although the work of production logistics managers has fewer implications for the final, internationally circulated images of the film, these individuals must develop an intimate understanding of the expected living conditions of the cast and crew members. Without this type of pragmatic work, maintaining the physical spaces of the Sino-US production ecosystem would be impossible. For example, Zhang Ai, the production logistics coordinator for *The Mummy 3* in Shanghai, was tasked with finding living space for the film's workers.[20]

Zhang was, in essence, responsible for facilitating the growth of a transnational community of more than a thousand media workers.[21] Where, how, and under what circumstances these people lived and worked was determined not only by the requests of her employers, but also by her own cultural knowledge of the needs of foreign production crews. One of Zhang's roles in the production process was to work with the proprietors of the Motel 168 located outside Chedun (the site of Shanghai Film Park) to create a living space that would meet the expectations of Chinese and international film crews.[22] Zhang's role in the film co-production process demonstrates how creating media via the international film co-production process develops new living communities of film workers who co-create international production standards. Production logistics coordinators establish a living space that supports the Sino-US collaboration process.

From the deployment of urban space for a shoot, to the repurposing of parts of a city into a miniature community of filmmakers, to the physical co-creation of Chinese set pieces, crew members who manage the physical components of the production ecosystem influence how film workers interact within the co-production's host country. Moreover, these practices form the space of the production ecosystem, from the living quarters for the cast and crew to the production sets where filming takes place. The cross-cultural work of this class of production labor leads to the development of a transnational media culture—not only on screen, but also in the context of the production community.

PRODUCTION MANAGEMENT

Production management is as much a part of the cultural dialogue as it is a pragmatic demand of the filmmaking process. Production managers ensure that logistics are executed smoothly. Those who work on co-productions typically divide their careers between domestic and co-produced films and are often local or overseas Chinese film workers.[23] This small group of individuals manages Sino-US co-productions and related Sino-US collaborations. The insularity of this group points to the ways in which Sino-US media is becoming its own discernible industrial structure. Lucy Lu, the Shanghai-born production manager for Spike Jonze's assisted production *Her*, was also a facilitator for the 2012 and 2016 seasons of the American television show *The Amazing Race*, which were shot in the PRC, and a production coordinator on the Sino-American animated television series *Flutemaster* (2003).[24] Drawing on her Shanghai roots, Lu is the executive producer of Gung-Ho Films, which bills itself as "the first Western-run production company in China."[25] Chiu Wah Lee, who is from Hong Kong, worked as production manager for the assisted production *Code 46* and the Sino-US co-production *Lust, Caution*. He moved up the production-management chain of command to be first assistant director for the Shanghai-based assisted production of Ronny Yu's *Fearless* and then worked as the second assistant director for China on the assisted production of Kurt Wimmer's *Ultraviolet*. Starting in 2008, Chiu Wah Lee began working as a China line producer on major international productions, including the co-productions *The Mummy 3* and *The Karate Kid* (dir. Harald Zwart 2010), the assisted production *Skyfall*, the faux-production *Transformers 4*, and the official co-production *Skiptrace* (dir. Renny Harlin 2016). Though a broad range of Hollywood directors now work on Chinese film collaborations, few production managers are capable of tackling the challenges involved when a foreign crew shoots in the PRC. As a result, a small number of cross-cultural workers are managing the ways in which Chinese spaces are appearing on international screens. The production ecosystem structures the repetition of local images that a foreign crew then circulates to Chinese film workers. Location selection by local location managers and foreign film workers creates a hierarchy with respect to who is allowed to "see" what a city looks like. Even though production managers are local, they must curate images of their cities to meet the demands of production partners.

A key corollary to the process of structuring transnational spaces in film co-productions is the rise of a subculture of transnational "assistants" who act as bridges between spaces, languages, and filmmaking cultures. Like interpreters, assistants (*zhuli* in Mandarin) supplement the linguistic and cultural knowledge of foreign film workers who come to the PRC to work on co-productions. Multilingual workers who reside in the PRC but have had experience abroad make up a large portion of the assistants in the film co-production process. These assistants primarily serve producers and directors, but they can also take on roles as coordinators between multiple groups on the film crew.

Cross-cultural competence is a requirement for most assistants on film co-productions. Indeed, cross-cultural knowledge can take precedence over a filmmaking background; this affirms the value of examining the below-the-line cultural collaboration that is necessary to co-produce a film. For example, Nick Critser, a University of California, Berkeley, graduate who traveled to the PRC to study Chinese at Peking University, was later hired to work as an interpreter for the stunt department on the set of Quentin Tarantino's *Kill Bill: Volume 1*, which was shot at the Beijing Film Studio.[26] Critser had no previous filmmaking experience, but by entering the production ecosystem in the role of a cultural laborer, and because of his ability to work with both the Chinese and American crews, he was eventually promoted from language assistant to stunt grip.

Jason Siu began his work on Rob Minkoff's *The Forbidden Kingdom* as a production assistant but later became third assistant director. Siu is Chinese British and studied film in Australia before relocating to Beijing. He met Minkoff through his father, a corporate executive in the PRC. Siu described his initial role in the filmmaking process as that of a "glorified translator," but "because [he] knew Excel and could make call sheets," he rapidly moved up the chain of command.[27] Based on a recommendation from the key second assistant director of *The Forbidden Kingdom*, Siu was then hired on as second second assistant director in the China action unit for *The Mummy 3*, which was shot at the same film studio in Hengdian.[28] Although the practice of film workers remaining on a film's site after it has been completed to work for a new production with similar technical requirements is hardly atypical, Siu's specific cultural role on the shoots makes his move from *The Forbidden Kingdom* to *The Mummy 3* significant in that it showcases the advancement of workers who have both a cultural and a filmmaking background throughout the Sino-US film co-production ecosystem. Like other workers profiled in this chapter, Siu ascended rapidly in the crew hierarchy because of his language skills and management abilities. Recall that Wang experienced a similar rise within the hierarchy of her film's crew for similar reasons. Merely being able to do the work required on a production is not sufficient for such advancement; film workers must have the capacity to address the needs of a dynamic and culturally complex workforce.

Siu's career development highlights the transferability of cross-cultural filmmaking skills across different productions. After his work on *The*

Forbidden Kingdom, Siu was hired as an assistant director for two independent American features shot in the Shanghai region, a role in which he relied on his experiences navigating between different languages and cultures.[29] Most significantly, he also worked in Hengdian and in Shanghai to support *The Mummy 3,* the next film co-production to be shot there.

Even unexpected aspects of the film-production process require dedicated cultural translation from assistants. Australian Henry Dray, head of the transportation department for Marc Forster's *The Kite Runner* (2007), which was shot in Xinjiang, recruited musician David Harris, a New Zealander living in Beijing, to be a transportation assistant.[30] Harris had no prior experience in film production, but Dray, who had already worked on transportation for three other international collaborations, said he chose Harris to be his assistant because of their shared cultural expectations and language and even promoted Harris during his tenure on set.[31] Like Wang, Siu, and Critser, Harris rose up the ranks because of his competence combined with cultural proficiency. The experiences of these production assistants reinforce the importance of the cross-cultural abilities of below-the-line workers in the genesis of Sino-US productions.

It is significant to note the precariousness of such roles. Siu eventually left film production to go into real estate after the 2008 financial crisis caused a number of Sino-US productions to pull their funding.[32] He had the chance to work on *The Karate Kid* in 2009 but already had started other, more stable employment.[33] Similarly, Critser left film production after moving to Los Angeles with the crew of *Kill Bill: Volume 1.* At the time of our interview, Harris, like Siu and Critser, did not plan to work on other film productions, though he did later work on the Sino-Korean co-production *Sophie's Revenge* (2009) with Chinese American director Eva Jin. The movement of workers into and out of the production ecosystem underscores that, even though these workers' skills can be used across productions, the inconsistency of job opportunities for below-the-line film workers is such that above-the-line workers miss out on crucial cross-cultural knowledge due to employee attrition. Further, as cultural critics Rosalind Gill and Andy Pratt assert, the relative precariousness of cultural labor—in this case, cultural labor on transnational productions—can also be a point of political protest with regard to questions of labor, citizenship, and migration.[34]

However, being able to move across physical borders as well as cultural ones is often an essential part of the job. Siu's and Harris's non-Chinese and non-American nationality points to an important phenomenon in the context of production coordination: third-party nationals working as facilitators on Sino-US co-productions. Yen San Michelle Lo worked as production manager for Malaysia on *Lust, Caution*, which led to a role as a production coordinator on *The Mummy 3*. Lo is a multilingual, culturally adaptable production worker who is from Malaysia and attended UCLA. She speaks English, Mandarin, and Cantonese and also worked on Chinese Malaysian director Tsai Ming-liang's *I Don't Want to Sleep Alone* (2006). On *The Mummy 3*, Lo coordinated American and Chinese crews across multiple languages and dialects. She later worked as assistant production coordinator on Harald Zwart's *The Karate Kid*, as the production coordinator for *Transformers 4*, and as production supervisor on *Skiptrace*.[35] Like Harris and Siu, Lo developed the cross-cultural skills to communicate across Sino-US production contexts, but her citizenship is neither Chinese nor American. Similarly, even though these third-country production workers are not "native" to the co-production site, they are essential to the operations of large-scale co-production activities. Unlike the compradors described in chapter 5, below-the-line workers who meet the cultural demands of co-productions are not in a position to structure deals from their inception, but these workers actively shape the way production ecosystems look and function on a daily basis.

The comparative mobility of Harris, Siu, Lo, and Critser underscores an incongruity of power in the production ecosystem for below-the-line workers. Because of restrictions on their *hukou* (residence permits), local workers Wang Fang and Zhang Ai could legally work only in their place of residence, while at the time of our first interview Chen Fenglei could legally work only within the PRC. Although working in a city without a *hukou* is a relatively common practice in China, doing so increases the likelihood that the labor market could exploit an individual worker.[36] Thus, the structure of the production ecosystem in the PRC relies on an already precarious system of contract-based employment layered on top of either an illegal labor market practice or the creation of a captive labor market.

The production-ecosystem model also demonstrates the inherent power inequities embedded in a system with fixed populations of workers in a new and transitory industry. An example of this phenomenon involves workers at Hengdian World Studios, Asia's largest film studio and one of the production locations of *The Mummy 3* and *The Forbidden Kingdom*. While visiting the studios in the summer of 2012, I spoke with a local tour guide who worked there, Hei Hei, who came from a family of farmers in Hengdian.[37] Despite having grown up in a farming community, Hei Hei and most of his family worked either part- or full-time in the film industry at Hengdian.[38] The new economy of the city now depends on tourist traffic and production activity, and the farming communities of Hengdian are no longer intact. Because of the PRC's *hukou* system, Hei Hei was not able to legally leave the city to find work. When faced with the conundrum of an unstable local industry and a geographically restricted *hukou*, many Chinese workers migrate to the cities to work, creating an underclass of illegal workers.[39] The economic growth and cultural collaboration that stem from the co-production process offer exciting new opportunities for Chinese workers, but it is essential to rigorously analyze the larger impact of these collaborations, particularly in industries that try to make transnational labor appear seamless.[40]

The combination of flexible and temporary work influences the types of cultural interactions that occur between workers on media production projects. Developing a taxonomy of the positions that integrate international film-production personnel within the larger Chinese film-production environment creates a rubric within which to better understand the cultural logic of groups moving into and out of production communities. It reveals how the power structures of film production play out in hierarchies of language, culture, citizenship, and residence.

CONCLUSION

Cultural policy researcher Chris Bilton defines an alternative cultural geography as "a range of informal networks of collaboration, expertise, and influence."[41] Bilton's alternative cultural geography cuts to the core of one of the main principles of the production ecosystem: namely, that like film co-production itself, the ecosystem is both hyperlocal and hyperglobal. It is created by the overlapping relationships of people and space—described by media sociologist Manuel Castells as the "space of flows."[42] Increasingly fluid work and employment practices make the contributions of cultural translators in the Sino-US production process essential. As below-the-line workers create an alternative cultural geography of production, they are also literally and figuratively shaping the image of Hollywood productions for Chinese partners and of Chinese productions for foreign workers. Below-the-line laborers tasked with translating production instructions and spaces establish an image of what collaboration looks like to the film workers—and potential film workers—within that market.

Below-the-line workers in the Sino-US production ecosystem quietly contend with the challenges of linguistic, cultural, and spatial translation. By contrast, above-the-line workers trade on the visibility of their work. Policymakers assert a vision of what they believe collaborative production should look like on an industry-wide scale. Media brandscapes market production brands to the public. Industry forums share strategic narratives of media production in China and the United States with a broad range of industry partners. The daily cultural translation work of below-the-line workers on Sino-US co-productions creates continuity within and between projects that shape understanding between global production partners. Taken together, all these elements shape how China understands Hollywood, how Hollywood understands China, and how these partners compete for influence in the increasingly cutthroat world of global media production.

Conclusion

Branded media co-ventures shape the Sino-US cultural relationship. Co-ventures influence high-level interactions between artists and media workers as well as between politicians and manufacturers. Thus, analyzing Sino-US media collaborations teaches us not only about media production in the PRC, but also about how to better understand our world on a fundamental level.

Film collaboration is a central feature of contemporary Sino-US media co-ventures. It offers a template of how cooperation between China and Hollywood works in media production because of the important role film plays both in the contemporary global mediascape and in the historical relationship between China and Hollywood. Film collaborations generate new expertise in the Chinese media industries and project images of contemporary China around the world. And yet collaboration limits the type of content that Chinese and US partners can jointly produce and distribute on the mainland. These collaborations thus both mark the changing boundaries of what content is acceptable and reveal the complex interactions between Chinese state-run film groups and Hollywood studios. For example, the deployment of revolutionary film studios in the service of Hollywood studio films, as suggested by the China Film Co-production

Corporation's *China-International Production Guide*, demonstrates the significant transitions taking place as Hollywood expands production in China.[1] Many participants in Sino-US film industry events have also become involved in other forms of collaboration, from investing in Oriental DreamWorks to developing digital distribution platform agreements. An understanding of film collaboration offers foundational insights into the changing relationship between China and Hollywood.

Sino-US film collaborations enrich the cultures of production that can emerge via cooperation between both above-the-line and below-the-line workers in the production process. The wide variety of cultural translators at all levels of the film-production process that are required for a successful Sino-US film collaboration dictate the need for extensive, continuous cooperation throughout the production process. Many of these workers also work in television or on commercials, or create digital content. As the previous chapters have demonstrated, both above-the-line and below-the-line workers facilitate cultural exchange within the film-production process, but they bring their ability to translate between cultures of production to any productions in which they are involved.

However, film collaborations are just one—albeit an extremely formative—way in which companies in China and Hollywood co-create media. Branded media worlds, or "brandscapes," based on Chinese government and private-sector collaboration with Hollywood media conglomerates both facilitate the process of film collaboration and expand beyond its reach. The Shanghai DreamCenter and the Shanghai Disney Resort create fresh markets for film collaborations by exposing consumers to new media brands. They also capitalize on audiences that have been cultivated through marketing efforts like the Disney English Schools. Such consumer-facing efforts to promote China-Hollywood co-ventures operate in parallel with industry-focused efforts to improve relations.

Media industry forums also expand the Sino-US collaboration process. Forums create and circulate strategic narratives that shape perception about the changing power relationship between China and Hollywood for industry insiders. The events create a space for dialogue between members of and aspirants to the industry "in group." The SIFFORUM, the BJIFF Sino-Foreign Film Co-production Forum, the Asia Society Southern California US-China Film Summit, and other such media-industry forums allow individuals to market their expertise in the area of Sino-US collaboration while establishing norms about what working in "Hollywood" or "China" really means. Although these forums may not re-create the reality of production on the ground, they are central to the Sino-US "discourse war" in the context of the media industries.[2]

China-Hollywood branded collaborations grounded in film production offer leading indicators of key challenges for other types of media. Because of rigorous regulatory restrictions, the substantial demand for interna-tional labor, and major spatial considerations, film collaboration offers a way of understanding Sino-US media co-ventures on a macro scale. Comparing other types of collaborations reveals important insights about the obstacles involved in the co-creation of Sino-US media.

Using film collaboration as a touchstone, I offer in this book a preliminary exploration of the co-creation of Sino-US media culture. Hollywood's invest-ment in post-WTO China has expanded to other types of media. While ear-lier chapters focused explicitly on the practice of Sino-US film co-production in conjunction with related brand-building endeavors, this conclusion exam-ines three additional modes of branded media collaboration: television, streaming video, and animation. Like film, television deploys the resources of the PRC's state-owned studios and therefore offers perspective on the various scales and types of collaboration that are possible with such studios. Streaming video, in contrast, is frequently the product of collaborations between private entities distributed almost entirely by domestic Chinese platforms. Animation, by contrast, requires substantial investment from an even wider range of partners. Sino-US animation collaborations thus most frequently include a wide range of stakeholders from the private sector in the United States and China, as well as from the Chinese public sector. Using Sino-US film collaboration as a baseline for comparisons of Sino-US collabo-rative media production in the post-WTO era makes visible the network of cultural relations across different modes of media production.

TELEVISION COLLABORATIONS

Using many of the same resources as film collaborations, but with differ-ent distribution standards, foreign and co-produced television content suggest an alternative to the collaborations that result from the PRC's film policies. Imported television content is not subject to the same quota system that governs imported film content. Provincial television stations in the PRC are well funded, have massive distribution networks, and constantly need new content. However, in the interest of national broadcasting sovereignty, Chinese television stations restrict both the time slots and total hours of foreign content they distribute.[3]

Unlike film co-production, Sino-US television collaboration is typically more limited (similar to assisted film productions). One example is the use of locations for footage in content distributed outside the PRC. For example, the Discovery Channel documentary *The Science of Star Wars* (2005) included images of locations and monks at the Shaolin Temple. A production such as *The Science of Star Wars* is analogous to a production-services arrangement in the field of film co-production in terms of the relationship between the media producers. *The Science of Star Wars* imposed a Western narrative onto Chinese content, even co-opting premodern Chinese martial arts practices and incorporating them into the larger narrative of George Lucas's ascent to Hollywood fame. The relationship between content and form for TV footage shot in China involves less direct collaboration and more deployment of Western narratives to subsume Chinese spaces.

Survivor: China (2007) is another incarnation of the production-services model of collaboration within the context of Chinese television. China served as the backdrop for a season of the popular American reality-television show. *Survivor: China* is a particularly interesting example of the co-creation of industrial culture, because the premise of the show mirrors the production challenges the show's crew faced in adapting to a new local culture, food, and landscape. On a plane from Shanghai to the United States in 2007, I saw the crew members of *Survivor: China* returning, wearily, from their sojourn abroad. Whereas the reality-television show focused on the cultural adjustment challenges with which the show's cast members grappled, the true reality of *Survivor: China* involved crew members navigating a new environment, albeit without the same level of celebrity attached. What the case of *Survivor: China* demonstrates—and what is pervasive throughout the production-services model of collaboration for both film and television—is the overlap of diegetic narrative discourses of cultural adaptation and industrial discourses of production that brand collaborative efforts for audiences, media workers, and policymakers. Notably, *Survivor: China* presaged an increase in Chinese reality-television shows that, like many American reality-television programs, adopt foreign formats but use local casts and crews.

US companies shoot American TV shows in Chinese spaces, but the reverse occurs in the domestic Chinese television market.[4] Chinese television shows have adapted American platforms to the domestic market but have used casts and crews made up either entirely or largely of PRC-based media workers. Examples of such productions include the *American Idol*–inspired *Super Girl (Chaoji Nüsheng)* (2004–2011) and *The Amazing Race: China Rush (Jisu Qianjin: Chongci Zhongguo)* (2010–2012), a reality show on International Channel Shanghai and DragonTV based on the US reality show *The Amazing Race*.[5] The show was followed by *The Amazing Race China (Jisu Qianjin)*, which premiered in 2014.[6] Media investment firm China Media Capital and the Shanghai Media Group achieved huge financial success in adapting the singing-reality-show-competition format with *The Voice of China (Zhongguo Hao Shengyin)* (2012–present).[7] New formats have transformed the cultures of media production in the PRC by internationalizing content produced by domestic production companies.[8] Unlike film collaborations that create a China-Hollywood composite or plaster a Hollywood brand onto a Chinese narrative, television formats obscure international cultural origins to create localized content.

Ultimately, the more localized televised content in mainland China requires less explicit collaboration between Chinese and American partners. Yet despite the comparatively limited cooperation between Chinese and American partners in foreign platform-based Chinese reality TV shows, in 2016 regulators still urged TV producers to move away from even this type of foreign influence. State media agency Xinhua reported on June 19, 2016, that SAPPRFT exhorted: "Only self-innovated TV programs with Chinese cultural inheritance and characteristics can better carry the Chinese Dream themes, the socialist core values, as well as patriotism and Chinese fine traditions." The regulation suggests that across platforms, Hollywood's position in the Chinese media industries is precarious.

New distribution options for content do provide additional opportunities for Hollywood studios to become involved in TV production for the Chinese market. As media and cultural studies scholar Michael Keane argues, foreign television content is also popular on other types of screens, including smartphones, tablets, and PCs.[9] Moreover, access is not limited to legal distribution patterns. Elites in China also use virtual private networks to access foreign content.[10] As viewers shift away from the television set, digital distribution will become increasingly essential for Hollywood in China.

STREAMING VIDEO

As with television, collaboration between Chinese firms and US media conglomerates in the production of streaming video is limited so as to protect the domestic industry and control the content that is available to mass audiences. Similarly, the data-gathering and mass-mobilization potential of social media platforms has prompted the Chinese government to limit market-access opportunities for foreign firms.[11] Convergence between film and digital media poses a challenge to foreign investors in China, given that digital media firms have encountered a much more restrictive foreign direct investment environment than have motion picture companies. Dominant US technology and media firm Facebook and its acquisition Instagram are blocked in China.[12] Only the Facebook acquisition WhatsApp is still available for use in China, but it has fewer active Chinese users than local firm WeChat. Owner of YouTube and global industry leader Google exited the Chinese market because of regulatory compliance issues.[13] The principles of cultural sovereignty in the production of television and streaming video are closely related to those influencing the regulation of film and other major brand collaborations, but in many ways the media present an even more challenging landscape for foreign investors.

Unlike film and television, the global streaming-video industry developed during the period of China's rapid economic liberalization. China already has successful digital distribution firms that do not require external technical expertise from American partners, and are already publicly traded in US capital markets.[14] As a result, rather than having to play catch-up with other global media markets, as in the film industry, Chinese firms started on a more even footing with international competitors like YouTube. Government restrictions that limited market-access opportunities for foreign companies further aided domestic video platforms. Chinese firms such as iQiyi and Youku have become global and regional leaders in terms of both platform features and user base.[15] With initial public offerings by media and technology companies such as Alibaba and Tencent forging the way for the growth of Chinese media and technology in the United States, cash-rich Chinese Internet companies have already begun to expand their presence in both Hollywood and the Silicon Valley.

Still, online streaming distribution of television programs provides Hollywood media conglomerates a space in which to brand properties for Chinese domestic audiences. For example, the American streaming-video company Netflix has begun exploring the possibility of formally entering the Chinese content-production market with its original programming. The company found an enthusiastic audience in the PRC for its drama *House of Cards*.[16] Netflix followed this success with the Chinese-themed *Marco Polo* serial, which had an extravagant budget of USD 90 million for its first ten-episode season, but little success in the market.[17] Like other networked platforms, the firm faces intense scrutiny and a high barrier to market entry. Netflix's struggles in China portend the difficulties that entrants into the streaming-video market will likely face without strong local partnerships. Investment in animation production, by contrast, has a potentially more optimistic forecast.

ANIMATION

Animation collaborations are similar to film co-productions in that they can jointly promote Chinese and Hollywood brands. Unlike the players in the social media space, Hollywood animators had a head start over Chinese animators in developing global animation brands, industry, and infrastructure. As a result, the incentive is stronger to continue branded collaborations between Chinese partners and Hollywood media conglomerates from the perspective of technology transfer, and also as a way of conveying Chinese content to a broader audience.

Oriental DreamWorks and the Shanghai DreamCenter—a major co-production studio and entertainment center, respectively—released *Kung Fu Panda 3* (2016), the first official Sino-US animated co-production. The film showcased Chinese culture, drove Chinese domestic animation production, and projected a major Hollywood brand. James Fong, CEO of Oriental DreamWorks, described the studio's mission as an effort to "marry [the] best of Chinese stories and [the] best of Western storytelling for audiences around the world," thereby creating content that leverages Hollywood expertise while promoting Chinese content.[18] Animated entertainment differs from live-action filmmaking in terms of how the medium supports cross-cultural narrative production. In an animated world, all characters can be the "other" by virtue of the medium. Fanciful lead characters of animated films like those in *Kung Fu Panda 3* evade difficult issues surrounding the race and nationality of actors.

Sino-US animation projects also allow for linguistic fluidity, avoiding one of the challenges of transnational spectatorship. Fong described the localization process for *Kung Fu Panda 3* as one that took advantage of the unique characteristics of animation to make the film as familiar as possible in both English- and Chinese-speaking markets.[19] For *Kung Fu Panda 3*, Oriental DreamWorks made both an English-language and a Chinese-language version of the film in which the characters' mouth movements matched the dialogue in the script.[20] The flexibility of animation as a medium made this type of adaptation feasible, but also reflects a best-case scenario for other types of collaborative production.

Screenwriters translated dialogue from English to Chinese for the Chinese release of the film, and Chinese writers then revised the dialogue to ensure that the film's jokes worked equally well in English and in Chinese.[21] Oriental DreamWorks also employed more than two hundred people in China to work on the film there, in addition to partners at the DreamWorks headquarters in Glendale, California.[22] Moreover, *Kung Fu Panda 3* had a United States–based and a China-based director, allowing for further sophistication in the localization process.[23] By contrast, live-action entertainment contends with making more realistic representations resonate with a wide range of audiences.

Animation also presents a unique challenge for foreign firms seeking to project their brand within the Chinese market. Children are the main target audience for animated entertainment, particularly in the PRC. Restrictions on foreign theatrical entertainment in Chinese cinemas during blackout periods that correspond to school breaks indicate that children's exposure to foreign media is an area of particular political sensitivity.[24] Regulators have also been careful to limit the amount of time foreign animation can be broadcast on Chinese television channels. To combat restrictions on foreign animated content, Oriental DreamWorks has focused on growing domestic Chinese animation with the DreamWorks brand.[25] But just because a media product is made in China does not mean it is free from scrutiny.

The emphasis on family entertainment suggests a move toward material that conforms to Chinese regulatory standards from its inception. Innocuous family-friendly animation collaborations offer regulator-friendly content. Animated films for children typically exclude political, sexual, or violent content that could present a challenge for Chinese regulators, while still attracting a large audience. Oriental DreamWorks and Disney's Chinese market investments reveal opportunities for the growth of animated family entertainment, but also market constraints.[26]

In addition to the family-entertainment emphasis of firms such as Oriental DreamWorks and Disney, other Hollywood producers who have worked in China on live-action films have also moved toward animation. Anecdotally, Bill Borden, the supervising producer of *Mission: Impossible 3*, opened the Los Angeles office of Mili Pictures, a Chinese studio focused on family entertainment.[27] *Mission: Impossible 3*, a Chinese assisted production, suffered substantial delays in its Chinese release because of changes required by regulators.[28] By contrast, family-oriented animation offers strong potential financial returns with lower regulatory risk.

HOLLYWOOD MADE FOR CHINA

As China's media market grows, foreign media companies will increasingly need to consider the Chinese market first when developing content. The power of the Chinese market is such that Hollywood producers will ignore the interests of Chinese audiences and regulators at great financial risk. "Made in China" will be a marketing strategy rather than a way to cut costs. If the market continues to grow, rather than simply being made in China, new productions will increasingly be made *for* China. Greater focus on the Chinese market in the development process will likely mean more China-related content for global audiences. The upside of Hollywood producing content for China is that it may diversify the type of stories that Hollywood studios produce, as well as the types of people represented on the screen. Yet greater focus on the Chinese market also may privilege content that is more likely to be accepted by Chinese regulators. As a result, Hollywood's accommodation of the Chinese market could substantially shift the type of media produced—not only for China, but also for other global markets. Compounding this trend, Chinese outbound capital has begun to have substantial influence in Hollywood.

Hollywood is increasingly a destination for media investment by Chinese companies in individual projects, in US-based offices, and even entire studios. Alibaba reportedly invested in the 2015 Hollywood film *Mission: Impossible—Rogue Nation* (dir. Christopher McQuarrie 2015).[29] The China Film Group has been linked as an investor to the record-breaking *Furious 7* movie (dir. James Wan 2015).[30] Chinese entertainment and technology firm LeTV established its US offices in Los Angeles in 2015.[31] In April 2015, Chinese film studio Huayi Bros. made an agreement with American motion picture company STX entertainment to co-produce and co-distribute 12 to 15 films.[32] In January 2016, the Dalian Wanda Group acquired American studio Legendary Pictures, making it the first Chinese firm to own a Hollywood studio.[33] Rather than made in China, Hollywood studio productions will also increasingly be made *by* China—or rather, by Chinese companies investing in Hollywood.[34]

If China's outbound investment in Hollywood increases, the Chinese government will have less need to accommodate Hollywood capital and technical investment in China. As more distribution moves to networked digital platforms, the incentive structure for Chinese collaborations with Hollywood is likely to shift from collaboration to competition. The increasing role of digital platforms in media distribution is poised to diminish the potential impact American companies can have within Chinese media markets.

Chinese media investment in the United States, by contrast, shows no signs of slowing down. Depending on its scope, Chinese FDI could reshape our understanding of the global cultural dominance of the US motion-picture industry, radically expanding what cultural critic Rey Chow termed Chinese cinema's "becoming-visible" to global audiences.[35] As this book has argued, Hollywood's relationship with China has already begun to leave a substantial global footprint as the result of collaborations on big-budget film releases and record-breaking shared theme park and studio investment.

The Chinese Dream and the Hollywood dream factory are becoming evermore entwined as Chinese media firms expand outward into the United States, and as the media and technology sectors continue to converge. But China and Hollywood remain in competition for global dominance—much as the United States and the PRC compete in the diplomatic realm. In parallel, as Chinese content regulations become more significant to international media production, global commercial media culture may become subject to more demanding content restrictions to which foreign producers may voluntarily agree because of their desire for access to the Chinese market. Collaborations advancing the Hollywood dream factory and the Chinese Dream may also crowd out content from other locales or in less commercial forms, thereby limiting rather than expanding the types of entertainment available to the global public. Although seemingly awash with an air of inevitability, Hollywood-China collaboration remains unpredictable. Regardless of the ultimate outcome, visual spectacles in the form of red-carpet events, theme parks, and blockbusters are poised to become only more dramatic as Hollywood and China negotiate their global media brands.

APPENDIX 1 Examples of Sino-US Film
Collaboration by Type

OFFICIAL CO-PRODUCTIONS (COMPLETED)

Restless (Julie Gilfillan, 2001)
Shanghai Red (Oscar L. Costo, 2006)
Lust, Caution (Ang Lee, 2007)
Shanghai Kiss (Kern Konweiser, David Ren, 2007)
The Kite Runner (Marc Forster, 2007)
The Forbidden Kingdom (Rob Minkoff, 2008)
The Mummy: Tomb of the Dragon Emperor (Rob Cohen, 2008)
Distance Runners (Robert Vicencio, 2009)
Disney High School Musical: China (Chen Shi-Zheng, 2010)
The Karate Kid (Harald Zwart, 2010)
Shanghai (Mikael Håfström, 2010)*
Shanghai Calling (Daniel Hsia, 2012)
Kung Fu Panda 3 (Alessandro Carloni and Jennifer Yuh, 2016)
Skiptrace (Renny Harlin, 2016)

* This film has the unique distinction of being both an official co-production and a faux-production. It started as a co-production, lost SARFT (later known as SAPPRFT) approval, and then regained approval prior to distribution.

167

FAUX-PRODUCTIONS

Shanghai (Mikael Håfström, 2010)
Cloud Atlas (Tom Tykwer, Andy Wachowski, and Lana Wachowski, 2012)
Looper (Rian Johnson, 2012)
Iron Man 3 (Shane Black, 2013)
Transformers: Age of Extinction (Michael Bay, 2014)
Transcendance (Wally Pfister, 2014)

ASSISTED PRODUCTIONS

Code 46 (Michael Winterbottom, 2003)
Kill Bill: Volume 1 (Quentin Tarantino, 2003)
The Painted Veil (John Curran, 2006)
Mission: Impossible III (J. J. Abrams, 2006)
Ultraviolet (Kurt Wimmer, 2006)
The Forbidden Kingdom (Rob Minkoff, 2008)
Skyfall (Sam Mendes, 2012)
Her (Spike Jonze, 2013)

CHINESE PRODUCTIONS WITH HOLLYWOOD-BASED
TALENT

Big Shot's Funeral (Feng Xiaogang, 2001)
The Pavilion of Women (Yim Ho, 2001)
Flowers of War (Zhang Yimou, 2011)
Inseparable (Dayyan Eng, 2012)
Back to 1942 (Feng Xiaogang, 2012)
My Lucky Star (Dennie Gordon, 2013)
Dragon Blade (Daniel Lee, 2015)
Hollywood Adventures (Timothy Kendall, 2015)

FOREIGN-BRANDED LOCAL PRODUCTIONS

Disney's *The Secret of the Magic Gourd* (Frankie Chung, 2007)
Disney's *Trail of the Panda* (Zhong Yu, 2009)

CHINESE CORPORATE INVESTMENTS IN HOLLYWOOD
STUDIO FILMS

Furious 7 (James Wan, 2015)
Mission: Impossible—Rogue Nation (Christopher McQuarrie 2015)
The Space between Us (Peter Chelsom, 2016)

Chinese Character
Glossary

FILMS AND TV TITLES

The glossary translations for film and television releases are not direct translations of the English-language title, but rather the names used for distribution in the Chinese market.

Amazing Race, The (Jisu Qianjin) 极速前进
Amazing Race, The: China Rush (Jisu Qianjin: Chongci Zhongguo)
　　极速前进: 冲刺! 中国
Amazing Spider-Man, The (Chaofan Zhizhixia) 超凡蜘蛛侠
Back to 1942 (Yi Jiu Si Er) 一九四二
Bait (3D) (Dahaixiao Zhi Shakou Taosheng) 大海啸之鲨口逃生
Big Shot's Funeral (Da Wan) 大腕
Black Coal, Thin Ice (Bai Ri, Yan Huo) 白日焰火
Blue Kite, The (Lan Fengzheng) 蓝风筝
Captain America: Civil War (Meiguo Duizhang 3) 美国队长3
Captain America: The Winter Soldier (Meiguo Duizhang 2) 美国队长2
Crouching Tiger, Hidden Dragon (Wo Hu Cang Long) 卧虎藏龙
Crouching Tiger, Hidden Dragon: The Sword of Destiny (Wo Hu Cang Long:
　　Qing Ming Bao Jian) 卧虎藏龙：青冥宝剑
Dark Knight Rises, The (Bianfuxia: Heian Qishi Jueqi) 蝙蝠侠：黑暗骑士崛起
Disney High School Musical: China (Ge Wu Qing Chun [Zhongguo Ban])
　　歌舞青春 [中国版]

Distance Runners (Zhui Meng Ren) 追梦人
Django Unchained (Bei Jiejiu de Jiangge) 被解救的姜戈
Dragon Blade (Tian Jiang Xiong Shi) 天将雄师
Eat Drink Man Woman (Yin Shi Nan Nü) 饮食男女
Expendables 2, The (Gansidui 2) 敢死队2
Expendables 3, The (Gansidui 3) 敢死队3
Fearless (Huo Yuanjia) 霍元甲
Finding Mr. Right (Beijing Yu Shang Xiyatu) 北京遇上西雅图
Forbidden Kingdom, The (Gongfu zhi Wang) 功夫之王
Founding of a Party, The (Jiandang Weiye) 建党伟业
Founding of a Republic, The (Jianguo Daye) 建国大业
Furious 7 (Sudu Yu Jiqing 7) 速度与激情7
Great Raid, The (Da Touxi) 大偷袭
Great Wall, The (Chang Cheng) 长城
Hollywood Adventures (Heng Chong Zhi Zhuang Hao Lai Wu) 横冲直撞好莱坞
I Don't Want to Sleep Alone (Hei Yan Quan) 黑眼圈
Inseparable (Xingying Bu Li) 形影不离
Iron Man 2 (Tiegang Xia 2) 钢铁侠2
Iron Man 3 (Tiegang Xia 3) 钢铁侠3
Jurassic World (Zhuluoji Shijie) 侏罗纪世界
Karate Kid, The (Gongfu Meng) 功夫梦
Kung Fu Hustle (Gongfu) 功夫
Kung Fu Panda 3 (Gongfu Xiongmao 3) 功夫熊猫3
Longest Night in Shanghai, The (Ye, Shanghai) 夜·上海
Lorax, The (Laoleisi de Gushi) 老雷斯的故事
Lost in Thailand (Ren Zai Jiongtu Zhi Tai Jiong) 人再囧途之泰囧
Lust, Caution (Se, Jie) 色·戒
Mermaid, The (Meirenyu) 美人鱼
Mission: Impossible III (Die Zhong Die 3) 碟中谍3
Mission: Impossible—Rogue Nation (Die Zhong Die 5: Shenmi Guodu)
    碟中谍5：神秘国度
Moon and the Sun, The (Riyuerenyu) 日月人鱼
Mummy: Tomb of the Dragon Emperor, The (Munaiyi 3: Longdi zhi Mu)
    木乃伊3:龙帝之墓
My Lucky Star (Feichang Xingyun) 非常幸运
Perhaps Love (Ruguo Ai) 如果爱
Prometheus (Puluomixiusi) 普罗米修斯
Secret of the Magic Gourd, The (Bao Hulu de Mimi) 宝葫芦的秘密
Shanghai (Die Hai Feng Yun) 谍海风云
Shanghai Calling (Niuyueke @ Shanghai) 纽约客@上海
Shanghai Red (Hong Meili) 红美丽
Skiptrace (Juedi Taowang) 绝地逃亡

Snow Flower and the Secret Fan (Xuehua Mishan) 雪花秘扇
Super Girl (Chaoji Nüsheng) 超级女声
Transformers: Age of Extinction (Bianxingjingang 4: Jueji Chongsheng)
   变形金刚4：绝迹重生
Trail of the Panda (Xiong Mao Hui Jia Lu) 熊猫回家路
Voice of China, The (Zhongguo Hao Shengyin) 中国好声音

TERMS, ORGANIZATIONS, AND NAMES

assistant *(zhuli)* 助理
assisted production *(xiepai dianying)* 协拍电影
buyout film *(jinkou maiduan pian)* 进口买断片
China Film Co-Production Corporation (Zhongguo Dianying Hezuo Zhipian
   Gongsi) 中国电影合作制片公司
China Film Group (Zhongguo Dianying Jituan Gongsi) 中国电影集团公司
Chinese Dream (Zhongguo Meng) 中国梦
comprador *(maiban)* 买办
dream passport *(mengxiang huzhao)* 梦想护照
Eileen Chang (Zhang Ailing) 张爱玲
farmer *(nongmin)* 农民
film co-production *(hepai dianying)* 合拍电影
going out policy *(zouchuqu zhanlüe)* 走出去战略
Hengdian World Studios (Hengdian Yingshi Cheng) 横店影视城
Hollywood *(haolaiwu)* 好莱坞
Huallywood *(hualaiwu)* 华莱坞
new mainstream cinema *(xin zhuliu dianying)* 新主流电影
propaganda *(xuanchuan)* 宣传
public relations *(gonggong guanxi)* 公共关系
residence permit *(hukou)* 户口
Shanghai Dongfang Media Company, Ltd. (Shanghai Dongfang Chuanmei
   Jituan Youxian Gongsi) 上海东方传媒有限集团公司
Shanghai DreamCenter (Meng Zhongxin) 梦中心
Shanghai International Tourism Resort District (Shanghai Guoji Lüyou
   Dujiaqu) 上海国际旅游度假区
Mandarin *(putonghua)* 普通话
State Administration of Press, Publication, Radio, Film and Television (Guojia
   Xinwen Chuban Guangdian Zongju) 国家新闻出版广电总局
State Administration of Radio, Film and Television (Zhongguo Guojia Guangbo
   Dianying Dianshi Zongju) 国家广播电影电视总局
West Bund Media Port (Xian Chuanmei Gang) 西安传媒港

Notes

PREFACE

1. Sherry Ortner, "Studying Sideways," in *Production Studies: Cultural Studies of Media Industries*, ed. Vicki Mayer, Miranda J. Banks, and John T. Caldwell (New York: Routledge, 2009).

2. Ibid., 176; Laura Nader, "Up the Anthropologist: Perspectives Gained from Studying Up," in *Reinventing Anthropology*, ed. Dell Hymes (New York: Pantheon Books, 1972).

3. Paul Schwartzman (agent for the Hong Kong–based director Wong Kar-Wai), interview with Aynne Kokas, July 30, 2009, Shanghai, China.

4. Gareth Wigan (former vice chairman of Columbia TriStar Pictures), interview by Aynne Kokas, December 17, 2009, Los Angeles, CA.

5. Ortner, "Studying Sideways."

6. Erin Hill, "Hollywood Assistanting," in *Production Studies: Cultural Studies of Media Industries*, ed. Vicki Mayer, Miranda J. Banks, and John T. Caldwell. (New York: Routledge, 2009); Erin Hill, *Never Done* (New Brunswick, NJ: Rutgers University Press, 2016.)

7. Xiaoling Zheng, "Chinese State Media Going Global," *East Asian Policy* 2, no. 1 (2010); Zhengrong Hu and Deqiang Ji, "Ambiguities in Communicating with the World: The 'Going-out' Policy of China's Media and Its Multilayered Contexts," *Chinese Journal of Communication* 5, no. 1 (2012).

INTRODUCTION

1. Ernst & Young, *Spotlight on China: Building a Roadmap for Success in Media and Entertainment* (Ernst & Young Media and Entertainment Center, 2012); Richard Gelfond, "National Committee on U.S.-China Relations, 2013 Gala Dinner, Part 2—National Committee on U.S.-China Relations," YouTube video, 54:08, posted by the National Committee on U.S.-China Relations, October 18, 2013.

2. Clifford Coonan, "China Box Office: 'Jurassic World' Grabs $100m as Blackout Looms," *Hollywood Reporter,* June 15, 2016, www.hollywoodreporter .com/news/china-box-office-jurassic-world-802660.

3. Michael Keane, "Once Were Peripheral: Creating Media Capacity in East Asia," *Media Culture Society* 28, no. 6 (2006); Michael Keane, *Creative Industries in China: Art, Design and Media* (Malden, MA: John Wiley and Sons, 2013); Ting Wei and Bao-lian Xia, "Analysis of the Current Situation and Reasons of China's Movie and TV Cultural Trade," *International Economics and Trade Research* 24, no. 3 (2008); Yu Chen and Baoming Zhang, "Film Trade Deficit Control Measures between China and USA Based on Gravity Model," *Advances in Applied Economics and Finance* 2, no. 4 (2012); Xin Zang, Zhu Lin, and Jun Shao, "Cultural Proximity, Economic Development and Export of Cultural Products," *Finance and Trade Economics* 10 (2012); Wendy Su, "Cultural Policy and Film Industry as Negotiation of Power: The Chinese State's Role and Strategies in Its Engagement with Global Hollywood 1994–2012," *Pacific Affairs* 87, no. 1 (2014).

4. Robert W. McChesney and John Bellamy Foster, *The Endless Crisis: How Monopoly-Finance Capital Produces Stagnation and Upheaval from the USA to China* (New York: NYU Press, 2012).

5. David Shambaugh, "China's Soft-Power Push," *Foreign Affairs* 94, no. 4 (2015): 103.

6. Darrell William Davis, "Market and Marketization in the China Film Business," *Cinema Journal* 49, no. 3 (2010): 124. Experts such as cultural studies professors Shao Peiren and Yong Xiang in China have also termed this idea "Hualiwood" or *hualaiwu,* a play on the character for ethnically Chinese people, or *hua,* and the second two characters of the Chinese transliteration of Hollywood, or *haolaiwu.*

7. Tom Gunning, "The Cinema of Attraction," *Wide Angle* 3, no. 4 (1986): 65.

8. James Jianxin Gong, Wim A. Van der Stede, and Mark S. Young, "Real Options in the Motion Picture Industry: Evidence from Film Marketing and Sequels," *Contemporary Accounting Research* 28, no. 5 (2011).

9. Thomas Schatz, "The New Hollywood," in *Movie Blockbusters,* ed. Julian Stringer (New York: Routledge, 2003).

10. Linden Dalecki, "Hollywood Media Synergy as Integrated Marketing Communications," *Journal of Integrated Marketing Communications* 8, no. 1 (2008).

11. Sylvia M. Chan-Olmsted, *Competitive Strategy for Media Firms: Strategic and Brand Management in Changing Media Markets* (New York: Routledge, 2006); Amelia H. Arsenault and Manuel Castells, "The Structure and Dynamics of Global Multi-Media Business Networks," *International Journal of Communication* 2 (2008).

12. Peter Li, "One-on-One: Peter Li, China Media Capital," presentation at the US-China Film and Television Industry Expo, Los Angeles, CA, September 28, 2015.

13. Wang Zheng, "The Chinese Dream: Concept and Context," *Journal of Chinese Political Science* 19, no. 1 (2013); Josef Gregory Mahoney, "Interpreting the Chinese Dream: An Exercise of Political Hermeneutics," *Journal of Chinese Political Science* 19, no. 1 (2013); Michael X.Y. Feng, "The 'Chinese Dream' Deconstructed: Values and Institutions," *Journal of Chinese Political Science* 20, no. 2 (2015).

14. Hortense Powdermaker, *Hollywood: The Dream Factory, an Anthropologist Looks at the Movie Makers* (London: Secker and Warburg, 1951); Magali Larson and Sherri Cavan, "Hollywood Dream Factory," *Society* 9, no. 10 (1972); Joss Lutz Marsh, "Fitzgerald, Gatsby, and the Last Tycoon: The 'American Dream' and the Hollywood Dream Factory," *Literature/Film Quarterly* 20, no. 1 (1992); J. Martin Corbett, "Reconstructing Human-Centred Technology: Lessons from the Hollywood Dream Factory," *AI and SOCIETY* 12, no. 3 (1998); Jan Lin, "Dream Factory Redux: Mass Culture, Symbolic Sites, and Redevelopment in Hollywood," in *Understanding the City: Contemporary and Future Perspectives,* ed. John Eade and Christopher Mele (Malden, MA: Wiley-Blackwell, 2002).

15. Kong Fuan (assistant department chief, Shanghai Commercial Affairs Committee Service and Trade Department), interview with Aynne Kokas, July 5, 2013, Shanghai, China.

16. Xiaowen Ren (director, Shanghai City Government News and Public Affairs Research Bureau), interview with Aynne Kokas, June 6, 2013, Shanghai, China.

17. Bloomberg News, "Disney's Already Expanding Its Shanghai Resort," *Bloomberg,* June 14, 2016, www.bloomberg.com/news/articles/2016-06-15/disney-to-make-shanghai-park-even-bigger-amid-china-potential.

18. Kui-yin Cheung and Ping Lin, "Spillover Effects of FDI on Innovation in China: Evidence from the Provincial Data," *China Economic Review* 15, no. 1 (2004); Jimmy Ran, Jan P. Voon, and Guangzhong Li, "How Does FDI Affect China? Evidence from Industries and Provinces," *Journal of Comparative*

Economics 35, no. 4 (2007); Banri Ito, Naomitsu Yashiro, Zhaoyuan Xu, Xiao-Hong Chen, and Ryuhei Wakasugi, "How Do Chinese Industries Benefit from FDI Spillovers?," *China Economic Review* 23, no. 2 (2012).

19. Linda Low, *Economics of Information Technology and the Media* (Singapore: Singapore University Press and World Scientific Press, 2000); Yongbok Jeon, Byung Il Park, and Pervez N. Ghauri, "Foreign Direct Investment Spillover Effects in China: Are They Different across Industries with Different Technological Levels?," *China Economic Review* 26 (2013).

20. Jintao Hu, "Full Text of Hu Jintao's Report at 17th Party Congress," *Scientific Outlook on Development, 17th Communist Party of China National Congress,* October 24, 2007.

21. Allen Scott, "The Other Hollywood: The Organizational and Geographic Bases of Television-Program Production," *Media, Culture and Society* 26, no. 2 (2004); Toby Miller, Richard Maxwell, Nitin Govil, John McMurria, and Ting Wang, *Global Hollywood: No. 2* (London: British Film Institute, 2008).

22. Paul Grainge, *Brand Hollywood: Selling Entertainment in a Global Media Age* (New York: Routledge, 2008).

23. David G. Brown and Kevin Scott, "China-Taiwan Relations: Cross-Strait Relations on Hold," *Comparative Connections: A Triannual E-Journal on East Asian Bilateral Relations* 16, no. 3 (2015).

24. Victoria Tin-bor Hui, "The Protests and Beyond," *Journal of Democracy* 26, no. 2 (2015).

25. Lucy Montgomery, *China's Creative Industries: Copyright, Social Network Markets and the Business of Culture in a Digital Age* (Northampton, MA: Edward Elgar Publishing, 2010), 56.

26. Ting Wang, "Hollywood's Crusade in China prior to China's WTO Accession," *Jump Cut: A Review of Contemporary Media,* no. 49 (2007).

27. Jihong Wan and Richard Kraus, "Hollywood and China as Adversaries and Allies," *Pacific Affairs* 75, no. 3 (2002); Christina Klein, "Kung Fu Hustle: Transnational Production and the Global Chinese-Language Film," *Journal of Chinese Cinemas* 1, no. 3 (2007); Silvia Lindtner, Bonnie Nardi, Yang Wang, Scott Mainwaring, He Jing, and Wenjing Liang, "A Hybrid Cultural Ecology: World of Warcraft in China," in *Proceedings of the 2008 ACM Conference on Computer-Supported Cooperative Work* (New York: ACM, 2008).

28. Kenneth Lieberthal and Jisi Wang, *Addressing U.S.-China Strategic Distrust* (Washington, DC: John L. Thornton China Center at Brookings, 2012).

29. Martine Durand and Haishan Fu, *Purchasing Power Parities and Real Expenditures of World Economies: Summary of Results and Findings of the 2011 International Comparison Program* (Washington, DC: International Bank for Reconstruction and Development, 2014); Joseph E. Stiglitz, "The Chinese Century," *Vanity Fair,* January 2015, www.vanityfair.com/news/2015/01/china-worlds-largest-economy

30. Kenneth Lieberthal, "The American Pivot to Asia," *Foreign Policy*, December 21, 2011; Mark E. Manyin, Stephen Daggett, Ben Dolven, Susan V. Lawrence, Michael F. Martin, Ronald O'Rourke, and Bruce Vaughn, *Pivot to the Pacific? The Obama Administration's Rebalancing toward Asia* (Fort Belvoir, VA: Defense Technical Information Center, 2012).

31. Motion Picture Association of America, *2015 Theatrical Market Statistics*, www.mpaa.org/wp-content/uploads/2016/04/MPAA-Theatrical-Market-Statistics-2015_Final.pdf, last modified April 2016.

32. Ernst & Young, "Spotlight on China."

33. Motion Picture Association of America, *2012 Theatrical Market Statistics*, www.mpaa.org/wp-content/uploads/2014/03/2012-Theatrical-Market-Statistics-Report.pdf, last modified 2013; *2013 Theatrical Market Statistics*, www.mpaa .org/wp-content/uploads/2014/03/MPAA-Theatrical-Market-Statistics-2013_ 032514-v2.pdf, last modified March 2014; *2014 Theatrical Statistics Summary*, www.mpaa.org/wp-content/uploads/2015/03/MPAA-Theatrical-Market-Statistics-2014.pdf, last modified March 2015; *2015 Theatrical Market Statistics*.

34. Motion Picture Association of America, *2015 Theatrical Market Statistics*.

35. Charles Rivkin, "2014 US-China Film Summit: Charles Rivkin," Asia Society video, 13:25, http://asiasociety.org/video/2014-us-china-film-summit-charles-rivkin, November 5, 2014.

36. Ernst & Young, "Spotlight on China."

37. Christopher Dodd, "Big Screen, Big Markets: U.S.-China Relations in the Film Business," keynote speech at the Beijing International Film Festival, Beijing, April 17, 2014, www.mpaa.org/wp-content/uploads/2014/04/Sino-Foreign-Co-Production-Forum-Remarks-As-Prepared-for-Delivery.pdf.

38. Michael Curtin, *Playing to the World's Biggest Audience: The Globalization of Chinese Film and TV* (Berkeley: University of California Press, 2007).

39. The Chinese translation of the book's title is *Zhongguo Zhizao de Haolaiwu*, as determined in conversation with Professor Li Daoxin and his students at the Peking University School of Art.

40. Yingchi Chu, "The Consumption of Cinema in Contemporary China," in *Media in China: Consumption, Content and Crisis*, ed. Stephanie Hemelryk Donald, Yin Hong, and Michael Keane (New York: Routledge, 2011); Ying Xiao, "'Leitmotif' State, Market, and Postsocialist Film Industry under Neoliberal Globalization," in *Neoliberalism and Global Cinema: Capital, Culture, and Marxist Critique*, ed. Jyotsna Kapur and Keith B. Wagner (New York: Routledge, 2011); Xiaobing Tang, *Visual Culture in Contemporary China: Paradigms and Shifts* (Cambridge, UK: Cambridge University Press, 2014).

41. Zhen Zhang, *The Urban Generation* (Durham, NC: Duke University Press, 2007).

42. Sharon LaFraniere, "Despite State Meddling, 'Avatar' Beats 'Confucius' in China," *New York Times*, January 29, 2010, www.nytimes.com/2010/01/30/business/global/30avatar.html.

43. Ibid.

44. Cameron Pace Group China, "Guanyu Women" 关于我们, www.cpgchina.com.cn/CPG/About/, last modified 2014.

45. Michael Keane, Anthony Y. H. Fung, and Albert Moran, *New Television, Globalisation, and the East Asian Cultural Imagination* (Hong Kong: Hong Kong University Press, 2007); Anthony Y. H. Fung, *Global Capital, Local Culture: Transnational Media Corporations in China* (New York: Peter Lang International Academic Publishers, 2008).

46. Wendy Su, "New Strategies of China's Film Industry as Soft Power," *Global Media and Communication* 6, no. 3 (2010); Wendy Su, "Resisting Cultural Imperialism, or Welcoming Cultural Globalization? China's Extensive Debate on Hollywood Cinema from 1994 to 2007," *Asian Journal of Communication* 21, no. 2 (2011); Su, "Cultural Policy and Film Industry."

47. Andrew Stewart, "Wanda Group Acquires AMC Entertainment," *Variety*, September 4, 2012, http://variety.com/2012/film/news/wanda-group-acquires-amc-entertainment-1118058647/; Ali Jaafar, "China's Le Vision Pictures Eyes Global Tentpoles with New LA Offshoot," *Deadline*, October 7, 2014, http://deadline.com/2014/10/china-le-vision-us-office-847216/; Patrick Frater, "China's Fosun Revealed as Leading Owner of Jeff Robinov's Studio 8 (Exclusive)," *Variety*, April 20, 2015, http://variety.com/2015/biz/asia/fosun-jeff-robinov-1201475704/; Patrick Frater, "China's Wanda Acquires Legendary Entertainment for $3.5 Billion," *Variety*, January 11, 2016, http://variety.com/2016/biz/asia/wanda-deal-with-legendary-1201676878/.

48. Anna Klingmann, *Brandscapes: Architecture in the Experience Economy* (Cambridge: Massachusetts Institute of Technology Press, 2007), 83.

49. Notable exceptions include Fung, *Global Capital;* Su, "Cultural Policy and Film Industry"; Nitin Govil, *Orienting Hollywood: A Century of Film Culture between Los Angeles and Bombay* (New York: New York University Press, 2015).

50. Edward Herrmann and Robert W. McChesney, *Global Media: The New Missionaries of Global Capitalism* (London: Continuum, 2004).

51. Brooks Barnes, "Theme Parks and Movies Propel Profit at Disney," *New York Times*, November 7, 2013, www.nytimes.com/2013/11/08/business/media/disney-and-netflix-in-deal-for-series-based-on-marvel-characters.html.

52. Su, "Cultural Policy and Film Industry."

53. Susan Christopherson and Michael Storper, "The Effects of Flexible Specialization on Industrial Politics and the Labor Market: The Motion Picture Industry," *Industrial and Labor Relations Review* 42, no. 3 (1989).

54. Ibid., 333.

1. POLICY AND SUPERHEROES

1. Joseph S. Nye, Jr., "Soft Power," *Foreign Policy* 80 (1990); "Chinese Soft Power in Latin America: A Case Study," *Joint Force Quarterly* 60, no. 1 (2011); Łukasz Fijałkowski, "China's 'Soft Power' in Africa?," *Journal of Contemporary African Studies* 29, no. 2 (2011); Gregory G. Holyk, "Paper Tiger? Chinese Soft Power in East Asia," *Political Science Quarterly* 126, no. 2 (2011); Xin Li and Verner Worm, "Building China's Soft Power for a Peaceful Rise," *Journal of Chinese Political Science* 16, no. 1 (2011); Deborah Bräutigam and Tang Xiaoyang, "Economic Statecraft in China's New Overseas Special Economic Zones: Soft Power, Business or Resource Security?," *International Affairs* 88, no. 4 (2012); Barthélémy Courmont, "What Implications for Chinese Soft Power: Charm Offensive or New Hegemony?," *Pacific Focus* 28, no. 3 (2013); Yuezhi Zhao, "China's Quest for 'Soft Power': Imperatives, Impediments and Irreconcilable Tensions?," *Javnost—The Public* 20, no. 4 (2013); Wendy Su, "Cultural Policy and Film Industry as Negotiation of Power: The Chinese State's Role and Strategies in Its Engagement with Global Hollywood 1994–2012," *Pacific Affairs* 87, no. 1 (2014); David Shambaugh, "China's Soft-Power Push," *Foreign Affairs* 94, no. 4 (2015): 103.

2. Matthew D. Johnson, "Propaganda and Censorship in Chinese Cinema," in *A Companion to Chinese Cinema*, ed. Yingjin Zhang (Malden, MA: Wiley-Blackwell, 2012), 175.

3. Ibid.

4. Keqiang Li, "Report on the Work of the Government," *National People's Congress*, March 18, 2014, http://english.gov.cn/premier/news/2016/03/17 /content_281475309417987.htm.

5. Su, "Cultural Policy and Film Industry."

6. "Xi Jinping: Jianshe Shehuizhuyi Wenhua Qiangguozheli Tigao Guojia Wenhua Ruanshili" (Build Socialist Culture to Strengthen the Nation, Focus on Improving the Country's Cultural Soft Power), *Xinhua*, January 1, 2014, http:// politics.people.com.cn/n/2014/0101/c1001-23994334.html (my translation).

7. Ibid.

8. World Trade Organization, "Accession of the People's Republic of China," *Accession Protocol WT/L/432* (2001), December 11, 2011, www.wto.org/english /thewto_e/acc_e/completeacc_e.htm.

9. U.S. Delegation to the WTO, "China—Measures Affecting Trading Rights and Distribution Services for Certain Publications and Audiovisual Entertainment Products, Request for Consultations by the United States," WT/DS363 /1 G/L/820 S/L/287 (2007), April 10, 2007, www.wto.org/english/tratop_e /dispu_e/cases_e/ds363_1.htm.

10. World Trade Organization, *Report of the Appellate Body, China—Measures Affecting Trading Rights and Distribution Services for Certain Publications and*

Audiovisual Entertainment Products, WT/DS363/AR, December 21, 2009, https://docs.wto.org/dol2fe/Pages/FE_Search/FE_S_S006.aspx?Query=(@Symbol=%20wt/ds363/ab/r*%20not%20rw*)&Language=ENGLISH&Context=FomerScriptedSearch&languageUIChanged=true#.

11. World Trade Organization, "Memorandum of Understanding between the People's Republic of China and the United States of America Regarding Films for Theatrical Release," April 25, 2012, www.state.gov/documents/organization/202987.pdf.

12. Ibid.

13. Office of the United States Trade Representative, *2014 Report to Congress on China's WTO Compliance* (Washington, DC: United States Trade Representative, 2014).

14. United States Trade Representative, *Public Hearing before the Trade Policy Staff Committee on China's WTO Compliance* (Washington, DC: United States Trade Representative, 2014).

15. Ibid.

16. Michael Berry, "Chinese Cinema with Hollywood Characteristics, or How the Karate Kid Became a Chinese Film," in *The Oxford Handbook of Chinese Cinemas,* ed. Carlos Rojas and Eileen Chow (New York: Oxford University Press, 2013); Qinyu Hao, "Development Report on the Film Industry (2011–2012)," in *China Cultural and Creative Industries Reports 2013,* ed. Hardy Yong Xiang and Patricia Ann Walker (Berlin: Springer 2014); Su, "Cultural Policy and Film Industry."

17. Motion Picture Association of America, *2015 Theatrical Market Statistics,* www.mpaa.org/wp-content/uploads/2016/04/MPAA-Theatrical-Market-Statistics-2015_Final.pdf, last modified April 2016.

18. Sandrine Cahn and Daniel Schimmel, "The Cultural Exception: Does It Exist in GATT and Frameworks—How Does It Affect or Is It Affected by the Agreement on TRIPS?," *Cardozo Arts and Entertainment Law Journal* 15 (1997); Caroline Pauwels and Jan Loisen, "The WTO and the Audiovisual Sector: Economic Free Trade vs Cultural Horse Trading?," *European Journal of Communication* 18, no. 3 (2003); Christoph Beat Graber, "The New UNESCO Convention on Cultural Diversity: A Counterbalance to the WTO?," *Journal of International Economic Law* 9, no. 3 (2006).

19. Tina W. Chao, "GATT's Cultural Exemption of Audiovisual Trade: The United States May Have Lost the Battle but Not the War," *University of Pennsylvania Journal of International Economics and Law* 17 (1996): 1127–54; Cahn and Schimmel, "Cultural Exception."

20. Emilie Yueh-yu Yeh and Darrell William Davis, "Re-Nationalizing China's Film Industry: Case Study on the China Film Group and Film Marketization," *Journal of Chinese Cinemas* 2, no. 1 (2008).

21. "The Outline of the 12th Five-Year Program for National Economic and Social Development of the People's Republic of China," *Xinhua*, March 16, 2001, www.asifma.org/uploadedFiles/Resources/PRC-12th-FYP%281%29.PDF.

22. Anna Klingmann, *Brandscapes: Architecture in the Experience Economy* (Cambridge: Massachusetts Institute of Technology Press, 2007).

23. "Outline of the 12th Five-Year Program," 42.

24. Ibid.

25. Ibid.

26. Michael Keane, *Creative Industries in China: Art, Design and Media* (Malden, MA: John Wiley and Sons, 2013).

27. Su, "Cultural Policy and Film Industry."

28. Hong Yu, "Reading the Twelfth Five-Year Plan: China's Communication-Driven Mode of Economic Restructuring," *International Journal of Communication* 5 (2011): 1045–57.

29. Jon Lewis, *Hollywood V. Hard Core: How the Struggle over Censorship Created the Modern Film Industry* (New York: New York University Press, 2002).

30. Ibid.

31. Ronald Brownstein, *The Power and the Glitter: The Hollywood-Washington Connection* (New York: Pantheon Books, 1990).

32. Kevin Lee, "Little State Department: Hollywood and the MPAA's Influence on US Trade Relations," *Northwestern Journal of International Law and Business* 28 (2007): 371–98.

33. Motion Picture Association of America, "Our Story," www.mpaa.org /our-story/, last modified 2016.

34. Paul Swann, "The Little State Department: Washington and Hollywood's Rhetoric of the Postwar Audience," in *Hollywood in Europe: Studies in a Cultural Hegemony*, edited by David Ellwood and Robert Kroes (Amsterdam: University of Utrecht Press, 1994); K. Lee, "Little State Department"; Hiroshi Kitamura, *Screening Enlightenment: Hollywood and the Cultural Reconstruction of Defeated Japan* (New York: Cornell University Press, 2010).

35. Yasheng Huang, Li Jin, and Yi Qian, "Does Ethnicity Pay? Evidence from Overseas Chinese FDI in China," *Review of Economics and Statistics* 95, no. 3 (2012).

36. World Trade Organization, "Memorandum of Understanding."

37. Ibid.

38. Anthony Vogels (senior vice president, International Development, IMAX), "The Art of Dealmaking," presentation at panel discussion, US-China Film and Television Industry Expo, Los Angeles, CA, September 28, 2015.

39. Jennifer Rubin, "Biden's Role in U.S. Companies' Deals with China," *Washington Post*, June 1, 2012, www.washingtonpost.com/blogs/right-turn/post /bidens-role-in-us-companies-deals-with-china/2012/06/01/gJQAEcSz7U_blog .html.

184   NOTES TO PAGES 29-33

40. Jeremy Page, "China's Xi Cultivates Relaxed Image on U.S. Trip," *Wall Street Journal*, February 19, 2012, www.wsj.com/articles/SB1000142405297020 4880404577231532208588976.

41. Feng-chao Liu, Denis Fred Simon, Yu-tao Sun, and Cong Cao, "China's Innovation Policies: Evolution, Institutional Structure, and Trajectory," *Research Policy* 40, no. 7 (2011); H. Yu, "Reading the Twelfth Five-Year Plan."

42. Anh Tran Hoang, "The Fragile and Vulnerable Foundation of the Sino-US Relationship," in *PacNet* 52 (Honolulu: Pacific Forum Center for Strategic and International Studies, 2013), www.csis.org/analysis/pacnet-52-fragile-and-vulnerable-foundation-sino-us-relationship.

43. Patrick Frater, "China Media Capital, Warner Bros. Seal Flagship Production Pact," *Variety*, September 20, 2015, http://variety.com/2015/film/asia/china-media-capital-warner-bros-seal-flagship-production-pact-1201597886/.

44. Veronica Toney, "Complete Guest List for the State Dinner in Honor of Chinese President Xi Jinping," *Washington Post*, September 25, 2015, www.washingtonpost.com/news/reliable-source/wp/2015/09/25/complete-guest-list-for-the-state-dinner-in-honor-of-chinese-president-xi-jinping/.

45. Ibid.

46. Ibid.

47. Ibid.

48. Veronica Toney, "The Combined Wealth of the Head Table at the Chinese State Dinner Is $49 Billion," *Washington Post*, September 25, 2015, www.washingtonpost.com/news/reliable-source/wp/2015/09/25/who-will-sit-at-the-head-table-at-the-chinese-state-dinner/.

49. Denise Mann, *Hollywood Independents: The Postwar Talent Takeover* (Minneapolis: University of Minnesota Press, 2008); Richard McGregor, *The Party: The Secret World of China's Communist Rulers* (New York: HarperCollins Publishers, 2010); David L. Shambaugh, *China's Communist Party: Atrophy and Adaptation* (Washington, DC: Woodrow Wilson Center Press, 2008).

50. Alexandra Cheney, "'Iron Man 3' Breaks Opening Day Records in China," *Speakeasy* (blog), *Wall Street Journal*, May 2, 2013, http://blogs.wsj.com/speakeasy/2013/05/02/iron-man-3-breaks-opening-day-records-in-china/.

51. Xiaying Xu, Tan See Kam, and Jiang Wei, "Of Goats, Lambs, Sheep and Wolves: Chinese Animation and Cultural Industries," *Asian Cinema* 24, no. 2 (2013).

52. Helen Pidd, "Sci-Fi Blockbuster Looper Achieves Chinese Box Office First," *The Guardian*, October 1, 2012, www.theguardian.com/film/2012/oct/01/looper-sci-fi-blockbuster-china.

53. James Daniel, "Iron Man 3 Execs 'Changed Film for Chinese Audience' by Adding Four Minutes to the Film with Chinese Actors," *Daily Mail*, May 13, 2013, www.dailymail.co.uk/news/article-2324077/Iron-Man-3-execs-changed-film-Chinese-audience-adding-4-minutes-Chinese-actors.html.

54. Heather Xiaoquan Zhang, Bin Wu, and Richard Sanders, *Marginalisation in China: Perspectives on Transition and Globalisation* (Burlington, VT: Ashgate Publishing, 2007).

55. Brian Ashcraft, "Why Many in China Hate Iron Man 3's Chinese Version," *Kotaku*, May 2, 2013, http://kotaku.com/why-many-in-china-hate-iron-man-3s-chinese-version-486840429.

56. Clarence Tsui, "'Iron Man 3' China-Only Scenes Draw Mixed Response," *Hollywood Reporter*, May 1, 2013, www.hollywoodreporter.com/news/iron-man-3-china-scenes-450184.

57. Grady Smith, "Box Office Update: 'Iron Man 3' Earns Huge $68.3 Million on Friday," *Entertainment Weekly*, May 4, 2013, http://insidemovies.ew.com/2013/05/04/box-office-update-iron-man-3/.

58. Germain Lussier, "Here's How the Chinese Cut of 'Iron Man 3' Is Different," *Slashfilm*, May 1, 2013, www.slashfilm.com/heres-how-the-chinese-cut-of-iron-man-3-is-different/.

59. Alyssa Sage, "Marvel Responds to *Doctor Strange* 'Whitewashing' Criticisms over Tilda Swinton Casting," *Variety*, April 27, 2016, http://variety.com/2016/film/news/doctor-strange-whitewashing-tilda-swinton-marvel-1201762267/.

60. Ibid.

61. Wheeler Winston Dixon and Gwendolyn Audrey Foster, *21st-Century Hollywood: Movies in the Era of Transformation* (New Brunswick, NJ: Rutgers University Press, 2011).

62. "Outline of the 12th Five-Year Program," 42.

63. Nancy Tartaglione, "Paramount Enters 'Cooperation Agreement' to Produce *Transformers* in China," *Deadline Hollywood*, April 2, 2013, http://deadline.com/2013/04/paramount-partner-china-produce-transformers-4-michael-bay-movie-channel-jiaflix-465746/.

64. Johannes Chan, "Hong Kong's Umbrella Movement," *The Round Table* 103, no. 6 (2014).

65. Scott Neumyer, "Exclusive Images: Take a Peek behind the Scenes of 'Transformers: Age of Extinction,'" *Tech Times*, September 12, 2015, www.techtimes.com/articles/16933/20141002/exclusive-images-transformers-age-of-extinction.htm.

2. HOLLYWOOD'S CHINA

1. Mary Forgione, "Nine Things You Need to Know about the World's Biggest Disney Store," *Los Angeles Times*, May 22, 2015, www.latimes.com/travel/la-trb-disney-store-china-20150521-htmlstory.html.

2. B. Joseph Pine II and James H. Gilmore, *The Experience Economy*, updated edition (Boston: Harvard Business Press, 2011), ix.

3. Ibid.

4. Nigel Thrift, *Knowing Capitalism* (Thousand Oaks, CA: SAGE, 2005).

5. Phil Hettema (president and creative executive, The Hettema Group), "China's Real Estate Investments," presentation at panel discussion, US-China Film and Television Industry Expo, Los Angeles, CA, September 29, 2015.

6. Pine and Gilmore, *The Experience Economy;* Mary Yoko Brannen, "When Mickey Loses Face: Recontextualization, Semantic Fit, and the Semiotics of Foreignness," *Academy of Management Review* 29, no. 4 (2004).

7. Anna Klingmann, *Brandscapes: Architecture in the Experience Economy* (Cambridge: Massachusetts Institute of Technology Press, 2007), 83.

8. Pine and Gilmore, *The Experience Economy*, ix.

9. Alexander Biel, "Converting Image into Equity," in *Brand Equity and Advertising: Advertising's Role in Building Strong Brands*, ed. David A. Aaker (New York: Psychology Press, 2013), 71.

10. Klingmann, *Brandscapes*, 83.

11. Philip J. Kitchen and Don E. Schultz, *Raising the Corporate Umbrella: Corporate Communications in the Twenty-First Century* (London: Palgrave Macmillan, 2001); Lynn Thorne, *Word-of-Mouth Advertising, Online and Off: How to Spark Buzz, Excitement, and Free Publicity for Your Business or Organization with Little or No Money* (Ocala, FL: Atlantic Publishing Company, 2008).

12. Scott A. Lukas, *Theme Park* (London: Reaktion Books, 2008).

13. Thomas Schatz, *The Genius of the System: Hollywood Filmmaking in the Studio Era* (New York: Henry Holt and Company, 1996); David Bordwell, Janet Staiger, and Kristin Thompson, *The Classical Hollywood Cinema: Film Style and Mode of Production to 1960* (New York: Routledge, 2003).

14. Douglas Gomery, "Economic Struggle and Hollywood Imperialism: Europe Converts to Sound," *Yale French Studies*, no. 60 (1980); Thomas Schatz, "The New Hollywood," in *Movie Blockbusters*, ed. Julian Stringer (New York: Routledge, 2003).

15. Michael Curtin, *Playing to the World's Biggest Audience: The Globalization of Chinese Film and TV* (Berkeley: University of California Press, 2007).

16. Ben Goldsmith and Tom O'Regan, *The Film Studio: Film Production in the Global Economy* (Lanham, MD: Rowman and Littlefield, 2005).

17. Allen J. Scott and Naomi E. Pope, "Hollywood, Vancouver, and the World: Employment Relocation and the Emergence of Satellite Production Centers in the Motion-Picture Industry," *Environment and Planning A* 39, no. 6 (2007).

18. Daragh O'Reilly and Finola Kerrigan, "A View to a Brand: Introducing the Film Brandscape," *European Journal of Marketing* 47, no. 5/6 (2013).

19. Salvador Anton Clavé, *The Global Theme Park Industry* (Cambridge, MA: CABI, 2007).

20. David Harvey, *Seventeen Contradictions and the End of Capitalism*, reprint edition (Oxford: Oxford University Press, 2015), 151.

21. "Shanghai Disney Resort Signs Alliance Agreement with Invengo," https://news.shanghaidisneyresort.com.cn/index.php?m=content&c=index&a=show&catid=8&id=326.

22. Bloomberg News, "Disney's Already Expanding Its Shanghai Resort," *Bloomberg*, June 14, 2016, www.bloomberg.com/news/articles/2016–06–15/disney-to-make-shanghai-park-even-bigger-amid-china-potential.

23. Victor Yip (director and general manager, Broadband Media, The Walt Disney Company, Shanghai), interview with Aynne Kokas, April 21, 2009, Shanghai, China.

24. Laikwan Pang, *Creativity and Its Discontents: China's Creative Industries and Intellectual Property Rights Offenses* (Durham, NC: Duke University Press, 2012).

25. Shanghai DreamCenter, "DreamCenter," www.dreamcentersh.com, last modified 2015.

26. "Guanyu Women" (About Us), *Xi An*, www.westbund.com/cn/index/On_the_West_Bund/Regional/DistrictOverview.html; "Shanghai Xian Kaifa [Jituan] Youxian Gongsi," *Shanghai Shi Xuhui Qu Youxian Zichanye Jiandu Guanli Weiyuanhui* (Shanghai West Development [Group] Limited Liability Company), http://xhgz.xh.sh.cn/SOE/?cid = 31&aid = 0e32fd50–7138–4bfb-8250–74b83c9bd3a2, last updated May 30, 2015.

27. Gabrielle Jaffe, "James Cameron's 3D China Venture," *Los Angeles Times*, August 8, 2012, http://articles.latimes.com/2012/aug/08/entertainment/la-et-ct-james-camerons-3d-china-venture-20120808; Motion Picture Association and China Film Co-Production Corporation, *China-International Film Co-Production Guide*, http://mpa-i.org/wp-content/uploads/2014/12/Co-Production_Handbook_English.pdf, last modified 2014.

28. Patrick Frater, "China's Wanda Acquires Legendary Entertainment for $3.5 Billion," *Variety*, January 11, 2016, http://variety.com/2016/biz/asia/wanda-deal-with-legendary-1201676878/.

29. Michael Keane, "Brave New World," *International Journal of Cultural Policy* 10, no. 3 (2004).

30. Hong Yu, "Reading the Twelfth Five-Year Plan: China's Communication-Driven Mode of Economic Restructuring," *International Journal of Communication* 5 (2011); Stephen Kline, *Out of the Garden: Toys and Children's Culture in the Age of TV Marketing* (New York: Verso, 1995); Janet Wasko, *Understanding Disney: The Manufacture of Fantasy* (Malden, MA: Polity Press, 2001); Edward Herrmann and Robert W. McChesney, *Global Media: The New Missionaries of*

Global Capitalism (London: Continuum, 2004); Edward W. Soja, "Inside Exopolis: Scenes from Orange County," in *Variations on a Theme Park: The New American City and the End of Public Space,* ed. Michael Sorkin (New York: Farrar, Straus, Giroux, 1992).

31. Christine Kessides, *The Contributions of Infrastructure to Economic Development: A Review of Experience and Policy Implications,* vol. 213 (Washington, DC: World Bank Publications, 1993).

32. Rémy Prud'Homme, *Annual World Bank Conference on Development Economics 2005: Lessons of Experience* (Washington, DC: World Bank Publications, 2005), 2.

33. Abid Rahman, "Shanghai Disneyland to Benefit from High-Speed Train Line," *The Hollywood Reporter,* July 30, 2014, www.hollywoodreporter.com /news/shanghai-disneyland-benefit-high-speed-722470.

34. James S. Lee, "Disney Research Harnesses the Synergy between Buildings and Infrastructure," *URBANLAND: The Magazine of the Urban Land Institute,* May 7, 2015, http://urbanland.uli.org/sustainability/disney-research-harnesses-synergy-buildings-infrastructure/.

35. John T. Caldwell, "Para-Industry, Shadow Academy," *Cultural Studies* 28, no. 4 (2014).

36. Richard Freeman, "The Work the Document Does: Research, Policy, and Equity in Health," *Journal of Health Politics, Policy and Law* 31, no. 1 (2006); Jane Davison, "Paratextual Framing of the Annual Report: Liminal Literary Conventions and Visual Devices," *Critical Perspectives on Accounting* 22, no. 2 (2011).

37. Davison, "Paratextual Framing of the Annual Report."

38. Aynne Kokas, "Building a Transparent Web in China," *Baker Institute Policy Report* 57 (2014), http://bakerinstitute.org/research/building-transparent-web-transnational-social-media-cybersecurity-and-sino-us-trade/.

39. Chwenchwen Chen and Vincenzo De Masi, "A Chinese Animation TV Production Industry: An Overview," *China Media Observatory Newsletter* 1, no. 9 (2009), www.academia.edu/6248826/A_Chinese_Animation_TV_Production_Industry_An_Overview.

40. Ulrike Rohn, *Cultural Barriers to the Success of Foreign Media Content: Western Media in China, India, and Japan* (Frankfurt am Main, Germany: Peter Lang, 2009), 260.

41. Yip, interview.

42. Guangwei Hu, "English Language Education in China: Policies, Progress, and Problems," *Language Policy* 4, no. 1 (2005).

43. David Buckingham, *Media Education: Literacy, Learning and Contemporary Culture* (Malden, MA: Blackwell, 2003); Renee Hobbs, *Digital and Media Literacy: Connecting Culture and Classroom* (Thousand Oaks, CA: Corwin Press, 2011); Tibor Koltay, "The Media and the Literacies: Media Literacy,

Information Literacy, Digital Literacy," *Media, Culture and Society* 33, no. 2 (2011); Frank W. Baker, *Media Literacy in the K-12 Classroom* (Arlington, VA: International Society for Technology in Education, 2012); James A. Brown, *Television "Critical Viewing Skills" Education: Major Media Literacy Projects in the United States and Selected Countries* (New York: Routledge, 2013); Jason Ohler, *Digital Storytelling in the Classroom: New Media Pathways to Literacy, Learning, and Creativity* (Thousand Oaks, CA: Corwin Press, 2013).

44. "Disney English: Home," Disney Careers, disneyenglish.disneycareers/en /default/, accessed September 19, 2015.

45. Ibid.

46. Su Yan Pan, "Confucius Institute Project: China's Cultural Diplomacy and Soft Power Projection," *Asian Education and Development Studies* 2, no. 1 (2013).

47. Hongqin Zhao and Jianbin Huang, "China's Policy of Chinese as a Foreign Language and the Use of Overseas Confucius Institutes," *Educational Research for Policy and Practice* 9, no. 2 (2010).

48. Terry Flew and Falk Hartig, "Confucius Institutes and the Network Communication Approach to Public Diplomacy," *IAFOR Journal of Asian Studies* 1, no. 1 (2014).

49. "FAQ," Disney Careers, http://disneyenglish.disneycareers.com/en/faq /general/, accessed May 30, 2016.

50. Dawn C. Chmielewski and Hugo Martin, "China OKs Disney Theme Park Plans," *Los Angeles Times*, November 4, 2009, http://articles.latimes.com/2009 /nov/04/business/fi-ct-disney4.

51. Yip, interview.

52. Mary Yoko Brannen, "'Bwana Mickey': Constructing Cultural Consumption at Tokyo Disneyland," in *Re-Made in Japan: Everyday Life and Consumer Taste in a Changing Society*, ed. Joseph Jay Tobin (New Haven, CT: Yale University Press, 1992); Susan Bennett and Marlis Schweitzer, "In the Window at Disney: A Lifetime of Brand Desire," *TDR/The Drama Review* 58, no. 4 (2014); Mary Yoko Brannen, "Cross-Cultural Materialism: Commodifying Culture in Japan," in *SV—Meaning, Measure, and Morality of Materialism*, ed. Floyd W. Rudmin and Marsha Richins (Provo, UT: Association for Consumer Research, 1992); John Van Maanen, "Displacing Disney: Some Notes on the Flow of Culture," *Qualitative Sociology* 15, no. 1 (1992); David Schalkwyk, "From the Globe to Globalisation: Shakespeare and Disney in the Postmodern World," *Journal of Literary Studies* 15, nos. 1–2 (1999); Christophe Bruchansky, "The Heterotopia of Disney World," *Philosophy Now* 77 (2010).

53. Xudong Zhang, "Shanghai Image: Critical Iconography, Minor Literature, and the Un-Making of a Modern Chinese Mythology," *New Literary History* 33, no. 1 (2002): 164.

54. Wendy Su, "Cultural Policy and Film Industry as Negotiation of Power: The Chinese State's Role and Strategies in Its Engagement with Global Hollywood 1994–2012," *Pacific Affairs* 87, no. 1 (2014).

55. Ben Schwegler (SVP/chief scientist, Walt Disney Imagineering), "Leaders in Sustainability," lecture, University of Calfornia, Los Angeles, Los Angeles, CA, April 14, 2010.

56. Hui Lu, "Disney's Shanghai Park to Be Unique, Says CEO," *Xinhua*, June 6, 2013, http://news.xinhuanet.com/english/china/2013-06-06/c_132435203 .htm.

57. Van Maanen, "Displacing Disney."

58. Jonathan Matusitz, "Disney's Successful Adaptation in Hong Kong: A Glocalization Perspective," *Asia Pacific Journal of Management* 28, no. 4 (2011).

59. Marie-Claire Bergère, *Shanghai: China's Gateway to Modernity*, trans. Janet Lloyd (Stanford: Stanford University Press, 2009).

60. Poshek Fu, *Between Shanghai and Hong Kong: The Politics of Chinese Cinemas* (Stanford: Stanford University Press, 2003).

61. Martha Bayless, "Disney's Castles and the Work of the Medieval in the Middle Ages," in *The Disney Middle Ages: A Fairy-Tale and Fantasy Past*, ed. Tison Pugh and Susan Aronstein (New York: Palgrave Macmillan, 2012). "Shanghai Disneyland Resort," Shanghai Disney Resort website, www.shanghaidisneyresort .com.cn/en/about/shanghai-disneyland/, accessed January 21, 2015. As of September 15, 2015, this page is no longer available and has instead become a general Shanghai Disney Resort page.

62. Ilan Mitchell-Smith, "The United Princesses of America: Ethnic Diversity and Cultural Purity in Disney's Medieval Past," in *The Disney Middle Ages: A Fairy-Tale and Fantasy Past*, ed. Tison Pugh and Susan Aronstein (New York: Palgrave Macmillan, 2012), 216.

63. "Shanghai Disneyland Resort."

64. Thomas Smith, "Sneak Peek: Enchanted Storybook Castle at Shanghai Disneyland," *DisneyParks* blog, August 19, 2011, http://disneyparks.disney.go .com/blog/2011/08/enchanted-storybook-castle-at-shanghai-disneyland/.

65. Pudong New Area Government "Vision and Targets," *Welcome to Pudong*, http://english.pudong.gov.cn/html/pden/pden_ap_oop_pi/2014-05-28/Detail_ 74364.htm, last modified May 28, 2014.

66. Patrick Frater, "China Online Giant Baidu Launches Film Funding Unit," *Variety*, September 20, 2014, http://variety.com/2014/film/news/china-online-giant-baidu-launches-film-funding-unit-1201310689/; Clifford Coonan, "Alibaba's Film Crowdfunding Service Swarmed by Chinese Investors, Sells Out in Five Days," *The Hollywood Reporter*, April 4, 2014, www.hollywoodreporter.com /news/alibabas-film-crowdfunding-service-swarmed-693683; Abid Rahman, "China's Wanda to Create Movie Fund to Attract Hollywood Productions," *The Hollywood Reporter*, www.hollywoodreporter.com/news/chinas-wanda-create-movie-fund-739111, October 7, 2014.

67. Kokas, "Building a Transparent Web."

68. Ernst & Young, *Spotlight on China: Building a Roadmap for Success in Media and Entertainment* (Ernst & Young Media and Entertainment Center, 2012).

69. Shujen Wang, "Piracy and the DVD/VCD Market: Contradictions and Paradoxes," in *Art, Politics, and Commerce in Chinese Cinema,* ed. Ying Zhu and Stanley Rosen (Hong Kong: Hong Kong University Press, 2010); Silvia Lindtner and Marcella Szablewicz, "China's Many Internets: Participation and Digital Game Play across a Changing Technology Landscape," in *Online Society in China: Creating, Celebrating, and Instrumentalising the Online Carnival,* ed. David Kurt Herold and Peter Marolt (New York: Routledge, 2011); Sung Wook Kim and Aziz Douai, "Google Vs. China's 'Great Firewall': Ethical Implications for Free Speech and Sovereignty," *Technology in Society* 34, no. 2 (2012).

3. SOFT POWER PLAYS

1. Asia Society, "US-China Film Summit: Zhang Xun," Asia Society video, 19:06, posted by the Asia Society, November 5, 2013, http://asiasociety.org /video/us-china-film-summit-zhang-xun.

2. Ibid.

3. Ibid.

4. Ibid.

5. Chris Berry, "'What's Big about the Big Film?': 'De-Westernizing' the Blockbuster in Korea and China," in *Movie Blockbusters,* ed. Julian Stringer (New York: Routledge, 2003).

6. Shujen Wang, "Piracy and the DVD/VCD Market: Contradictions and Paradoxes," in *Art, Politics, and Commerce in Chinese Cinema,* ed. Ying Zhu and Stanley Rosen (Hong Kong: Hong Kong University Press, 2010).

7. Ibid.; Marc Gareton (executive vice president, Warner Bros. Entertainment), interview with Aynne Kokas, March 1, 2012, Los Angeles, CA.

8. Sophie Hardach and Ian Ransom, "Shanghai to Be Shot in Thailand after China Ban," *Reuters,* March 19, 2008, www.reuters.com/article/2008/03/19 /us-china-hollywood-idUST27055320080319.

9. Janet Yang (executive producer of *Disney High School Musical: China*), interview with Aynne Kokas, October 21, 2011, Los Angeles, CA.

10. Michael Keane, Anthony Y. H. Fung, and Albert Moran, *New Television, Globalisation, and the East Asian Cultural Imagination* (Hong Kong: Hong Kong University Press, 2007); Hong Yu, "Reading the Twelfth Five-Year Plan: China's Communication-Driven Mode of Economic Restructuring," *International Journal of Communication* 5 (2011); Michael Keane, *Creative Industries*

in China: Art, Design and Media (Malden, MA: John Wiley and Sons, 2013); Wendy Su, "Cultural Policy and Film Industry as Negotiation of Power: The Chinese State's Role and Strategies in Its Engagement with Global Hollywood 1994–2012," *Pacific Affairs* 87, no. 1 (2014).

11. Stephanie DeBoer, *Coproducing Asia: Locating Japanese-Chinese Regional Film and Media* (Minneapolis: University of Minnesota Press, 2014); Michael Curtin, *Playing to the World's Biggest Audience: The Globalization of Chinese Film and TV* (Berkeley: University of California Press, 2007); Toby Miller, Richard Maxwell, Nitin Govil, John McMurria, and Ting Wang, *Global Hollywood: No. 2* (London: British Film Institute, 2008); Ben Goldsmith and Tom O'Regan, *The Film Studio: Film Production in the Global Economy* (Lanham, MD: Rowman and Littlefield Publishers, 2005).

12. Arthur Andersen, *The European Film Production Guide: Finance—Tax—Legislation France—Germany—Italy—Spain—UK* (London: Routledge, 1996); Albert Moran, *Film Policy: International, National and Regional Perspectives* (New York: Routledge, 1996); Mark Litwak, *Contracts for the Film and Television Industry,* 3rd edition (Beverly Hills, CA: Silman-James Press, 2012).

13. Doris Baltruschat, *Global Media Ecologies: Networked Production in Film and Television* (New York: Routledge, 2010), 6.

14. Seio Nakajima, "Re-Imagining Civil Society in Contemporary Urban China: Actor-Network-Theory and Chinese Independent Film Consumption," *Qualitative Sociology* 36, no. 4 (2013).

15. State Administration of Radio, Film and Television, "The Stipulation of Administration on Chinese-Foreign Film Co-Production," July 6, 2004, www .cfcc-film.com.cn/policeg/content/id/1.html.

16. Motion Picture Association and China Film Co-Production Corporation, *China-International Film Co-Production Guide,* http://mpa-i.org/wp-content /uploads/2014/12/Co-Production_Handbook_English.pdf, last modified 2014, accessed May 30, 2016.

17. James Schamus (executive producer and screenwriter for *Lust, Caution*), interview with Aynne Kokas, December 18, 2009, New York, NY; Gareth Wigan (former vice chairman of Columbia TriStar), interview with Aynne Kokas, December 17, 2009, Los Angeles, CA.

18. Yingjin Zhang, *Cinema and Urban Culture in Shanghai, 1922–1943* (Stanford: Stanford University Press, 1999).

19. Yuezhi Zhao, "Transnational Capital, the Chinese State, and China's Communication Industries in a Fractured Society," *Javnost—The Public* 10, no. 4 (2003); Wendy Su, "New Strategies of China's Film Industry as Soft Power," *Global Media and Communication* 6, no. 3 (2010); Wendy Su, *China's Encounter with Global Hollywood: Cultural Policy and the Film Industry, 1994–2013* (Lexington: University Press of Kentucky, 2016).

20. Yingchi Chu, "The Consumption of Cinema in Contemporary China," in *Media in China: Consumption, Content and Crisis,* ed. Stephanie Donald, Michael Keane, and Yin Hong (London: Routledge, 2013).

21. Ibid.; Su, *China's Encounter with Global Hollywood.*

22. World Trade Organization, "Memorandum of Understanding between the People's Republic of China and the United States of America Regarding Films for Theatrical Release," April 25, 2012, www.state.gov/documents/organization /202987.pdf.

23. United States Trade Representative, *2014 Report to Congress on China's WTO Compliance* (Washington, DC: United States Trade Representative, 2014).

24. World Trade Organization, "Memorandum of Understanding"; M. Berry, "Chinese Cinema"; Chuck Tryon, *On-Demand Culture: Digital Delivery and the Future of Movies* (New Brunswick, NJ: Rutgers University Press, 2013); Su, "Cultural Policy and Film Industry."

25. Motion Picture Association of America, *2015 Theatrical Market Statistics,* www.mpaa.org/wp-content/uploads/2016/04/MPAA-Theatrical-Market-Statistics-2015_Final.pdf, last modified April 2016.

26. Sharon LaFraniere, "Despite State Meddling, 'Avatar' Beats 'Confucius' in China," *New York Times,* January 29, 2010, www.nytimes.com/2010/01/30 /business/global/30avatar.html.

27. Rob Cain, "China's Censors Ride into the Old West and Castrate 'Django,'" *China Film Biz,* April 11, 2013, http://chinafilmbiz.com/2013/04/11/chinas-censors-ride-into-the-old-west-and-castrate-django/; Ying Zhu, "Will China Unchain Django?," *CNN,* April 17, 2013, http://globalpublicsquare.blogs.cnn .com/2013/04/17/will-china-unchain-django/.

28. Daniel Miller, "After the Controversy, 'Django Unchained' Flops in China," *Los Angeles Times,* June 4, 2013, www.latimes.com/entertainment/envelope /cotown/la-et-ct-django-unchained-china-20130603-story.html.

29. Ben Fritz and Amy Kaufman, "'Ice Age' Clobbers 'The Lorax' in China Face-Off," *Los Angeles Times,* July 30, 2012, http://articles.latimes.com/2012 /jul/30/entertainment/la-et-ct-ice-age-lorax-china-20120730.

30. Ben Fritz, "'Dark Knight,' 'Spider-Man,' 'Prometheus' to Open Close in China," *Los Angeles Times,* August 13, 2012, http://articles.latimes.com/2012 /aug/13/entertainment/la-et-ct-china-dark-knight-spider-man-prometheus-20120813.

31. State Administration of Radio, Film and Television, "Stipulation of Administration."

32. Motion Picture Association and China Film Co-production Corporation, *China-International Film Co-Production Guide.*

33. Asia Society, "2013 US-China Film Summit: Zhang Xun."

34. Ibid.

35. State Administration of Radio, Film and Television, "Stipulation of Administration."

36. Wenxia Fu (Shanghai International Film Festival executive general secretary), interview with Aynne Kokas, July 3, 2013, Shanghai, China; State Administration of Radio, Film and Television, "Stipulation of Administration"; Asia Society, "2013 US-China Film Summit."

37. W. Fu, interview; Asia Society, "2013 US-China Film Summit: Zhang Xun."

38. Janet Yang (president of Janet Yang Production), "Bridging the Creative Gap," presentation at panel discussion, 2011 Asia Society US-China Film Summit, Los Angeles, CA, November 1, 2011.

39. Yoshiharu Tezuka, *Japanese Cinema Goes Global: Filmworkers' Journeys* (Hong Kong: Hong Kong University Press, 2011).

40. Ibid., 12.

41. Trista Marie, "Behind Shanghai Calling: The Real Stories that Inspired the Movie," *City Weekend,* August 10, 2012, www.cityweekend.com.cn/shanghai /blog/the-stories-behind-shanghai-calling/.

42. Patrick Frater, "Oliver Stone Spars with Chinese Film Official at Beijing Film Festival," *Variety,* April 16, 2014, http://variety.com/2014/film/news /oliver-stone-disses-international-co-productions-1201158657/; Christopher Dodd (chairman and CEO of the Motion Picture Association of America), "Big Screen, Big Markets: U.S.-China Relations in the Film Business," keynote speech at the Beijing International Film Festival, Beijing, China, April 17, 2014, www .mpaa.org/wp-content/uploads/2014/04/Sino-Foreign-Co-Production-Forum-Remarks-As-Prepared-for-Delivery.pdf.

43. Clifford Coonan, "Oliver Stone Slams Chinese Film Industry at Beijing Festival," *The Hollywood Reporter,* April 17, 2014, www.hollywoodreporter.com /news/oliver-stone-slams-chinese-film-697058.

44. Jing Meng, "Prohibition and Production of the Past: Representation of the Cultural Revolution in TV Dramas," *Media, Culture & Society* 37, no. 5 (2015).

45. State Administration of Radio, Film and Television, "Stipulation of Administration."

46. Ibid.

47. Production liaison, interview with Aynne Kokas, August 27, 2009, Shanghai, China. This interviewee requested anonymity because of the sensitive nature of the disclosure.

48. CBC Arts, "Censored Mission: Impossible III Opens in China," *CBC News,* July 21, 2006, www.cbc.ca/news/arts/censored-mission-impossible-iii-opens-in-china-1.592989.

49. BBC News, "Censored Bond Film Skyfall Opens in China," *BBC News,* January 21, 2013, www.bbc.com/news/world-asia-china-21115987.

50. Asia Society, "2013 US-China Film Summit: Zhang Xun."

51. Ana Swanson, "Stephen Colbert's 'Pander Express' Is a Brilliant Takedown of How Hollywood Sucks Up to China," *Washington Post*, October 10, 2015, www .washingtonpost.com/news/wonkblog/wp/2015/10/10/stephen-colberts-pander-express-is-a-brilliant-takedown-of-how-hollywood-sucks-up-to-china/.

52. David Palumbo-Liu, *Asian/American: Historical Crossings of a Racial Frontier* (Stanford: Stanford University Press, 1999); Jachinson W. Chan, "Bruce Lee's Fictional Models of Masculinity," *Men and Masculinities* 2, no. 4 (2000); Karen Fang, "Globalization, Masculinity, and the Changing Stakes of Hollywood Cinema for Asian American Studies," *Asian American Literary Studies* 79 (2005); Brian Locke, *Racial Stigma on the Hollywood Screen from World War II to the Present: The Orientalist Buddy Film* (New York: Macmillan, 2009); Celine Shimizu, *Straitjacket Sexualities: Unbinding Asian American Manhoods in the Movies* (Stanford: Stanford University Press, 2012).

53. Dennie Gordon (director, *My Lucky Star*), interview with Aynne Kokas, Los Angeles, CA, November 15, 2013; Margy Rochlin, "Her Lucky Star," *Director's Guild of America*, Fall 2013, www.dga.org/Craft/DGAQ/All-Articles/1304-Fall-2013/Dennie-Gordon.aspx.

54. Schamus, interview; James Fong (CEO of OrientalDreamWorks), "The Art of Dealmaking," presentation at panel discussion, US-China Film and Television Industry Expo, Los Angeles, CA, September 28, 2015.

55. Liz Shackleton, "Oriental Dreamworks Unveils Slate," *Screen International*, June 16, 2014, www.screendaily.com/territories/asia-pacific/oriental-dreamworks-unveils-slate/5073199.article.

56. Cindy Mi Lin (CEO, Infotainment China), interview with Aynne Kokas, January 27, 2016, Beijing, China.

57. Ibid.

58. Clifford Coonan, "China's LeVision Sets Up U.S. Unit with $200 Million War Chest," *Hollywood Reporter*, October 7, 2014, www.hollywoodreporter.com /news/chinas-levision-sets-up-us-738718.

59. "EURIMAGES—European Cinema Support Fund: Co-production Support," Council of Europe website, www.coe.int/t/dg4/eurimages/support /supportcoprod_EN.asp, last modified 2014.

60. "European Convention on Cinematographic Co-Production," Council of Europe website, www.coe.int/en/web/conventions/full-list/-/conventions /treaty/147, last modified February 10, 1992.

61. Motion Picture Association and China Film Co-production Corporation, *China-International Film Co-Production Guide*.

62. Ibid.

63. Jonathan Landreth, "China, France Sign Co-Production Treaty," *The Hollywood Reporter*, April 29, 2010, www.hollywoodreporter.com/news/china-france-sign-co-production-23114; Gouvernement de la Communaute francaise de Belgique et Gouvernement de la Republique populaire de China, "Accord

Cinematographique Entre le Gouvernement de la Communauté Française de Belgique et la Republique Populaire de Chine," April 17, 2012, pp. 1–12, www .bridgingthedragon.com/download/belgium.pdf; Ministero dei Beni e delle Attività Culturali del Turismo; "Accordo Di Coproduzione Cinematograpica Con La Repubblica Popolare Cinese" (2013), December 1, 2006. http://documenti .camera.it/Leg14/dossier/Testi/es0450.htm; Pamela Rolfe, "Spain and China Ink Co-Production Deal," The Hollywood Reporter, October 1, 2014, www .hollywoodreporter.com/news/spain-china-ink-production-deal-737143; Government of the United Kingdom of Great Britain and Northern Ireland and Government of the People's Republic of China, "Film Co-Production Agreement between the Government of the United Kingdom of Great Britain and Northern Ireland and the Government of the People's Republic of China," April 23, 2014, www.bfi.org.uk/sites/bfi.org.uk/files/downloads/bfi-uk-china-films-coproduction-agreement-2015-03-23.pdf.

64. "International Co-Production Program Guidelines," Screen Australia and Australian Government, www.screenaustralia.gov.au/getmedia/16f6b32b-7785-42a5-b08d-0058a47131d5/Guidelines-co-production.pdf?ext=.pdf, last modified November 12, 2015.

65. Ibid.

66. Government of Australia and Government of People's Republic of China, Film Co-production Agreement between the Government of Australia and the Government of the People's Republic of China, August 27, 2007, www .screenaustralia.gov.au/getmedia/3f5797f6-30dd-4654-86f2-d549e1b564c7 /Agreement-China.pdf.

67. Ibid.

68. Ibid.

69. Weiyu Peng, "China Film Coproduction and Soft Power Competition" (PhD diss., Queensland University of Technology, 2015).

4. WHISPERS IN THE GALLERY

1. "2013 U.S.-China Film Summit and Gala Dinner," Asia Society website, August 15, 2013, http://asiasociety.org/southern-california/events/2013-us-china-film-summit-and-gala-dinner.

2. "2010 US-China Film Co-Production Summit," USC US-China Institute website, November 2, 2010, http://china.usc.edu/calendar/2010-us-china-film-co-production-summit.

3. "2013 U.S.-China Film Summit and Gala Dinner."

4. Ernst & Young, The Ernst & Young Guide to International Film Production (Phoenix, AZ: Ernst & Young, 2001).

5. Andreas Antoniades, Alister Miskimmon, and Ben O'Loughlin, "Great Power Politics and Strategic Narratives," in *Working Paper No. 7* (Brighton, UK: Center for Global Political Economy at the University of Sussex, 2010), 5.

6. Ibid., 12.

7. Ibid., 15.

8. Aynne Kokas, "American Media and China's Blended Public Sphere," in *Connected Viewing: Selling, Streaming and Sharing Media in the Digital Age*, ed. Jennifer Holt and Kevin Sanson (New York: Routledge, 2014).

9. Patricia G. Lange, "Publicly Private and Privately Public: Social Networking on YouTube," *Journal of Computer-Mediated Communication* 13, no. 1 (2007): 368.

10. Heide Fehrenbach, *Cinema in Democratizing Germany: Reconstructing National Identity after Hitler* (Chapel Hill: University of North Carolina Press, 1995); Lucy Mazdon, "Transnational 'French' Cinema: The Cannes Film Festival," *Modern and Contemporary France* 15, no. 1 (2007); Onookome Okome, "Nollywood: Spectatorship, Audience and the Sites of Consumption," *Postcolonial Text* 3, no. 2 (2007); Vanessa R. Schwartz, *It's So French! Hollywood, Paris, and the Making of Cosmopolitan Film Culture* (Chicago: University of Chicago Press, 2007); Marijke de Valck, *Film Festivals: From European Geopolitics to Global Cinephilia* (Amsterdam: Amsterdam University Press, 2008); SooJeong Ahn, *The Pusan International Film Festival, South Korean Cinema and Globalization* (Hong Kong: Hong Kong University Press, 2011); Cindy Hing-Yuk Wong, *Film Festivals: Culture, People, and Power on the Global Screen* (New Brunswick, NJ: Rutgers University Press, 2011); Darae Kim, Dina Iordanova, and Chris Berry, "The Busan International Film Festival in Crisis or, What Should a Film Festival Be?," *Film Quarterly* 69, no. 1 (2015); Lydia Papadimitriou, "The Hindered Drive toward Internationalization: Thessaloniki (International) Film Festival," *New Review of Film and Television Studies* 14, no. 1 (2016).

11. Julian Stringer, "Global Cities and the International Film Festival Economy," in *Cinema and the City: Film and Urban Societies in a Global Context*, ed. Mark Shiel and Tony Fitzmaurice (Malden, MA: Wiley-Blackwell, 2001); Thomas Elsaesser, "Film Festival Networks: The New Topographies of Cinema in Europe," *European Cinema: Face to Face with Hollywood* 82 (2005); Lucy Mazdon, "The Cannes Film Festival as Transnational Space," *Post Script* 25, no. 2 (2006); Owen Evans, "Border Exchanges: The Role of the European Film Festival," *Journal of Contemporary European Studies* 15, no. 1 (2007); Dina Iordanova and Ragan Rhyne, *The Festival Circuit* (St. Andrews, UK: St. Andrews Film Studies, 2009); Dina Iordanova and Ruby Cheung, *Film Festival Yearbook 3: Film Festivals and East Asia* (St. Andrews, UK: St Andrews Film Studies, 2011); Marijke de Valck, Brendan Kredell, and Skadi Loist, *Film Festivals: History, Theory, Method, Practice* (New York: Routledge, 2016).

12. Wong, *Film Festivals.*

13. John Thornton Caldwell, *Production Culture: Industrial Reflexivity and Critical Practice in Film and Television* (Durham, NC: Duke University Press, 2008).

14. Ibid., 48.

15. Though red-carpet events are not discussion forums in the traditional sense, as this chapter later argues, they present key opportunities for the highest-level players—from the head of the Shanghai Film Group, to two-time Academy Award-winning director Ang Lee, to feared Hollywood producer Harvey Weinstein—to publicly present the results of their collaborative filmmaking process.

16. "2014 U.S.-China Film Summit and Gala Dinner," Asia Society website, http://asiasociety.org/southern-california/photosvideos-2014-us-china-film-summit-gala-1, last modified November 12, 2014.

17. Mihalis Kavaratzis, "From City Marketing to City Branding: Towards a Theoretical Framework for Developing City Brands," *Place Branding* 1, no. 1 (2004).

18. "Forum Brief: 17th Shanghai International Film Festival," Shanghai International Film Festival website, www.siff.com/InformationEn/ViewNews.aspx?CategoryID=0959078b-5f74-446d-a218-b19187440e56&ParentCategoryID=f2ecbd5e-4c83-4358-8ba0-137abd8c4076, last modified June 2014.

19. "2004 Jin Jue International Film Forum," Shanghai International Film Festival website, www.siff.com/InformationEn/ViewDetail.aspx?ParentCategoryID=765439c3-8020-4e9d-9738-1e0e914991ce&InfoGuid=0228ee4a-f1f5-4917-9f31-f6ece899bbdf, last modified January 16, 2009.

20. Ibid.

21. Ibid.

22. "Winston Baker to Host First Ever Film Finance Forum in China," Marketwired website, www.marketwired.com/press-release/Winston-Baker-to-Host-First-Ever-Film-Finance-Forum-in-China-1797898.htm, last modified June 4, 2013.

23. Ibid.

24. Ibid.

25. Caldwell, *Production Culture.*

26. C. Lin, "CEO Infotainment China," interview.

27. Ibid.

28. Ran Ma, "Celebrating the International, Disremembering Shanghai: The Curious Case of the Shanghai International Film Festival," *Culture Unbound* 4 (2012).

29. Cindy Mi Lin (CEO, Infotainment China), interview with Aynne Kokas via WeChat, January 27, 2016.

30. Fan Zhang, "China Brings Cultural Feast to Berlin," *Xinhua,* May 17, 2015, http://news.xinhuanet.com/english/2015-05/17/c_134246598.htm.

31. Ahn, *Pusan International Film Festival.*

32. de Valck, *Film Festivals;* Wong, *Film Festivals;* Ahn, *Pusan International Film Festival.*

33. Jeeyoung Shin, "Negotiating Local, Regional, and Global: Nationalism, Hybridity, and Transnationalism in New Korean Cinema" (PhD diss., Indiana University, 2008).

34. Teresa Brawner Bevis, *A History of Higher Education Exchange: China and America* (New York: Routledge, 2013).

35. "Tallin Industry Days 2012: The Golden Triangle—Funding and Co-production Markets in East-Asia," YouTube video, 1:06:03, posted by PÖFF, January 13, 2013, https://www.youtube.com/watch?v=aWka8kBzuMo.

36. Ibid.

37. Ku6, "DMG Lianshou Dishini *Tiegangxia 3* Zhongmei Hepai," Ku6 video, April 18, 2012, http://baidu.ku6.com/watch/7242064773369640591.html?page = videoMultiNeed.

38. Ibid.

39. Ibid.

40. Vivian Norris, "Cannes: China Arrives on and off the Red Carpet," *BBC News,* May 27, 2014, www.bbc.co.uk/news/business-18226801.

41. Liu Yang, "Shanghai International Film Festival Kicks Off," *CRIENGLISH. com,* June 13, 2010, http://english.cri.cn/6666/2010/06/13/2483s576451.htm; Benjamin Wright, "Remember 'Shanghai' Starring John Cusack & Chow Yun-Fat? Well, It's Going Straight to Blu-ray . . . in England," *The Playlist* (blog), Indiewire.com, May 10, 2012, http://blogs.indiewire.com/theplaylist /remember-shanghai-starring-john-cusack-chow-yun-fat-well-its-going-straight-to-blu-ray-in-england-20120510.

42. Ma, "Celebrating the International."

43. Xiaowen Ren (director, Shanghai City Government News and Public Affairs Research Bureau), interview with Aynne Kokas, June 6, 2013, Shanghai, China.

5. COMPRADORS

1. Pierre Bourdieu, *Distinction: A Social Critique of the Judgement of Taste,* trans. Richard Nice (Cambridge, MA: Harvard University Press, 1984).

2. Peter Miller and Nikolas Rose, "Mobilizing the Consumer Assembling the Subject of Consumption," *Theory, Culture and Society* 14, no. 1 (1997); Paul du Gay and Michael Pryke, *Cultural Economy: Cultural Analysis and Commercial Life* (Thousand Oaks, CA: SAGE, 2002); Sean Nixon and Paul Du Gay, "Who Needs Cultural Intermediaries?," *Cultural Studies* 16, no. 4 (2002); David Wright, "Mediating Production and Consumption: Cultural Capital and 'Cultural Workers,'" *The British Journal of Sociology* 56, no. 1 (2005); Steven

McGuire and Michael Smith, *The European Union and the United States: Competition and Convergence in the Global Arena* (New York: Palgrave Macmillan, 2008).

3. Mike Featherstone, *Global Culture: Nationalism, Globalization and Modernity* (Thousand Oaks, CA: SAGE, 1990); Sean Nixon, *Advertising Cultures: Gender, Commerce, Creativity* (Thousand Oaks, CA: SAGE, 2003); Joanne Entwistle, *The Aesthetic Economy of Fashion: Markets and Value in Clothing and Modelling* (New York: Berg, 2009).

4. Entwistle, *Aesthetic Economy*.

5. David Hesmondhalgh, *The Cultural Industries*, 3rd ed. (London: SAGE, 2012).

6. Allen J. Scott and Naomi E. Pope, "Hollywood, Vancouver, and the World: Employment Relocation and the Emergence of Satellite Production Centers in the Motion-Picture Industry," *Environment and Planning A* 39, no. 6 (2007).

7. For further discussion of Sino-US cultural relations in the late Qing period (1700–1911), including the role of the comprador, see Theodore Huters, *Bringing the World Home: Appropriating the West in Late Qing and Early Republican China* (Honolulu: University of Hawaii Press, 2005). Further explorations of the usage of the term *comprador* can be found in John King Fairbank, *Trade and Diplomacy on the China Coast: The Opening of Treaty Ports, 1842–1854* (Cambridge, MA: Harvard University Press, 1953); Yanping Hao (Yen-p'ing Hao), *The Comprador in Nineteenth Century China: Bridge between East and West* (Cambridge, MA: Harvard University Press, 1970); and David Meyer, *Hong Kong as a Global Metropolis* (Cambridge UK: Cambridge University Press, 2000).

8. Julean Herbert Arnold and the United States Bureau of Foreign Domestic Commerce, *Commercial Handbook of China* (Washington, DC: Government Printing Office, 1919–1920).

9. Herbert I. Schiller, *Mass Communications and American Empire* (Boulder, CO: Westview Press, 1992); Dallas Smythe, "Foreword," in *Canadian Dreams and American Control: The Political Economy of the Canadian Film Industry*, ed. Manjunath Pendakur (Detroit, MI: Wayne State University Press, 1990).

10. Smythe, "Foreword," 17.

11. Wen-Hsin Yeh, *Becoming Chinese: Passages to Modernity and Beyond* (Berkeley: University of California Press, 2000)

12. Jinhua Dai, "Jijie, Xingbie yu Shehuixiuci" (Class, Gender, and Social Rhetoric), in *Kuawenhua Yanjiu: Shenme Shi Bijiao Wenxue* (Transcultural Research: What Is Comparative Literature), ed. Shaodang Yan and Sihe Chen (Beijing: Beijing Daxue Chuban She, 2007).

13. Xiaowen Ren (director, Shanghai City Government News and Public Affairs Research Bureau), interview with Aynne Kokas, June 6, 2013, Shanghai, China.

14. Sara Rubenfeld, Richard Clément, Jessica Vinograd, Denise Lussier, Valérie Amireault, Réjean Auger, and Monique Lebrun, "Becoming a Cultural

Intermediary a Further Social Corollary of Second-Language Learning," *Journal of Language and Social Psychology* 26, no. 2 (2007).

15. Jason Siu (second second assistant director, action unit–China, *The Mummy: Tomb of the Dragon Emperor*), interview with Aynne Kokas, Beijing, China, August 7, 2009.

16. Matthew Feitshans (key second assistant director, *The Forbidden Kingdom*), interview with Aynne Kokas, August 12, 2008. Los Angeles, CA.

17. Ibid.

18. Ibid.

19. Jiansheng Lü (head of set building department, Shanghai Film Studios), interview with Aynne Kokas, Shanghai, China, February 17, 2009.

20. Eileen Chang—Zhang Ailing in Mandarin—was an iconic twentieth-century Chinese writer born in Shanghai who divided her later years between Hong Kong and the United States. Zhang came to prominence during Shanghai's highly international semicolonial period; see Peng-Hsiang Chen and Whitney Crothers Dilley, *Feminism/femininity in Chinese Literature* (New York: Rodopi, 2001).

21. Eileen Chang, Hui-ling Wang, and James Schamus, *Lust, Caution: The Story, the Screenplay, and the Making of the Film* (New York: Pantheon Books, 2007).

22. Ibid.

23. Ibid.

24. Sheila Roberts, "Ang Lee Interview *Lust, Caution*," Moviesonline.ca, www.moviesonline.ca/movienews_13127.html, accessed October 18, 2015 (site no longer available).

25. Paul McDonald, *The Star System: Hollywood's Production of Popular Identities* (New York: Wallflower Press, 2000), 1.

26. "Production Notes—*Lust, Caution*," Focus Features website, www.focusfeatures.com/article/production_notes___lust__caution?film%20=%20lust__caution, last modified September 28, 2007.

27. Ibid.

28. Brad Balfour, "Ang Lee Expresses Lust with Little Caution," PopEntertainment.com, September 23, 2007, www.popentertainment.com/anglee.htm.

29. Rob Carnevale, "Lust, Caution—Ang Lee Interview," IndieLondon.co.uk, n.d., www.indielondon.co.uk/Film-Review/lust-caution-ang-lee-interview, accessed January 23, 2015.

30. Chang, Wang, and Schamus, *Lust, Caution*.

31. James Schamus (executive producer and screenwriter for *Lust, Caution*), phone interview with Aynne Kokas, December 18, 2009.

32. Ian Balfour and Atom Egoyan, eds., *Subtitles: On the Foreignness of Film* (Cambridge, MA: MIT Press, 2004).

33. Schamus, interview.

34. Ibid.

35. Chang, Wang, and Schamus, *Lust, Caution*.

36. Ibid.

37. Ibid.

38. China-US Motion Picture Summit, "Zhang Xun Biography," http://china-us-summit.com/xun_zhang, last modified 2016.

39. Sen-lun Yu, "The Mummy 3 Has Strong Opening in Mainland China," *Screen International*, September 5, 2008, www.screendaily.com/the-mummy-3-has-strong-opening-in-mainland-china/4040623.article.

40. Anecdotally, Hong Kong auteur Wong Kar-Wai's 2004 film *2046* played at the NuArt Theater, a small art cinema in Los Angeles. In contrast, NC-17–rated *Lust, Caution* played in art theaters throughout Los Angeles and in commercial theaters throughout the city's heavily Chinese San Gabriel Valley. By the numbers, *Lust, Caution*'s widest release was at 143 theaters, despite the limiting factor of its NC-17 rating, compared with 61 theaters for *2046*, according to industry trade website Box Office Mojo on September 19, 2015.

41. *Crouching Tiger, Hidden Dragon* differed dramatically from *Lust, Caution* in the types of cultural boundaries it needed to overcome. Chinese martial arts cinema has a history of playing relatively successfully to commercial American audiences, both in narrative form (such as Bruce Lee's successful films of the 1970s) and as an important hybrid element in Hollywood action choreography.

42. "Production Notes—*Lust, Caution*," Focus Features website, www.focus-features.com/article/production_notes___lust__caution?film = lust__caution, last modified September 28, 2007.

43. Chang, Wang, and Schamus, *Lust, Caution*.

44. Ibid., 51.

45. Ibid.

46. Orlando Parfitt, "Lust, Caution Q&A: Producer James Schamus on Ang Lee's Controversial New Drama," IGN website, January 2, 2008, http://movies.ign.com/articles/843/843268p1.html (page no longer active).

47. Brian Hu, "Lust, Caution and Tony Leung's Eyes," *Asia Pacific Arts*, October 5, 2007, www.international.ucla.edu/asia/article/79221.

48. Dan Fainaru, "Review: *Lust, Caution (Se Jie)*," *Screen International*, August 30, 2007, www.screendaily.com/lust-caution-se-jie/4034220.article.

49. "Director Ang Lee on the Making of 'Lust, Caution,'" YouTube video, 5:16, posted by the Asia Society, December 7, 2007.

6. FARM LABOR, FILM LABOR

1. Kongzi, *Lunyu Quanji*, ed. Ruo Kong Man (Beijing: Zhongyang Bianyi Chubanshe, 2011); Edward Slingerland, trans., *Analects: With Selections from*

Traditional Commentaries (Indianapolis, IN: Hackett Publishing Company, 2003).

2. Pierre Bourdieu, *Distinction: A Social Critique of the Judgement of Taste*, trans. Richard Nice (Cambridge, MA: Harvard University Press, 1984).

3. Susan Christopherson, "Project Work in Context: Regulatory Change and the New Geography of Media," *Environment and Planning A* 34 (2002); Allen Scott, "The Other Hollywood: The Organizational and Geographic Bases of Television-Program Production," *Media, Culture and Society* 26, no. 2 (2004).

4. Doris Baltruschat, *Global Media Ecologies: Networked Production in Film and Television* (New York: Routledge, 2010), 3; Ben Goldsmith and Tom O'Regan, *The Film Studio: Film Production in the Global Economy* (Lanham, MD: Rowman and Littlefield, 2005).

5. Goldsmith and O'Regan, *The Film Studio;* Baltruschat, *Global Media Ecologies.*

6. James F. Moore, "Predators and Prey: A New Ecology of Competition," *Harvard Business Review* 71, no. 3 (1993): 76.

7. Wei Li and Hua Zhu, "Voices from the Diaspora: Changing Hierarchies and Dynamics of Chinese Multilingualism," *International Journal of the Sociology of Language* 205 (2010); Robert Vicencio (director, *Distance Runners*), interview with Aynne Kokas, July 28, 2009, Shanghai, China; Cindy Mi Lin (CEO, Infotainment China), interview with Aynne Kokas, June 25, 2013, Beijing, China.

8. Emily Honig, "Invisible Inequalities: The Status of Subei People in Contemporary Shanghai," *The China Quarterly* 122 (June 1990); Jos Gamble, *Shanghai in Transition: Changing Perspectives and Social Contours of a Chinese Metropolis* (New York: Routledge, 2005); Yuwei Xie, "Language and Development of City: The Linguistic Triangle of English, Mandarin, and the Shanghai Dialect," *The Trinity Papers* (2011), http://digitalrepository.trincoll.edu/cgi/viewcontent .cgi?article = 1002&context = trinitypapers.

9. Peter Chan (producer, *Bodyguards and Assassins*) press junket, Shanghai, China, 14, 2009.

10. Ibid.

11. Li and Zhu, "Voices from the Diaspora."

12. Jiansheng Lü (head of set building department, Shanghai Film Studios), interview with Aynne Kokas, Shanghai, China, February 17, 2009.

13. Ibid.; "2013 U.S.-China Film Summit and Gala Dinner," Asia Society website, August 15, 2013, http://asiasociety.org/southern-california/events/2013-us-china-film-summit-and-gala-dinner, accessed September 18, 2015; Asia Society, "US-China Film Summit: Zhang Xun," Asia Society video, 19:06, posted by the Asia Society, November 5, 2013, http://asiasociety.org/video/us-china-film-summit-zhang-xun.

14. Fang Wang (translator and stand-in, *The Mummy: Tomb of the Dragon Emperor*), interview with Aynne Kokas, August 2008, Shanghai, China.

15. Ibid.; Jason Siu (second second assistant director, action unit–China, *The Mummy: Tomb of the Dragon Emperor*), interview with Aynne Kokas, Beijing, China, August 7, 2009.

16. Fang Wang, interview.

17. Mark Deuze, *Media Work* (Malden, MA: Polity, 2007).

18. Goldsmith and O'Regan, *The Film Studio*.

19. Fenglei Chen (location manager, *The Mummy: Tomb of the Dragon Emperor*), interview with Aynne Kokas, December 14, 2008, Shanghai, China.

20. Ai Zhang (production logistics coordinator, *The Mummy: Tomb of the Dragon Emperor*), interview with Aynne Kokas, June 26, 2009, Shanghai, China.

21. Ibid.

22. Ibid.

23. F. Chen, interview.

24. "Lucy Lu," IMDb, n.d., www.imdb.com/name/nm3283143/.

25. "About Us," Gung-Ho Films website, www.gunghofilms.com, last modified 2016.

26. Nick Critser (translator and grip, *Kill Bill: Volume 1*), interview with Aynne Kokas, July 24, 2007, Beijing, China.

27. Siu, interview, 2009.

28. Ibid.; Jason Siu (marketing director at Benchmark Marketing and Management), email communication with Aynne Kokas, May 25, 2016.

29. Siu, interview, 2009.

30. David Harris (transportation assistant, *The Kite Runner*), interview with Aynne Kokas, November 25, 2008, Beijing, China.

31. Henry Dray (transportation coordinator and unit manager, *The Kite Runner*), email and Skype communication with Aynne Kokas, December 9, 2008; "Henry Dray," IMDb, www.imdb.com/name/nm1806049/. Both sources referenced here indicate that Dray was head of the transportation department for *The Great Raid* (2005), *Ultraviolet* (2006), and *Mission: Impossible III* (2006).

32. Siu, interview, 2009.

33. Siu, email communication, 2016.

34. Rosalind Gill and Andy Pratt, "In the Social Factory? Immaterial Labour, Precariousness and Cultural Work," *Theory, Culture and Society* 25, nos. 7–8 (2008).

35. "Yen San Michelle Lo," IMDb, www.imdb.com/name/nm2652324 /?ref_=fn_al_nm_1.

36. Yang Song, "What Should Economists Know about the Current Chinese Hukou System?," *China Economic Review* 29 (June 2014).

37. Hei Hei (tour guide and production assistant), interview by Aynne Kokas, August 24, 2011, Hengdian, China.

38. Ibid.

39. Heather Xiaoquan Zhang, Bin Wu, and Richard Sanders, *Marginalisation in China: Perspectives on Transition and Globalisation* (Burlington, VT: Ashgate, 2007).

40. Hye Jean Chung, "Media Heterotopia and Transnational Filmmaking: Mapping Real and Virtual Worlds," *Cinema Journal* 51, no. 4 (2012).

41. Chris Bilton, *Management and Creativity: From Creative Industries to Creative Management* (Malden, MA: Blackwell, 2007), 46.

42. Manuel Castells, *The Rise of the Network Society: The Information Age: Economy, Society, and Culture* (Malden, MA: John Wiley and Sons, 2011).

CONCLUSION

1. Motion Picture Association and China Film Co-Production Corporation, *China-International Film Co-Production Guide*, http://mpa-i.org/wp-content/uploads/2014/12/Co-Production_Handbook_English.pdf, last modified 2014,.

2. David Shambaugh, "China's Soft-Power Push," *Foreign Affairs* 94, no. 4 (July/August 2015): 99–107.

3. Xin Li, "Michael Barr, Who's Afraid of China? The Challenge of Chinese Soft Power," *The Copenhagen Journal of Asian Studies* 30, no. 1 (2013).

4. Keane, *The Chinese Television Industry* (London: British Film Institute, 2015).

5. An excellent example of the comparatively liberal environment of provincial television production, the show *Super Girl (Chaoji Nüsheng)*, produced by Hunan Satellite Television, was hugely popular, but it became controversial because it allowed direct participation by its audience in the form of a "vote." For more on the *Super Girl* phenomenon, see Bingchun Meng, "Who Needs Democracy if We Can Pick Our Favorite Girl? *Super Girl* as Media Spectacle," *Chinese Journal of Communication* 2, no. 3 (2009).

6. Min Zhou, "Zhongguoban *Jinsu Qianci* yu Meiguoban *The Amazing Race* Bijiao Fenxi," *Shengbing Shijie* 3 (2015).

7. Peter Li (managing director, China Media Capital), "One-on-One: Peter Li, China Media Capital," presentation at US-China Film and Television Industry Expo, Los Angeles, CA, September 28, 2015.

8. Michael Keane, *Created in China: The Great New Leap Forward* (New York: Routledge, 2007); Minghua Xu, "Television Reform in the Era of Globalization: New Trends and Patterns in Post-WTO China," *Telematics and Informatics* 30, no. 4 (2013); Xie Shuang, "Similarities and Differences or Similarities in Differences? China's TV Programming in Global Trend of Neo-Liberal Imperialism," *China Media Research* 10, no. 1 (2014).

9. Keane, *The Chinese Television Industry*.

10. Rebecca MacKinnon, "China's 'Networked Authoritarianism,'" *Journal of Democracy* 22, no. 2 (2011); Aynne Kokas, "American Media and China's Blended Public Sphere," in *Connected Viewing: Selling, Streaming and Sharing Media in the Digital Age,* ed. Jennifer Holt and Kevin Sanson, 144–57 (New York: Routledge, 2014); Jinying Li, "China: The Techno-Politics of the Wall," in *Geoblocking and Global Video Culture,* ed. Ramon Lobato and James Meese, 110–19 (Amsterdam: Institute of Network Cultures, 2016).

11. Gary King, Jennifer Pan, and Margaret E. Roberts, "How Censorship in China Allows Government Criticism but Silences Collective Expression," *American Political Science Review* 107, no. 2 (2013).

12. Guopeng Yin, Ling Zhu, and Xusen Cheng, "Continuance Usage of Localized Social Networking Services: A Conceptual Model and Lessons from China," *Journal of Global Information Technology Management* 16, no. 3 (2013).

13. Siva Vaidhyanathan, *The Googlization of Everything* (Berkeley: University of California Press, 2011).

14. Aynne Kokas, "Building a Transparent Web in China," *Baker Institute Policy Report* 57 (2014), http://bakerinstitute.org/research/building-transparent-web-transnational-social-media-cybersecurity-and-sino-us-trade/.

15. Andrew Pearson, "China's Social and Mobile Companies Set to Shake the Tech World," *Journal of Digital and Social Media Marketing* 3, no. 2 (2015).

16. Zachary Boren, "House of Cards Season 3: China Is Pirating Netflix Series," *The Independent,* March 2, 2015, www.independent.co.uk/arts-entertainment/tv/news/house-of-cards-season-3-china-is-pirating-netflix-series-10080057.htmlfiles/3372/ygurys.html.

17. Mike Ayers, "Inside 'Marco Polo,' Netflix's $90 Million Epic," *Speakeasy* (blog), *Wall Street Journal,* December 12, 2014, http://blogs.wsj.com/speakeasy/2014/12/12/marco-polo-netflix/.

18. James Fong (CEO of OrientalDreamWorks), "The Art of Dealmaking," presentation at panel discussion, US-China Film and Television Industry Expo, Los Angeles, CA, September 28, 2015.

19. Ibid.

20. Ibid.

21. Ibid.

22. Ibid.

23. Ibid.

24. Emilie Yueh-yu Yeh and Darrell William Davis, "Re-Nationalizing China's Film Industry: Case Study on the China Film Group and Film Marketization," *Journal of Chinese Cinemas* 2, no. 1 (2008).

25. "Shanghai Dream Center," Shanghai DreamCenter website, www.dreamcentersh.com/, accessed January 7, 2015.

26. Fei Wang, "The Need for a Film Rating System in China: The Case of Ang Lee's Lust, Caution (2007)," *New Review of Film and Television Studies* 12, no. 4 (2014).

27. Wei Xu, "Hollywood Veterans See Bright Future in Chinese Animation," *Shanghai Daily*, July 17, 2015, www.shanghaidaily.com/feature/people /Hollywood-veterans-see-bright-future-in-Chinese-animation/shdaily.shtml.

28. CBC Arts, "Censored Mission: Impossible III Opens in China," *CBC News*, July 21, 2006, www.cbc.ca/news/arts/censored-mission-impossible-iii-opens-in-china-1.592989.

29. Abid Rahman and Georg Szalai, "China's Alibaba Pictures Investing in Paramount's 'Mission: Impossible 5,'" *The Hollywood Reporter*, June 24, 2015, www.hollywoodreporter.com/news/chinas-alibaba-pictures-investing-paramounts-804709.

30. Stanley Rosen, "Hollywood in China: Selling Out or Cashing In?," *The Diplomat*, May 26, 2015, http://thediplomat.com/2015/05/hollywood-in-china-selling-out-or-cashing-in/.

31. Julie Makinen, "China's LeTV Launches Smartphone, Inks Production Deals," *Los Angeles Times*, April 14, 2015, www.latimes.com/entertainment /envelope/cotown/la-et-ct-chinas-letv-launches-smartphone-inks-production-deals-20150414-story.html.

32. Richard Verrier, "China's Huayi Bros. Approves Deal with Robert Simonds STX," *Los Angeles Times*. April 1, 2015. http://www.latimes.com/entertainment /envelope/cotown/la-et-ct-china-huayi-stx-deal-20150402-story.html.

33. Patrick Frater, "China's Wanda Acquires Legendary Entertainment for $3.5 Billion," *Variety*, January 11, 2016, http://variety.com/2016/biz/asia /wanda-deal-with-legendary-1201676878/.

34. A substantial uptick in the prevalence of filmmaking by US companies in China and by Chinese companies in the United States could also challenge the power of US-based craft guilds such as the Writers Guild of America, the Producers Guild of America, and the Directors Guild of America.

35. Rey Chow, *Sentimental Fabulations, Contemporary Chinese Films: Attachment in the Age of Global Visibility* (New York: Columbia University Press, 2007), 14.

Filmography

For films released in China, where available the Chinese title is added in pinyin. For Chinese characters, please see Appendix 2: Chinese Character Glossary.

Amazing Spider-Man, The (Chaofan Zhizhixia). 2012. Directed by Marc Web. United States: Columbia Pictures.

Avatar. 2009. Directed by James Cameron. United States: Twentieth Century Fox.

Back to 1942 (Yi Jiu Si Er). 2012. Directed by Feng Xiaogang. United States: China Lion Distribution.

Bait (3D) (Dahaixiao Zhi Shakou Taosheng). 2012. Directed by Kimble Rendall. China: Enlight Pictures.

Big Shot's Funeral (Da Wan). 2001. Directed by Feng Xiaogang. United States: Sony Pictures Classics.

Black Coal, Thin Ice (Bai Ri, Yan Huo). 2014. Directed by Diao Yinan. United States: Fortissimo Films.

Blue Kite, The (Lan Fengzheng). 1994. Directed by Tian Zhuangzhuang. United States: Kino International.

Bodyguards and Assassins (Shi Yue Wei Cheng). 2009. Directed by Teddy Chan. United States: Indomina Releasing.

Brokeback Mountain. 2005. Directed by Ang Lee. United States: Focus Features.

Captain America: Civil War (Meiguo Duizhang 3: Neizhan). 2016. Directed by Anthony Russo and Joe Russo. United States: Walt Disney Studios Motion Pictures.

Captain America: The First Avenger. 2011. Directed by Joe Johnston. United States: Paramount Pictures.

Captain America: The Winter Soldier (Meiguo Duizhang 2). 2014. Directed by Anthony Russo and Joe Russo. United States: Walt Disney Studios Motion Pictures.

Charlie's Angels. 2000. Directed by McG. United States: Columbia Pictures.

Code 46. 2003. Directed by Michael Winterbottom. United States: United Artists.

Confucius (Kongzi). 2010. Directed by Hu Mei. China: China Film Group.

Crouching Tiger, Hidden Dragon (Wo Hu Cang Long). 2000. Directed by Ang Lee. United States: Sony Pictures Classics.

Crouching Tiger, Hidden Dragon: The Sword of Destiny (Wo Hu Cang Long: Qing Ming Bao Jian). 2016. Directed by Yuen Woo-ping. United States: The Weinstein Company.

Dark Knight Rises, The (Bianfuxia: Heian Qishi Jueqi). 2012. Directed by Christopher Nolan. United States: Warner Bros. Entertainment.

Disney High School Musical: China (Ge Wu Qing Chun [Zhongguo Ban]). 2010. Directed by Chen Shi-Zheng. China: Huayi Television Media and Shanghai Television Media.

Distance Runners (Zhui Meng Ren). 2009. Directed by Robert Vicencio. China: China Venture Films.

Django Unchained (Bei Jiejiu de Jiangge). 2012. Directed by Quentin Tarantino. United States: The Weinstein Company.

Doctor Strange (Qiyi Boshi). 2016. Directed by Scott Derrickson.

Dragon Blade (Tian Jiang Xiong Shi). 2015. Directed by Daniel Lee. China: Shanghai Film Group.

Eat Drink Man Woman (Yin Shi Nan Nü). 1994. Directed by Ang Lee. United States: Good Machine.

Expendables, The (Gansidui). 2010. Directed by Sylvester Stallone. United States: Lionsgate.

Expendables 2, The (Gansidui 2). 2012. Directed by Simon West. United States: Lionsgate.

Expendables 3, The (Gansidui 3). 2014. Directed by Patrick Hughes. United States: Lionsgate.

Fearless (Huo Yuanjia). 2006. Directed by Ronny Yu. United States: Rogue Pictures.

Finding Mr. Right (Beijing Yu Shang Xiyatu). 2013. Directed by Xue Xiaolu. China: Edko Films.

Forbidden Kingdom, The (Gongfu zhi Wang). 2008. Directed by Rob Minkoff. United States: Casey Silver Productions.

Founding of a Party, The, or *Beginning of the Great Revival (Jiandang Weiye).* 2011. Directed by Han Sanping and Huang Jianxin. United States: China Lion Film Distribution.

Founding of a Republic, The (Jianguo Daye). 2009. Directed by Han Sanping and Huang Jianxin. China: China Film Group, CCTV Movie Channel, and Shanghai Film Group.

Furious 7 (Sudu Yu Jiqing 7). 2015. Directed by James Wan. United States: Universal Pictures.

Great Raid, The (Da Touxi). 2005. Directed by John Dahl. United States: Miramax.

Great Wall, The (Chang Cheng). 2016. Directed by Zhang Yimou. United States: Universal Pictures.

Harold and Kumar Go to White Castle. 2004. Directed by Danny Leiner. United States: New Line Cinema.

Her. 2013. Directed by Spike Jonze. United States: Warner Bros. Entertainment.

Hollywood Adventures (Heng Chong Zhi Zhuang Hao Lai Wu). 2015. Directed by Timothy Kendall. China: Enlight Pictures.

I Don't Want to Sleep Alone (Hei Yan Quan). 2006. Directed by Tsai Ming-liang. United States: Strand Releasing.

Ice Age: Continental Drift (Binghe Shiji 4: Dalu Piaoyi). 2012. Directed by Steve Martino and Michael Thurmeier. United States: Twentieth Century Fox Film Corporation.

Independence Day. 1996. Directed by Roland Emmerich. United States: Twentieth Century Fox Film Corporation.

Inseparable (Xingying Bu Li). 2012. Directed by Dayyan Eng. China: Fantawild Pictures.

Iron Man. 2008. Directed by Jon Favreau. United States: Paramount Pictures.

Iron Man 2 (Tiegang Xia 2). 2010. Directed by Jon Favreau. United States: Paramount Pictures.

Iron Man 3 (Tiegang Xia 3). 2013. Directed by Shane Black. United States: Marvel Studios.

Jurassic World (Zhuluoji Shijie). 2015. Directed by Colin Trevorrow. United States: Universal Studios.

Karate Kid, The (Gongfu Meng). 2010. Directed by Harald Zwart. United States: Columbia Pictures.

Kill Bill: Volume 1. 2003. Directed by Quentin Tarantino. United States: Miramax.

King's Daughter, The (Riyuerenyu). 2016. Directed by Sean McNamara. United States: Picturehouse Entertainment.

Kite Runner, The. 2007. Directed by Marc Forster. United States: DreamWorks SKG.

Kung Fu Hustle (Gongfu). 2005. Directed by Stephen Chow. United States: Sony Pictures Classics.

Kung Fu Panda 3 (Gongfu Xiongmao 3). 2016. Directed by Alessandro Carloni and Jennifer Yuh. United States: Twentieth Century Fox Film Corporation.

Longest Night in Shanghai, The (Ye, Shanghai). 2007. Directed by Zhang Yibai. China: China Film Group.

Looper (Huanxing Shizhe). 2012. Directed by Rian Johnson. China: DMG Entertainment; United States: Sony Pictures Releasing.

Lorax, The (Laoleisi de Gushi). 2012. Directed by Chris Renaud and Kyle Balda. United States: Universal Studios.

Lost in Thailand (Ren Zai Jiongtu Zhi Tai Jiong). 2012. Directed by Xu Zheng. China: Enlight Pictures.

Lost in Translation. 2003. Directed by Sofia Coppola. United States: Focus Features.

Lust, Caution (Se, Jie). 2007. Directed by Ang Lee. United States: Focus Features.

Matrix, The. 1999. Directed by Andy Wachowski and Lana Wachowski. United States: Warner Bros.

Mermaid, The (Meirenyu). 2016. Directed by Stephen Chow. United States: Sony Pictures Releasing.

Mission: Impossible III (Die Zhong Die 3). 2006. Directed by J. J. Abrams. United States: Paramount Pictures.

Mission: Impossible—Rogue Nation (Die Zhong Die 5: Shenmi Guodu). 2015. Directed by Christopher McQuarrie. United States: Paramount Pictures.

Monkey King, The (Xi You Ji: Da Nao Tian Gong). 2014. Directed by Cheang Pou-soi. China: China Film Group Corporation.

Mummy: Tomb of the Dragon Emperor, The (Munaiyi 3: Longdi zhi Mu). 2008. Directed by Rob Cohen. United States: Universal Pictures.

My Lucky Star (Feichang Xingyun). 2013. Directed by Dennie Gordon. United States: China Lion Film Distribution.

Painted Veil, The. 2006. Directed by John Curran. United States: Warner Independent Pictures.

Pavilion of Women. 2001. Directed by Yim Ho. China: Beijing Film Studio.

Perhaps Love (Ruguo Ai). 2005. Directed by Peter Chan. Hong Kong: Celestial Pictures.

Prometheus (Puluomixiusi). 2012. Directed by Ridley Scott. United States: Twentieth Century Fox Film Corporation.

Rush Hour. 1998. Directed by Brett Ratner. United States: New Line Cinema.

Rush Hour 2. 2001. Directed by Brett Ratner. United States: New Line Cinema.

Science of Star Wars. 2005. Television miniseries. United States: Discovery Channel.

Secret of the Magic Gourd, The (Bao Hulu de Mimi). 2007. Directed by Frankie Chung. United States: Walt Disney Studios.

Shanghai (Die Hai Feng Yun). 2010. Directed by Mikael Håfström. United States: The Weinstein Company.

Shanghai Baby. 2007. Directed by Berengar Pfahl. United States: Arclight Films.

Shanghai Calling (Niuyueke @ Shanghai). 2012. Directed by Daniel Hsia. China: China Film Group Corporation.

Shanghai Kiss. 2007. Directed by David Ren and Kern Konwiser. United States: Starz Home Entertainment.

Shanghai Red (Hong Meili). 2006. Directed by Oscar Costo. China: Shanghai MARdeORO Films and Television.

Shanghai Trance. 2008. Directed by David Verbeek. France: Les Petites Lumières.

Skiptrace (Juedi Taowang). 2016. Directed by Renny Harlin. China: Talent International Media.

Skyfall. 2012. Directed by Sam Mendes. United States: Columbia Pictures.

Snow Flower and the Secret Fan (Xuehua Mishan). 2011. Directed by Wayne Wang. United States: Fox Searchlight Pictures.

Space between Us, The. 2016. Directed by Peter Chelsom. Singapore: Golden Village Pictures.

Tortilla Soup. 2001. Directed by Maria Ripoll. United States: Samuel Goldwyn Films.

Trail of the Panda (Xiong Mao Hui Jia Lu). 2009. Directed by Zhong Yu. China: Castle Hero Pictures.

Transformers: Age of Extinction (Bianxingjingang 4: Jueji Chongsheng). 2014. Directed by Michael Bay. United States: Paramount Pictures.

2046. 2004. Directed by Wong Kar-wai. United States: Sony Pictures Classics.

Ultraviolet. 2006. Directed by Kurt Wimmer. United States: Screen Gems.

White Countess, The. 2005. Directed by James Ivory. United States: Sony Pictures Classics.

Bibliography

Ahn, SooJeong. *The Pusan International Film Festival, South Korean Cinema and Globalization.* Hong Kong: Hong Kong University Press, 2011.

Andersen, Arthur. *The European Film Production Guide: Finance—Tax—Legislation France—Germany—Italy—Spain—UK.* London: Routledge, 1996.

Antoniades, Andreas, Alister Miskimmon, and Ben O'Loughlin. "Great Power Politics and Strategic Narratives." In *Working Paper No. 7,* 1–26. Brighton, UK: Center for Global Political Economy at the University of Sussex, 2010.

Arnold, Julean Herbert, and the United States Bureau of Foreign Domestic Commerce. *Commercial Handbook of China.* Washington, DC: Government Printing Office, 1919–1920.

Arsenault, Amelia H., and Manuel Castells. "The Structure and Dynamics of Global Multi-Media Business Networks." *International Journal of Communication* 2 (2008): 707–48.

Ashcraft, Brian. "Why Many in China Hate *Iron Man 3*'s Chinese Version." *Kotaku,* May 2, 2013. http://kotaku.com/why-many-in-china-hate-iron-man-3s-chinese-version-486840429.

Asia Society. "US-China Film Summit: Zhang Xun." Asia Society video, 19:06. November 5, 2013. http://asiasociety.org/video/us-china-film-summit-zhang-xun.

Baker, Frank W. *Media Literacy in the K-12 Classroom.* Arlington, VA: International Society for Technology in Education, 2012.

Balfour, Ian, and Atom Egoyan, eds. *Subtitles: On the Foreignness of Film.* Cambridge, MA: Massachusetts Institute of Technology Press, 2004.

Baltruschat, Doris. *Global Media Ecologies: Networked Production in Film and Television.* New York: Routledge, 2010.

Barr, Michael D. *Who's Afraid of China? The Challenge of Chinese Soft Power.* London: Zed Books, 2011.

Bayless, Martha. "Disney's Castles and the Work of the Medieval in the Middle Ages." In *The Disney Middle Ages: A Fairy-Tale and Fantasy Past,* edited by Tison Pugh and Susan Aronstein, 39–57. New York: Palgrave Macmillan, 2012.

Bennett, Susan, and Marlis Schweitzer. "In the Window at Disney: A Lifetime of Brand Desire." *TDR/The Drama Review* 58, no. 4 (2014): 23–31.

Bergère, Marie-Claire. *Shanghai: China's Gateway to Modernity.* Translated by Janet Lloyd. Stanford: Stanford University Press, 2009.

Berry, Chris. "'What's Big about the Big Film?' 'De-Westernizing' the Blockbuster in Korea and China." In *Movie Blockbusters,* edited by Julian Stringer, 217–29. New York: Routledge, 2003.

Berry, Michael. "Chinese Cinema with Hollywood Characteristics, or How *The Karate Kid* Became a Chinese Film." In *The Oxford Handbook of Chinese Cinemas,* edited by Carlos Rojas and Eileen Chow, 170–89. New York: Oxford University Press, 2013.

Bevis, Teresa Brawner. *A History of Higher Education Exchange: China and America.* New York: Routledge, 2013.

Biel, Alexander. "Converting Image into Equity." In *Brand Equity and Advertising: Advertising's Role in Building Strong Brands,* edited by David A. Aaker, 67–82. New York: Psychology Press, 2013.

Bilton, Chris. *Management and Creativity: From Creative Industries to Creative Management.* Malden, MA: Blackwell, 2007.

Bordwell, David, Janet Staiger, and Kristin Thompson. *The Classical Hollywood Cinema: Film Style and Mode of Production to 1960.* New York: Routledge, 2003.

Bourdieu, Pierre. *Distinction: A Social Critique of the Judgement of Taste.* Translated by Richard Nice. Cambridge, MA: Harvard University Press, 1984.

boyd, danah m., and Nicole B. Ellison. "Social Network Sites: Definition, History, and Scholarship." *Journal of Computer-Mediated Communication* 13, no. 1 (2007): 210–30.

Brannen, Mary Yoko. "'Bwana Mickey': Constructing Cultural Consumption at Tokyo Disneyland." In *Re-Made in Japan: Everyday Life and Consumer Taste in a Changing Society,* edited by Joseph Jay Tobin, 216–34. New Haven, CT: Yale University Press, 1992.

———. "Cross-Cultural Materialism: Commodifying Culture in Japan." In *Meaning, Measure, and Morality of Materialism,* edited by Floyd Rudmin and Marsha Richins, 167–80. Provo, UT: The Association for Consumer Research, 1992.

———. "When Mickey Loses Face: Recontextualization, Semantic Fit, and the Semiotics of Foreignness." *Academy of Management Review* 29, no. 4 (2004): 593–616.

Bräutigam, Deborah, and Tang Xiaoyang. "Economic Statecraft in China's New Overseas Special Economic Zones: Soft Power, Business or Resource Security?" *International Affairs* 88, no. 4 (2012): 799–816.

Brown, David G., and Kevin Scott. "China-Taiwan Relations: Cross-Strait Relations on Hold." *Comparative Connections: A Triannual E-Journal on East Asian Bilateral Relations* 16, no. 3 (2015): 67–74.

Brown, James A. *Television "Critical Viewing Skills" Education: Major Media Literacy Projects in the United States and Selected Countries.* New York: Routledge, 2013.

Brownstein, Ronald. *The Power and the Glitter: The Hollywood-Washington Connection.* New York: Pantheon, 1990.

Bruchansky, Christophe. "The Heterotopia of Disney World." *Philosophy Now* 77 (2010): 15–17.

Buckingham, David. *Media Education: Literacy, Learning and Contemporary Culture.* Malden, MA: Blackwell, 2003.

Cahn, Sandrine, and Daniel Schimmel. "The Cultural Exception: Does It Exist in GATT and GATS Frameworks—How Does It Affect or Is It Affected by the Agreement on TRIPS? *Cardozo Arts and Entertainment Law Journal* 15 (1997): 281–314.

Cain, Rob. "China's Censors Ride into the Old West and Castrate 'Django.'" China Film Biz website, April 11, 2013. http://chinafilmbiz.com/2013/04/11 /chinas-censors-ride-into-the-old-west-and-castrate-django/.

Caldwell, John T. "Para-Industry, Shadow Academy." *Cultural Studies* 28, no. 4 (2014): 720–40.

———. *Production Culture: Industrial Reflexivity and Critical Practice in Film and Television.* Durham, NC: Duke University Press, 2008.

Castells, Manuel. *The Rise of the Network Society: The Information Age: Economy, Society, and Culture.* Malden, MA: John Wiley and Sons, 2011.

Chan, Jachinson W. "Bruce Lee's Fictional Models of Masculinity." *Men and Masculinities* 2, no. 4 (2000): 371–87.

Chan, Johannes. "Hong Kong's Umbrella Movement." *The Round Table* 103, no. 6 (2014): 571–80.

Chan-Olmsted, Sylvia M. *Competitive Strategy for Media Firms: Strategic and Brand Management in Changing Media Markets.* New York: Routledge, 2006.

Chang, Eileen, Hui-ling Wang, and James Schamus. *Lust, Caution: The Story, the Screenplay, and the Making of the Film.* New York: Pantheon Books, 2007.

Chao, T. W. "GATT's Cultural Exemption of Audiovisual Trade: The United States May Have Lost the Battle but Not the War." *University of Pennsylvania Journal of International Economic Law* 17 (1996).

Chen, Chwenchwen, and Vincenzo De Masi. "A Chinese Animation TV Production Industry: An Overview." *China Media Observatory Newsletter* 1, no. 9 (2009). https://www.academia.edu/6248826/A_Chinese_Animation_TV_Production_ Industry_An_Overview.

Chen, Peng-Hsiang, and Whitney Crothers Dilley. *Feminism/femininity in Chinese Literature.* New York: Rodopi, 2002.

Chen, Yu, and Baoming Zhang. "Film Trade Deficit Control Measures between China and USA Based on Gravity Model." *Advances in Applied Economics and Finance* 2, no. 4 (2012): 456–61.

Cheung, Kui-yin, and Ping Lin. "Spillover Effects of FDI on Innovation in China: Evidence from the Provincial Data." *China Economic Review* 15, no. 1 (2004): 25–44.

China-US Motion Picture Summit. "Zhang Xun Biography." 2016. http:// china-us-summit.com/xun_zhang.

Chow, Rey. *Sentimental Fabulations, Contemporary Chinese Films: Attachment in the Age of Global Visibility.* New York: Columbia University Press, 2007.

Christopherson, Susan. "Project Work in Context: Regulatory Change and the New Geography of Media." *Environment and Planning A.* 34 (2002): 2003–16.

Christopherson, Susan, and Michael Storper. "The Effects of Flexible Specialization on Industrial Politics and the Labor Market: The Motion Picture Industry." *Industrial and Labor Relations Review* 42, no. 3 (1989): 331–47.

Chu, Yingchi. "The Consumption of Cinema in Contemporary China." In *Media in China: Consumption, Content and Crisis,* edited by Stephanie Hemelryk Donald, Yin Hong, and Michael Keane, 43–54. New York: Routledge, 2013.

Chung, Hye Jean. "Media Heterotopia and Transnational Filmmaking: Mapping Real and Virtual Worlds." *Cinema Journal* 51, no. 4 (2012): 87–109.

Clavé, Salvador Anton. *The Global Theme Park Industry.* Cambridge, MA: CABI, 2007.

Coonan, Clifford. "Alibaba's Film Crowdfunding Service Swarmed by Chinese Investors, Sells Out in Five Days." *The Hollywood Reporter,* April 4, 2014. www.hollywoodreporter.com/news/alibabas-film-crowdfunding-service- swarmed-693683.

———. "China's Levision Sets Up U.S. Unit with $200 Million War Chest." *The Hollywood Reporter,* October 7, 2014. www.hollywoodreporter.com/news /chinas-levision-sets-up-us-738718.

———. "Oliver Stone Slams Chinese Film Industry at Beijing Festival." *The Hollywood Reporter,* April 17, 2014. www.hollywoodreporter.com/news /oliver-stone-slams-chinese-film-697058.

Corbett, J. Martin. "Reconstructing Human-Centred Technology: Lessons from the Hollywood Dream Factory." *AI and Society* 12, no. 3 (1998): 214–30.

Courmont, Barthélémy. "What Implications for Chinese Soft Power: Charm Offensive or New Hegemony?" *Pacific Focus* 28, no. 3 (2013): 343–64.

Curtin, Michael. *Playing to the World's Biggest Audience: The Globalization of Chinese Film and TV.* Berkeley: University of California Press, 2007.

Dai, Jinhua. "Jijie, Xingbie yu Shehuixiuci" (Class, Gender, and Social Rhetoric). In *Kuawenhua Yanjiu: Shenme Shi Bijiao Wenxue* (Transcultural Research: What Is Comparative Literature), edited by Shaodang Yan and Sihe Chen, 355–71. Beijing: Beijing Daxue Chubanshe, 2007.

Dalecki, Linden. "Hollywood Media Synergy as Integrated Marketing Communications." *Journal of Integrated Marketing Communications* 8, no. 1 (2008): 47–52.

Davis, Darrell William. "Market and Marketization in the China Film Business." *Cinema Journal* 49, no. 3 (2010): 121–25.

———. "Marketization, Hollywood, Global China." *Modern Chinese Literature and Culture* 26, no. 1 (Spring 2014): 191–241.

Davison, Jane. "Paratextual Framing of the Annual Report: Liminal Literary Conventions and Visual Devices." *Critical Perspectives on Accounting* 22, no. 2 (2011): 118–34.

DeBoer, Stephanie. *Coproducing Asia: Locating Japanese-Chinese Regional Film and Media.* Minneapolis: University of Minnesota Press, 2014.

Deuze, Mark. *Media Work.* Malden, MA: Polity, 2007.

de Valck, Marijke. *Film Festivals: From European Geopolitics to Global Cinephilia.* Amsterdam: Amsterdam University Press, 2008.

de Valck, Marijke, Brendan Kredell, and Skadi Loist. *Film Festivals: History, Theory, Method, Practice.* New York: Routledge, 2016.

"Director Ang Lee on the Making of 'Lust, Caution.'" YouTube video, 5:16. December 7, 2007. www.youtube.com/watch?v = irSY5l3BecU&feature = youtube_gdata_player.

Dixon, Wheeler Winston, and Gwendolyn Audrey Foster. *21st-Century Hollywood: Movies in the Era of Transformation.* New Brunswick, NJ: Rutgers University Press, 2011.

Donald, Stephanie, and John G. Gammack. *Tourism and the Branded City: Film and Identity on the Pacific Rim.* Burlington, VT: Ashgate Publishing, 2007.

du Gay, Paul, and Michael Pryke. *Cultural Economy: Cultural Analysis and Commercial Life.* Thousand Oaks, CA: SAGE, 2002.

Durand, Martine, and Haishan Fu. *Purchasing Power Parities and Real Expenditures of World Economies: Summary of Results and Findings of the 2011 International Comparison Program.* Washington, DC: International Bank for Reconstruction and Development, 2014.

Ellis, R. Evan. "Chinese Soft Power in Latin America: A Case Study." *Joint Force Quarterly* 60, no. 1 (2011): 85–91.

Elsaesser, Thomas. "Film Festival Networks: The New Topographies of Cinema in Europe." *European Cinema: Face to Face with Hollywood* 82 (2005): 82–106.

Entwistle, Joanne. *The Aesthetic Economy of Fashion: Markets and Value in Clothing and Modelling.* New York: Berg, 2009.

Ernst & Young. *The Ernst & Young Guide to International Film Production.* Phoenix, AZ: Ernst & Young, 2001.

Evans, Owen. "Border Exchanges: The Role of the European Film Festival." *Journal of Contemporary European Studies* 15, no. 1 (2007): 23–33.

Fainaru, Dan. "Review: *Lust, Caution (Se Jie)*." *Screen International,* August 30, 2007. www.screendaily.com/lust-caution-se-jie/4034220 .article.

Fairbank, John King. *Trade and Diplomacy on the China Coast: The Opening of Treaty Ports, 1842–1854.* Cambridge, MA: Harvard University Press, 1953.

Fang, Karen. "Globalization, Masculinity, and the Changing Stakes of Hollywood Cinema for Asian American Studies." *Asian American Literary Studies* 79 (2005): 79–108.

Featherstone, Mike. *Global Culture: Nationalism, Globalization and Modernity.* Thousand Oaks, CA: SAGE, 1990.

Fehrenbach, Heide. *Cinema in Democratizing Germany: Reconstructing National Identity after Hitler.* Chapel Hill: University of North Carolina Press, 1995.

Feng, Michael X.Y. "The 'Chinese Dream' Deconstructed: Values and Institutions." *Journal of Chinese Political Science* 20, no. 2 (2015): 163–83.

Fijałkowski, Łukasz. "China's 'Soft Power' in Africa?" *Journal of Contemporary African Studies* 29, no. 2 (2011): 223–32.

Flew, Terry, and Falk Hartig. "Confucius Institutes and the Network Communication Approach to Public Diplomacy." *IAFOR Journal of Asian Studies* 1, no. 1 (2014): 27–44.

Frater, Patrick. "China's Fosun Revealed as Leading Owner of Jeff Robinov's Studio 8 (Exclusive)." *Variety,* April 20, 2015. http://variety.com/2015/biz /asia/fosun-jeff-robinov-1201475704/.

———. "China Media Capital, Warner Bros. Seal Flagship Production Pact." *Variety,* September 20, 2015. http://variety.com/2015/film/asia/china-media-capital-warner-bros-seal-flagship-production-pact-1201597886/.

———. "China Online Giant Baidu Launches Film Funding Unit." *Variety*, September 20, 2014. http://variety.com/2014/film/news/ china-online-giant-baidu-launches-film-funding-unit-1201310689/.

———. "China's Wanda Acquires Legendary Entertainment for $3.5 Billion." *Variety*, January 11, 2016. http://variety.com/2016/biz/asia/wanda-deal- with-legendary-1201676878/.

———. "Oliver Stone Spars with Chinese Film Official at Beijing Film Festival." *Variety*, April 16, 2014. http://variety.com/2014/film/news/oliver-stone- disses-international-co-productions-1201158657/.

Freeman, Richard. "The Work the Document Does: Research, Policy, and Equity in Health." *Journal of Health Politics, Policy and Law* 31, no. 1 (2006): 51–70.

Fu, Poshek. *Between Shanghai and Hong Kong: The Politics of Chinese Cin- emas.* Stanford: Stanford University Press, 2003.

Fung, Anthony Y. H. *Global Capital, Local Culture: Transnational Media Corporations in China.* New York: Peter Lang, 2008.

Gamble, Jos. *Shanghai in Transition: Changing Perspectives and Social Contours of a Chinese Metropolis.* New York: Routledge, 2005.

Gelfond, Richard. "National Committee on U.S. China Relations, 2013 Gala Dinner, Part 2." *National Committee on U.S.-China Relations.* YouTube video, 54:03. October 18, 2013. https://www.youtube.com/watch?v = CCprcFSq-uw.

Gill, Rosalind, and Andy Pratt. "In the Social Factory? Immaterial Labour, Precariousness and Cultural Work." *Theory, Culture and Society* 25, nos. 7–8 (2008): 1–30.

Goldsmith, Ben, and Tom O'Regan. *The Film Studio: Film Production in the Global Economy.* Lanham, MD: Rowman and Littlefield, 2005.

Gomery, Douglas. "Economic Struggle and Hollywood Imperialism: Europe Converts to Sound." *Yale French Studies*, no. 60 (1980): 80–93.

Gong, James Jianxin, Wim A. Van der Stede, and Mark S. Young. "Real Options in the Motion Picture Industry: Evidence from Film Marketing and Sequels." *Contemporary Accounting Research* 28, no. 5 (2011): 1438–66.

Government of Australia and Government of People's Republic of China. *Film Co-production Agreement Between the Government of Australia and the Government of the People's Republic of China.* August 27, 2007. www .screenaustralia.gov.au/getmedia/3f5797f6–30dd-4654–86f2-d549e1b564c7 /Agreement-China.pdf.

Govil, Nitin. *Orienting Hollywood: A Century of Film Culture between Los Angeles and Bombay.* New York: New York University Press, 2015.

Graber, Christoph Beat. "The New UNESCO Convention on Cultural Diversity: A Counterbalance to the WTO?" *Journal of International Economic Law* 9, no. 3 (2006): 553–74.

Grainge, Paul. *Brand Hollywood: Selling Entertainment in a Global Media Age.* New York: Routledge, 2008.

Gunning, Tom. "The Cinema of Attraction: Early Film, Its Spectator, and the Avant-Garde." *Wide Angle* 3, no. 4 (1986): 63–70.

Hao, Qinyu. "Development Report on the Film Industry (2011–2012)." In *China Cultural and Creative Industries Reports 2013,* edited by Hardy Yong Xiang and Patricia Ann Walker, 11–25. Berlin: Springer, 2014.

Hao, Yanping (Hao, Yen-p'ing). *The Comprador in Nineteenth Century China: Bridge between East and West.* Cambridge, MA: Harvard University Press, 1970.

Harvey, David. *Seventeen Contradictions and the End of Capitalism.* Reprint edition. Oxford: Oxford University Press, 2015.

Herrmann, Edward, and Robert W. McChesney. *Global Media: The New Missionaries of Global Capitalism.* London: Continuum, 2004.

Hesmondhalgh, David. *The Cultural Industries.* 3rd ed. London: SAGE, 2012.

Hill, Erin. "Hollywood Assistanting." In *Production Studies: Cultural Studies of Media Industries,* edited by Vicki Mayer, Miranda J. Banks, and John T. Caldwell, 220–23. New York: Routledge, 2010.

———. *Never Done.* New Brunswick, NJ: Rutgers University Press, 2016.

Hoang, Anh Tran. "The Fragile and Vulnerable Foundation of the Sino-US Relationship." In *PacNet* 52. Honolulu: Pacific Forum Center for Strategic and International Studies, 2013. www.csis.org/analysis/pacnet-52-fragile-and-vulnerable-foundation-sino-us-relationship.

Hobbs, Renee. *Digital and Media Literacy: Connecting Culture and Classroom.* Thousand Oaks, CA: Corwin Press, 2011.

Holyk, Gregory G. "Paper Tiger? Chinese Soft Power in East Asia." *Political Science Quarterly* 126, no. 2 (2011): 223–54.

Honig, Emily. "Invisible Inequalities: The Status of Subei People in Contemporary Shanghai." *The China Quarterly* 122 (June 1990): 273–92.

Hu, Brian. "Lust, Caution and Tony Leung's Eyes." *Asia-Pacific Arts,* October 5, 2007. http://asiapacificarts.usc.edu/w_apa/showarticle.aspx?articleID = 10011&AspxAutoDetectCookieSupport = 1.

Hu, Guangwei. "English Language Education in China: Policies, Progress, and Problems." *Language Policy* 4, no. 1 (2005): 5–24.

Hu, Jintao. "Full Text of Hu Jintao's Report at 17th Party Congress." *Scientific Outlook on Development, 17th Communist Party of China Congress.* October 24, 2007. http://news.xinhuanet.com/english/2007-10/24/content_6938749 .htm.

Hu, Zhengrong, and Deqiang Ji. "Ambiguities in Communicating with the World: The 'Going-out' Policy of China's Media and Its Multilayered Contexts." *Chinese Journal of Communication* 5, no. 1 (2012): 32–37.

Huang, Yasheng, Li Jin, and Yi Qian. "Does Ethnicity Pay? Evidence from Overseas Chinese FDI in China." *Review of Economics and Statistics* 95, no. 3 (2012): 868–83.

Hui, Victoria Tin-bor. "The Protests and Beyond." *Journal of Democracy* 26, no. 2 (2015): 111–21.

Huters, Theodore. *Bringing the World Home: Appropriating the West in Late Qing and Early Republican China.* Honolulu: University of Hawaii Press, 2005.

Iordanova, Dina, and Ruby Cheung. *Film Festival Yearbook 3: Film Festivals and East Asia.* St. Andrews, UK: St. Andrews Film Studies, 2011.

Iordanova, Dina, and Ragan Rhyne. *The Festival Circuit.* St. Andrews, UK: St. Andrews Film Studies, 2009.

Ito, Banri, Naomitsu Yashiro, Zhaoyuan Xu, XiaoHong Chen, and Ryuhei Wakasugi. "How Do Chinese Industries Benefit from FDI Spillovers?" *China Economic Review* 23, no. 2 (2012): 342–56.

Jaafar, Ali. "China's Le Vision Pictures Eyes Global Tentpoles with New LA Offshoot." *Deadline,* October 7, 2014. http://deadline.com/2014/10/china-le-vision-us-office-847216/.

Jeon, Yongbok, Byung Il Park, and Pervez N. Ghauri. "Foreign Direct Investment Spillover Effects in China: Are They Different across Industries with Different Technological Levels?" *China Economic Review* 26 (2013): 105–17.

Johnson, Matthew D. "Propaganda and Censorship in Chinese Cinema." In *A Companion to Chinese Cinema,* edited by Yingjin Zhang, 151–78. Malden, MA: Wiley-Blackwell, 2012.

Kavaratzis, Mihalis. "From City Marketing to City Branding: Towards a Theoretical Framework for Developing City Brands." *Place Branding* 1, no. 1 (2004): 58–73.

Keane, Michael. "Brave New World." *International Journal of Cultural Policy* 10, no. 3 (2004): 265–79.

———. *The Chinese Television Industry.* London: British Film Institute, 2015.

———. *Created in China: The Great New Leap Forward.* New York: Routledge, 2007.

———. *Creative Industries in China: Art, Design and Media.* Malden, MA: John Wiley and Sons, 2013.

———. "Once Were Peripheral: Creating Media Capacity in East Asia." *Media Culture Society* 28, no. 6 (2006): 835–55.

Keane, Michael, Anthony Y. H. Fung, and Albert Moran. *New Television, Globalisation, and the East Asian Cultural Imagination.* Hong Kong: Hong Kong University Press, 2007.

Kessides, Christine. *The Contributions of Infrastructure to Economic Development: A Review of Experience and Policy Implications.* Vol. 213. Washington, DC: World Bank Publications, 1993.

Kim, Darae, Dina Iordanova, and Chris Berry. "The Busan International Film Festival in Crisis or, What Should a Film Festival Be?" *Film Quarterly* 69, no. 1 (2015): 80–89.

Kim, Sung Wook, and Aziz Douai. "Google Vs. China's 'Great Firewall': Ethical Implications for Free Speech and Sovereignty." *Technology in Society* 34, no. 2 (2012): 174–81.

King, Gary, Jennifer Pan, and Margaret E. Roberts. "How Censorship in China Allows Government Criticism but Silences Collective Expression." *American Political Science Review* 107, no. 2 (2013): 326–43.

———. "Reverse-Engineering Censorship in China: Randomized Experimentation and Participant Observation." *Science* 345, no. 6199 (2014): 891–901.

Kitamura, Hiroshi. *Screening Enlightenment: Hollywood and the Cultural Reconstruction of Defeated Japan.* New York: Cornell University Press, 2010.

Kitchen, Philip J., and Don E. Schultz. *Raising the Corporate Umbrella: Corporate Communications in the Twenty-First Century.* London: Palgrave Macmillan, 2001.

Klein, Christina. "Kung Fu Hustle: Transnational Production and the Global Chinese-Language Film." *Journal of Chinese Cinemas* 1, no. 3 (2007): 189–208.

Kline, Stephen. *Out of the Garden: Toys and Children's Culture in the Age of TV Marketing.* New York: Verso, 1995.

Klingmann, Anna. *Brandscapes: Architecture in the Experience Economy.* Cambridge: Massachusetts Institute of Technology Press, 2007.

Kokas, Aynne. "American Media and China's Blended Public Sphere." In *Connected Viewing: Selling, Streaming and Sharing Media in the Digital Age,* edited by Jennifer Holt and Kevin Sanson, 144–57. New York: Routledge, 2014.

———. "Building a Transparent Web in China." *Baker Institute Policy Report* 57 (2014): 1–7. http://bakerinstitute.org/research/building-transparent-web-transnational-social-media-cybersecurity-and-sino-us-trade/.

Koltay, Tibor. "The Media and the Literacies: Media Literacy, Information Literacy, Digital Literacy." *Media, Culture and Society* 33, no. 2 (2011): 211–21.

Kongzi. *Lunyu Quanji* (The Analects of Confucius). Edited by Ruokong Man. Beijing: Zhongyang Bianyi Chubanshe, 2011.

Ku6. "DMG Lianshou Dishini *Tiegangxia 3* Zhongmei Hepai" (DMG Joins Hands with Disney in *Ironman 3* Sino-US Co-production). Ku6 video, 4:40. April 18, 2012. http://baidu.ku6.com/watch/7242064773369640591.html?page = videoMultiNeed.

Landreth, Jonathan. "China, France Sign Co-Production Treaty." *The Hollywood Reporter,* April 29, 2010. www.hollywoodreporter.com/news/china-france-sign-co-production-23114.

Lange, Patricia G. "Publicly Private and Privately Public: Social Networking on YouTube." *Journal of Computer-Mediated Communication* 13, no. 1 (2007): 361–80.

Larson, Magali, and Sherri Cavan. "Hollywood Dream Factory." *Society* 9, no. 10 (1972): 68–70.

Lau, Tuen-Yu, and Axel Kwok. "A Case Study of Business Model Innovation and Tranformation in China's Film Industry." In *International Perspectives on Business Innovation and Disruption in the Creative Industries: Film, Video and Photography*, edited by Robert DeFillippi and Patrik Wikström, 37–49. Northampton, MA: Edward Elgar Publishing, 2014.

Lee, James S. "Disney Research Harnesses the Synergy between Buildings and Infrastructure." *URBANLAND: The Magazine of the Urban Land Institute*, May 7, 2015. http://urbanland.uli.org/sustainability/disney-research-harnesses-synergy-buildings-infrastructure/.

Lee, Kevin. "The Little State Department: Hollywood and the MPAA's Influence on US Trade Relations." *Northwestern Journal of International Law and Business* 28, no. 371 (2007): 371–98.

Lewis, Jon. *Hollywood V. Hard Core: How the Struggle over Censorship Created the Modern Film Industry.* New York: New York University Press, 2002.

Li, Jinying. "China: The Techno-Politics of the Wall." In *Geoblocking and Global Video Culture*, ed. Ramon Lobato and James Meese, 110–19. Amsterdam: Institute of Network Cultures, 2016.

Li, Wei, and Hua Zhu. "Voices from the Diaspora: Changing Hierarchies and Dynamics of Chinese Multilingualism." *International Journal of the Sociology of Language*, no. 205 (2010): 155–71.

Li, Xin. "Michael Barr, Who's Afraid of China? The Challenge of Chinese Soft Power." *The Copenhagen Journal of Asian Studies* 30, no. 1 (2013): 117–19.

Li, Xin, and Verner Worm. "Building China's Soft Power for a Peaceful Rise." *Journal of Chinese Political Science* 16, no. 1 (2011): 69–89.

Lieberthal, Kenneth. "The American Pivot to Asia." *Foreign Policy*, December 21, 2011. http://foreignpolicy.com/2011/12/21/the-american-pivot-to-asia/.

Lieberthal, Kenneth, and Jisi Wang. *Addressing U.S.-China Strategic Distrust.* Monograph 4. Washington, DC: John L. Thornton China Center at Brookings, 2012.

Lin, Jan. "Dream Factory Redux: Mass Culture, Symbolic Sites, and Redevelopment in Hollywood." In *Understanding the City: Contemporary and Future Perspectives*, edited by John Eade and Christopher Mele, 397–418. Malden, MA: Wiley-Blackwell, 2002.

Lindtner, Silvia, Bonnie Nardi, Yang Wang, Scott Mainwaring, He Jing, and Wenjing Liang. "A Hybrid Cultural Ecology: World of Warcraft in China." In

Proceedings of the ACM Conference on Computer-Supported Cooperative Work, 371–82. New York: ACM, 2008.

Lindtner, Silvia, and Marcella Szablewicz. "China's Many Internets: Participation and Digital Game Play across a Changing Technology Landscape." In *Online Society in China: Creating, Celebrating, and Instrumentalising the Online Carnival*, edited by David Kurt Herold and Peter Marolt, 89–105. New York: Routledge, 2011.

Litwak, Mark. *Contracts for the Film and Television Industry*. 3rd edition. Beverly Hills, CA: Silman-James Press, 2012.

Liu, Feng-chao, Denis Fred Simon, Yu-tao Sun, and Cong Cao. "China's Innovation Policies: Evolution, Institutional Structure, and Trajectory." *Research Policy* 40, no. 7 (2011): 917–31.

Locke, Brian. *Racial Stigma on the Hollywood Screen from World War II to the Present: The Orientalist Buddy Film*. New York: Macmillan, 2009.

Low, Linda. *Economics of Information Technology and the Media*. Singapore: Singapore University Press, 2000.

Lukas, Scott A. *Theme Park*. London: Reaktion Books, 2008.

Lussier, Germain. "Here's How the Chinese Cut of 'Iron Man 3' Is Different." *Slashfilm*. May 1, 2013. www.slashfilm.com/heres-how-the-chinese-cut-of-iron-man-3-is-different/.

Ma, Ran. "Celebrating the International, Disremembering Shanghai: The Curious Case of the Shanghai International Film Festival." *Culture Unbound* 4 (2012): 147–68.

MacKinnon, Rebecca. "China's 'Networked Authoritarianism.'" *Journal of Democracy* 22, no. 2 (2011): 32–46.

Mahoney, Josef Gregory. "Interpreting the Chinese Dream: An Exercise of Political Hermeneutics." *Journal of Chinese Political Science* 19, no. 1 (2013): 15–34.

Mann, Denise. *Hollywood Independents: The Postwar Talent Takeover*. Minneapolis: University of Minnesota Press, 2008.

Manyin, Mark E., Stephen Daggett, Ben Dolven, Susan V. Lawrence, Michael F. Martin, Ronald O'Rourke, and Bruce Vaughn. *Pivot to the Pacific? The Obama Administration's Rebalancing toward Asia*. Fort Belvoir, VA: Defense Technical Information Center, 2012.

Marsh, Joss Lutz. "Fitzgerald, Gatsby, and the Last Tycoon: The 'American Dream' and the Hollywood Dream Factory." *Literature/Film Quarterly* 20, no. 1 (1992): 3–13.

Matusitz, Jonathan. "Disney's Successful Adaptation in Hong Kong: A Glocalization Perspective." *Asia Pacific Journal of Management* 28, no. 4 (2011): 667–81.

Mazdon, Lucy. "The Cannes Film Festival as Transnational Space." *Post Script* 25, no. 2 (2006): 19–30.

———. "Transnational 'French' Cinema: The Cannes Film Festival." *Modern and Contemporary France* 15, no. 1 (2007): 9–20.

McChesney, Robert W., and John Bellamy Foster. *The Endless Crisis: How Monopoly-Finance Capital Produces Stagnation and Upheaval from the USA to China.* New York: New York University Press, 2012.

McDonald, Paul. *The Star System: Hollywood's Production of Popular Identities.* New York: Wallflower Press, 2000.

McGregor, Richard. *The Party: The Secret World of China's Communist Rulers.* New York: HarperCollins, 2010.

McGuire, Steven, and Michael Smith. *The European Union and the United States: Competition and Convergence in the Global Arena.* New York: Palgrave Macmillan, 2008.

Meng, Bingchun. "Who Needs Democracy if We Can Pick Our Favorite Girl? *Super Girl* as Media Spectacle." *Chinese Journal of Communication* 2, no. 3 (2009): 257–72.

Meng, Jing. "Prohibition and Production of the Past: Representation of the Cultural Revolution in TV Dramas." *Media, Culture and Society* 37, no. 5 (2015): 671–85.

Meyer, David. *Hong Kong as a Global Metropolis.* Cambridge, UK: Cambridge University Press, 2000.

Miller, Peter, and Nikolas Rose. "Mobilizing the Consumer Assembling the Subject of Consumption." *Theory, Culture and Society* 14, no. 1 (1997): 1–36.

Miller, Toby, Richard Maxwell, Nitin Govil, John McMurria, and Ting Wang. *Global Hollywood: No. 2.* London: British Film Institute, 2008.

Mitchell-Smith, Ilan. "The United Princesses of America: Ethnic Diversity and Cultural Purity in Disney's Medieval Past." In *The Disney Middle Ages: A Fairy-Tale and Fantasy Past,* edited by Tison Pugh and Susan Aronstein, 209–24. New York: Palgrave Macmillan, 2012.

Montgomery, Lucy. *China's Creative Industries: Copyright, Social Network Markets and the Business of Culture in a Digital Age.* Northampton, MA: Edward Elgar, 2010.

Moore, James F. "Predators and Prey: A New Ecology of Competition." *Harvard Business Review* 71, no. 3 (1993): 75–86.

Moran, Albert. *Film Policy: International, National and Regional Perspectives.* New York: Routledge, 1996.

Nader, Laura. "Up the Anthropologist: Perspectives Gained from Studying Up." In *Reinventing Anthropology,* edited by Dell Hymes, 284–311. New York: Pantheon Books, 1972.

Nakajima, Seio. "Re-Imagining Civil Society in Contemporary Urban China: Actor-Network-Theory and Chinese Independent Film Consumption." *Qualitative Sociology* 36, no. 4 (2013): 383–402.

———. "The Genesis, Structure and Transformation of the Contemporary Chinese Cinematic Field: Global Linkages and National Refractions." *Global Media and Communication* 12, no. 1 (2016): 85–108.

Neumyer, Scott. "Exclusive Images: Take a Peek behind the Scenes of 'Transformers: Age of Extinction.'" *Tech Times*, September 12, 2015. www .techtimes.com/articles/16933/20141002/exclusive-images-transformers-age-of-extinction.htm.

Nixon, Sean. *Advertising Cultures: Gender, Commerce, Creativity*. Thousand Oaks, CA: SAGE, 2003.

Nixon, Sean, and Paul Du Gay. "Who Needs Cultural Intermediaries?" *Cultural Studies* 16, no. 4 (2002): 495–500.

Nye, Joseph S., Jr. "Soft Power." *Foreign Policy*, no. 80 (Autumn 1990): 153–71.

Ohler, Jason. *Digital Storytelling in the Classroom: New Media Pathways to Literacy, Learning, and Creativity*. Thousand Oaks, CA: Corwin Press, 2013.

Okome, Onookome. "Nollywood: Spectatorship, Audience and the Sites of Consumption." *Postcolonial Text* 3, no. 2 (2007): 1–21.

O'Reilly, Daragh, and Finola Kerrigan. "A View to a Brand: Introducing the Film Brandscape." *European Journal of Marketing* 47, nos. 5/6 (2013): 769–89.

Ortner, Sherry. "Studying Sideways." In *Production Studies: Cultural Studies of Media Industries*, edited by Vicki Mayer, Miranda J. Banks, and John T. Caldwell, 175–89. New York: Routledge, 2009.

Palumbo-Liu, David. *Asian/American: Historical Crossings of a Racial Frontier*. Stanford: Stanford University Press, 1999.

Pan, Su Yan. "Confucius Institute Project: China's Cultural Diplomacy and Soft Power Projection." *Asian Education and Development Studies* 2, no. 1 (2013): 22–33.

Pang, Laikwan. *Creativity and Its Discontents: China's Creative Industries and Intellectual Property Rights Offenses*. Durham, NC: Duke University Press, 2012.

Papadimitriou, Lydia. "The Hindered Drive toward Internationalization: Thessaloniki (International) Film Festival." *New Review of Film and Television Studies* 14, no. 1 (2016): 93–111.

Pauwels, Caroline, and Jan Loisen. "The WTO and the Audiovisual Sector: Economic Free Trade vs Cultural Horse Trading?" *European Journal of Communication* 18, no. 3 (2003): 291–313.

Pearson, Andrew. "China's Social and Mobile Companies Set to Shake the Tech World." *Journal of Digital and Social Media Marketing* 3, no. 2 (2015): 135–50.

Peng, Weiyu. "China Film Coproduction and Soft Power Competition." PhD diss., Queensland University of Technology, 2015.

Pine, B. Joseph, II, and James H. Gilmore. *The Experience Economy.* Updated edition. Boston: Harvard Business Press, 2011.

PÖFF. "Tallin Industry Days 2012: The Golden Triangle—Funding and Co-production Markets in East-Asia." YouTube video, 1:06:05. January 13, 2013. https://www.youtube.com/watch?v = aWka8kBzuMo&list = PLTMX-F4YO5DU-fs2-6-BRGtM_ihhChiQYa&index = 7.

Potter, W. James. *Media Literacy.* Thousand Oaks, CA: SAGE, 2013.

Powdermaker, Hortense. *Hollywood: The Dream Factory, an Anthropologist Looks at the Movie Makers.* London: Secker and Warburg, 1951.

Prud'Homme, Rémy. *Annual World Bank Conference on Development Economics 2005: Lessons of Experience.* Washington, DC: World Bank Publications, 2005.

Rahman, Abid. "China's Wanda to Create Movie Fund to Attract Hollywood Productions." *The Hollywood Reporter,* October 7, 2014. www.hollywood reporter.com/news/chinas-wanda-create-movie-fund-739111.

———. "Shanghai Disneyland to Benefit from High-Speed Train Line." *The Hollywood Reporter,* July 30, 2014. www.hollywoodreporter.com/news /shanghai-disneyland-benefit-high-speed-722470.

Rahman, Abid, and Georg Szalai. "China's Alibaba Pictures Investing in Paramount's 'Mission: Impossible 5." *The Hollywood Reporter,* June 24, 2015. www.hollywoodreporter.com/news/chinas-alibaba-pictures-investing-paramounts-804709.

Ran, Jimmy, Jan P. Voon, and Guangzhong Li. "How Does FDI Affect China? Evidence from Industries and Provinces." *Journal of Comparative Economics* 35, no. 4 (2007): 774–99.

Rivkin, Charles. "2014 US-China Film Summit: Charles Rivkin." Asia Society video, 13:25. November 5, 2014. http://asiasociety.org/video/2014-us-china-film-summit-charles-rivkin.

Rochlin, Margy. "Her Lucky Star." *Director's Guild of America,* Fall 2013. www.dga.org/Craft/DGAQ/All-Articles/1304-Fall-2013/Dennie-Gordon .aspx.

Rohn, Ulrike. *Cultural Barriers to the Success of Foreign Media Content: Western Media in China, India, and Japan.* Frankfurt am Main, Germany: Peter Lang, 2009.

Rolfe, Pamela. "Spain and China Ink Co-Production Deal." *The Hollywood Reporter,* October 1, 2014. www.hollywoodreporter.com/news/spain-china-ink-production-deal-737143.

Rosen, Stanley. "Hollywood in China: Selling Out or Cashing In?" *The Diplomat,* May 26, 2015. http://thediplomat.com/2015/05/hollywood-in-china-selling-out-or-cashing-in/.

Rubenfeld, Sara, Richard Clément, Jessica Vinograd, Denise Lussier, Valérie Amireault, Réjean Auger, and Monique Lebrun. "Becoming a Cultural

Intermediary a Further Social Corollary of Second-Language Learning."
Journal of Language and Social Psychology 26, no. 2 (2007): 182–203.

Schalkwyk, David. "From the Globe to Globalisation: Shakespeare and Disney in the Postmodern World." *Journal of Literary Studies* 15, nos. 1–2 (1999): 33–65.

Schatz, Thomas. *The Genius of the System: Hollywood Filmmaking in the Studio Era*. New York: Henry Holt, 1996.

———. "The New Hollywood." In *Movie Blockbusters,* edited by Julian Stringer, 15–44. New York: Routledge, 2003.

Schiller, Herbert I. *Mass Communications and American Empire*. Boulder, CO: Westview Press, 1992.

Schwartz, Vanessa R. *It's So French! Hollywood, Paris, and the Making of Cosmopolitan Film Culture*. Chicago: University of Chicago Press, 2007.

Scott, Allen. "The Other Hollywood: The Organizational and Geographic Bases of Television-Program Production." *Media, Culture and Society* 26, no. 2 (2004): 183–205.

Scott, Allen J., and Naomi E. Pope. "Hollywood, Vancouver, and the World: Employment Relocation and the Emergence of Satellite Production Centers in the Motion-Picture Industry." *Environment and Planning A* 39, no. 6 (2007): 1364–81.

Screen Australia, and Australian Government. "International Co-Production Program Guidelines." November 12, 2015. https://www.screenaustralia.gov .au/getmedia/05f7de49-ac13-46fe-8840-37dab5a1b394/Glines_Copro.pdf.

Shackleton, Liz. "Oriental Dreamworks Unveils Slate." *Screen International,* June 16, 2014. www.screendaily.com/territories/asia-pacific/oriental-dreamworks-unveils-slate/5073199.article.

Shambaugh, David L. *China's Communist Party: Atrophy and Adaptation*. Washington, DC: Woodrow Wilson Center Press, 2008.

———. "China's Soft-Power Push." *Foreign Affairs* 94, no. 4 (July/August 2015): 99–107.

Shao, Peiren. "A New Horizon of Huallywood Cinema Studies: Preface to Huallywood Cinema Studies Book Series." *China Media Report Oversease* 11, no. 3 (2015): 1–4.

Shimizu, Celine. *Straitjacket Sexualities: Unbinding Asian American Manhoods in the Movies*. Stanford: Stanford University Press, 2012.

Shin, Jeeyoung. *Negotiating Local, Regional, and Global: Nationalism, Hybridity, and Transnationalism in New Korean Cinema*. PhD diss., Indiana University, Bloomington, 2008.

Shuang, Xie. "Similarities and Differences or Similarities in Differences? China's TV Programming in Global Trend of Neo-Liberal Imperialism." *China Media Research* 10, no. 1 (2014): 91–102.

Slingerland, Ted, trans. *Analects: With Selections from Traditional Commentaries*. Indianapolis, IN: Hackett, 2003.

Smith, Grady. "Box Office Update: 'Iron Man 3' Earns Huge $68.3 Million on Friday." *Entertainment Weekly*, May 4, 2013. http://insidemovies.ew.com/2013/05/04/box-office-update-iron-man-3/.

Smythe, Dallas. "Foreword." In *Canadian Dreams and American Control: The Political Economy of the Canadian Film Industry*, edited by Manjunath Pendakur, 15–26. Detroit: Wayne State University Press, 1990.

Soja, Edward W. "Inside Exopolis: Scenes from Orange County." In *Variations on a Theme Park: The New American City and the End of Public Space*, edited by Michael Sorkin, 94–122. New York: Farrar, Straus, and Giroux, 1992.

Song, Yang. "What Should Economists Know about the Current Chinese Hukou System?" *China Economic Review* 29 (June 2014): 200–212.

State Administration of Radio, Film and Television. "The Stipulation of Administration on Chinese-Foreign Film Co-Production." China Film Co-Production Corporation website. www.cfcc-film.com.cn/policeg/content/id/1.html.

Stewart, Andrew. "Wanda Group Acquires AMC Entertainment." *Variety*, September 4, 2012. http://variety.com/2012/film/news/wanda-group-acquires-amc-entertainment-1118058647/.

Straubhaar, "Beyond Media Imperialism: Assymetrical Interdependence and Cultural Proximity." *Critical Studies in Media Communication* 8, no. 1 (1991): 39–59.

Stringer, Julian. "Global Cities and the International Film Festival Economy." In *Cinema and the City: Film and Urban Societies in a Global Context*, edited by Mark Shiel and Tony Fitzmaurice, 134–44. Malden, MA: Wiley-Blackwell, 2001.

Su, Wendy. *China's Encounter with Global Hollywood: Cultural Policy and the Film Industry, 1994–2013*. Lexington: University Press of Kentucky, 2016.

———. "Cultural Policy and Film Industry as Negotiation of Power: The Chinese State's Role and Strategies in Its Engagement with Global Hollywood 1994–2012." *Pacific Affairs* 87, no. 1 (2014): 93–114.

———. "New Strategies of China's Film Industry as Soft Power." *Global Media and Communication* 6, no. 3 (2010): 317–22.

———. "Resisting Cultural Imperialism, or Welcoming Cultural Globalization? China's Extensive Debate on Hollywood Cinema from 1994 to 2007." *Asian Journal of Communication* 21, no. 2 (2011): 186–201.

Swann, Paul. "The Little State Department: Washington and Hollywood's Rhetoric of the Postwar Audience." In *Hollywood in Europe: Studies in a Cultural Hegemony*, edited by David Ellwood and Robert Kroes, 176–96. Amsterdam: University of Utrecht Press, 1994.

Tammen, Ronald L. "The Organski Legacy: A Fifty-Year Research Program." *International Interactions* 34, no. 4 (2008): 314–32.

Tang, Xiaobing. *Visual Culture in Contemporary China: Paradigms and Shifts.* Cambridge, UK: Cambridge University Press, 2014.

Tezuka, Yoshiharu. *Japanese Cinema Goes Global: Filmworkers' Journeys.* Hong Kong: Hong Kong University Press, 2011.

Thorne, Lynn. *Word-of-Mouth Advertising, Online and Off: How to Spark Buzz, Excitement, and Free Publicity for Your Business or Organization with Little or No Money.* Ocala, FL: Atlantic Publishing Company, 2008.

Thrift, Nigel. *Knowing Capitalism.* Thousand Oaks, CA: SAGE, 2005.

Tryon, Chuck. *On-Demand Culture: Digital Delivery and the Future of Movies.* New Brunswick, NJ: Rutgers University Press, 2013.

Tsui, Clarence. "'Iron Man 3' China-Only Scenes Draw Mixed Response." *The Hollywood Reporter,* May 1, 2013. www.hollywoodreporter.com/news /iron-man-3-china-scenes-450184.

Vaidhyanathan, Siva. *The Googlization of Everything.* Berkeley: University of California Press, 2011.

Van Maanen, John. "Displacing Disney: Some Notes on the Flow of Culture." *Qualitative Sociology* 15, no. 1 (1992): 5–35.

Wan, Jihong, and Richard Kraus. "Hollywood and China as Adversaries and Allies." *Pacific Affairs* 75, no. 3 (2002): 419–34.

Wang, Fei. "The Need for a Film Rating System in China: The Case of Ang Lee's *Lust, Caution* (2007)." *New Review of Film and Television Studies* 12, no. 4 (2014): 400–411.

Wang, Shujen. "Piracy and the DVD/VCD Market: Contradictions and Para-doxes." In *Art, Politics, and Commerce in Chinese Cinema,* edited by Ying Zhu and Stanley Rosen, 71–84. Hong Kong: Hong Kong University Press, 2010.

Wang, Ting. "Hollywood's Crusade in China prior to China's WTO Accession." *Jump Cut: A Review of Contemporary Media* 49 (2007).

Wasko, Janet. *Understanding Disney: The Manufacture of Fantasy.* Malden, MA: Polity Press, 2001.

Wasserstrom, Jeffrey. *Global Shanghai, 1850–2010: A History in Fragments.* New York: Routledge, 2008.

Wei, Ting, and Bao-lian Xia. "Analysis of the Current Situation and Reasons of China's Movie and TV Cultural Trade." *International Economics and Trade Research* 24, no. 3 (2008).

Wong, Cindy Hing-Yuk. *Film Festivals: Culture, People, and Power on the Global Screen.* New Brunswick, NJ: Rutgers University Press, 2011.

Wright, Benjamin. "Remember 'Shanghai' Starring John Cusack and Chow Yun-Fat? Well, It's Going Straight to Blu-ray . . . in England." *Playlist* (blog). *Indiewire,* May 10, 2012. http://blogs.indiewire.com/theplaylist/remember-shanghai-starring-john-cusack-chow-yun-fat-well-its-going-straight-to-blu-ray-in-england-20120510.

Wright, David. "Mediating Production and Consumption: Cultural Capital and 'Cultural Workers.'" *The British Journal of Sociology* 56, no. 1 (2005): 105–21.

Xiao, Ying. "'Leitmotif' State, Market, and Postsocialist Film Industry under Neoliberal Globalization." In *Neoliberalism and Global Cinema: Capital, Culture, and Marxist Critique,* edited by Jyotsna Kapur and Keith B. Wagner, 157–79. New York: Routledge, 2011.

Xie, Yuwei. "Language and Development of City: The Linguistic Triangle of English, Mandarin, and the Shanghai Dialect." *The Trinity Papers* (2011). Trinity College Digital Repository, Hartford, CT. http://digitalrepository .trincoll.edu/trinitypapers/3/.

Xu, Minghua. "Television Reform in the Era of Globalization: New Trends and Patterns in Post-WTO China." *Telematics and Informatics* 30, no. 4 (2013): 370–80.

Xu, Xiaying, Tan See Kam, and Jiang Wei. "Of Goats, Lambs, Sheep and Wolves: Chinese Animation and Cultural Industries." *Asian Cinema* 24, no. 2 (2013): 239–58.

Yang, Liu. "Shanghai Int'l Film Festival Kicks Off." *CRIENGLISH.com,* June 13, 2010, http://english.cri.cn/6666/2010/06/13/2483s576451.htm.

Yeh, Emilie Yueh-yu. "Montage of Attractions: Juxtaposing Lust, Caution." In *Lust/Caution from Eileen Chang to Ang Lee,* edited by Peng Xiao-yen and Whitney, 15–34. New York: Routledge.

Yeh, Emilie Yueh-yu, and Darrell William Davis. "Re-Nationalizing China's Film Industry: Case Study on the China Film Group and Film Marketization." *Journal of Chinese Cinemas* 2, no. 1 (2008): 37–51.

Yeh, Wen-Hsin. *Becoming Chinese: Passages to Modernity and Beyond.* Berkeley: University of California Press, 2000.

Yin, Guopeng, Ling Zhu, and Xusen Cheng. "Continuance Usage of Localized Social Networking Services: A Conceptual Model and Lessons from China." *Journal of Global Information Technology Management* 16, no. 3 (2013): 7–30.

Yu, Hong. "Reading the Twelfth Five-Year Plan: China's Communication-Driven Mode of Economic Restructuring." *International Journal of Communication* 5 (2011): 1045–57.

Yu, Sen-lun. "*The Mummy 3* Has Strong Opening in Mainland China." *Screen International,* September 5, 2008. www.screendaily.com/the-mummy-3-has-strong-opening-in-mainland-china/4040623.article.

Zang, Xin, Zhu Lin, and Jun Shao. "Cultural Proximity, Economic Development and Export of Cultural Products." *Finance and Trade Economics* 10 (2012).

Zeng, Ke, Wenli Liu, Xiao Wang, and Songhang Chen. "Traffic Congestion and Social Media in China." *IEEE Intelligent Systems* 28, no. 1 (2013): 72–77.

Zhang, Heather Xiaoquan, Bin Wu, and Richard Sanders. *Marginalisation in China: Perspectives on Transition and Globalisation.* Burlington, VT: Ashgate, 2007.

Zhang, Xudong. "Shanghai Image: Critical Iconography, Minor Literature, and the Un-Making of a Modern Chinese Mythology." *New Literary History* 33, no. 1 (2002): 137–67.

Zhang, Yingjin. *Cinema and Urban Culture in Shanghai, 1922–1943*. Stanford: Stanford University Press, 1999.

Zhang, Zhen. *The Urban Generation*. Durham, NC: Duke University Press, 2007.

Zhao, Hongqin, and Jianbin Huang. "China's Policy of Chinese as a Foreign Language and the Use of Overseas Confucius Institutes." *Educational Research for Policy and Practice* 9, no. 2 (2010): 127–42.

Zhao, Yuezhi. "China's Quest for 'Soft Power': Imperatives, Impediments and Irreconcilable Tensions?" *Javnost—The Public* 20, no. 4 (2013): 17–29.

———. "Transnational Capital, the Chinese State, and China's Communication Industries in a Fractured Society." *Javnost—The Public* 10, no. 4 (2003): 53–74.

Zheng, Wang. "The Chinese Dream: Concept and Context." *Journal of Chinese Political Science* 19, no. 1 (2013): 1–13.

Zheng, Xiaoling. "Chinese State Media Going Global." *East Asian Policy* 2, no. 1 (2010): 42–50.

Zhou, Min. "Zhongguoban *Jinsu Qianci* yu Meiguoban *The Amazing Race* Bijiao Fenxi" (A Comparative Analysis of the American and Chinese Versions of *The Amazing Race*). *Shengbing Shijie* 3 (2015): 67–68.

Index

Aaker, David, 41
above-the-line media workers, 14, 84, 95, 130, 154; as brokers and translators of culture, 113; complex demands placed on, 110; cultural exchange and, 156; defined, 17; media studies scholars and, 134; strategic narratives and, 107. *See also* compradors; cultural intermediaries
Abrams, J.J., 77
actors, 17, 78–79, 117–18; Asian American, 79; Chinese actors in Hollywood films, 79–80
Aipai.com website, 105
Air Force Entertainment Liaison Office, 25
Alibaba, 60, 61, 161, 164
Amazing Race, The (American TV show), 149, 159
Amazing Race China, The [*Jisu Qianjin*] (TV show, 2014), 159
Amazing Spider-Man, The (2012), 70
AMC Theaters, 13
American Film Institute Festival, 93
American Film Market, 93
animation, 15, 18, 24, 157, 161–63
Annenberg Foundation, 29
Antoniades, Andreas, 90
Arnold, Julean, 112

Asia Pacific Arts magazine, 127
Asia Society Southern California, 70, 89, 93, 97, 129, 156; Entertainment/Media Asia Group, 96; industry forums and, 104. *See also* US-China Film Summit
assistants (*zhuli*), transnational, 149–153
assisted productions, 66, 76–77, 88, 149
audiences, American, 34, 116, 127, 130
audiences, Chinese, 10, 62, 72, 88; children as target audience, 162–63; *Iron Man 3* and, 33
audiences, global/international, 64, 110, 124; China-related content for, 164; visibility of Chinese cinema to, 165
Australia, 17, 81, 85–86, 134, 150
Avatar (2009), 12, 69

Back to 1942 (2012), 78
Bai, Samantha, 80
Baidu search engine, 60, 61
Bait (3D) (2012), 81
Balda, Kyle, 69
Baltruschat, Doris, 67, 134, 135–36
Bay, Michael, 1, 11, 37, 38, 80
Beijing, 8, 34, 136, 137
Beijing Film Market, 94
Beijing Film Studio, 150

market, 163; Qing-period compradors, 112. *See also* Greater China region

China, mainland, 8, 11, 72, 121, 124, 141

China, People's Republic of (PRC), 10, 61, 94; balance of power with the United States, 90, 165; Chinese dialects spoken in, 113–14; "cultural trade deficit" of, 2, 3, 61–62; entertainment market, 95; film distribution in, 5, 21, 22; *hukou* (residence permits), 152, 153; industrial relations with the United States, 42–43, 118; international influence of, 2, 5; intersection of policy and product in, 21–25; "One China" policy, 7; service industry, 16; television stations in, 158; tensions with Japan, 121; theatrical exhibition market, 16, 90; twelfth five-year plan (2011), 24–25, 35–36, 45; US financial dependence on, 128. *See also* film import quotas, in PRC; WTO, China's accession to

China Film Co-Production Corporation, 64, 155–56

China Film Group Corporation, 11, 14, 103, 164

China Film Pitch and Catch (CFPC) forum, 101–102

China–Hollywood collaboration. *See* Sino-US film collaborations

China-International Production Guide, 156

China Media Capital, 4, 29, 30, 159

"Chinawood," 2

"Chinese Dream" (*Zhongguo Meng*), 4, 11, 20; Hollywood dream factory commingled with, 37, 41, 109, 165; public advertising for, *21*; television programs and, 159

Chinese film industry: growth of, 106; Hollywood intertwined with, 88; international film festivals and, 103; "preservation" of, 63–64; privatization of, 97; state-controlled monopoly of (before 1984), 68

Chinese film market, 2, 9, 65, 80, 88

Chinese language, 8, 30, 113–14, 120, 127; production ecosystem and spoken dialects of, 136–37; translated dialogue, 162. *See also* Cantonese; Mandarin (*putonghua*)

Cho, John, 79

Chow, Rey, 165

Chow, Stephen, 88, 141

Christopherson, Susan, 17

Chu, Judy, 30

Chu, Karen, 94

Chung, Frankie, 80

citizenship, 132, 136, 151, 152, 153

Code 46 (2003), 77, 149

Cohen, Rob, 74, 123, 131, 141

Colligan, Megan, 37

commissioned productions, 80–81

Communist Party, Chinese, 2, 20

compradors, 112–13, 129–130, 152; Ang Lee as comprador director, 116–18; Bill Kong as comprador dealmaker, 121–22; challenges faced by, 113–15; David Lee as comprador producer, 118–19; James Schamus as comprador screenwriter, 119–120; media co-productions and, 123–29; Zhang Xun as comprador regulator, 122–23

Confucius, 131, 132

Confucius (2010), 12, 69

Confucius Institutes, 52–54, 104

consumerism, 56

Coonan, Clifford, 10

Coppola, Sofia, 78

Co-Production Film Pitch Forum (Co-FPC), 102

co-productions, 23, 32–33, 61; Australian, 85–86; Chinese style, 70–71; compradors and, 123–29; co-production forums, 94; European, 82–85; Hollywood style, 71–74; industrial culture of, 132–33; as "local" films for distribution purposes, 68; as most publicly visible mode of collaboration, 67; PRC government approval and, 66, 67; production management, 148–153; Sino-Korean, 151

Costo, Oscar L., 72, 74

Council of Europe, 82, 83

Coupe, Eliza, 73

Craig, Daniel, 77

Critser, Nick, 150, 151

Crouching Tiger, Hidden Dragon (2000), 80, 121, 124, 127, 202n41

cultural imperialism, 15, 37, 56

cultural intermediaries, 111, 112, 133

Cultural Revolution, 75, 147

culture industries, 2, 11, 23, 45, 111, 113

Curtin, Michael, 10, 42

Cusack, John, 78, 106

Dafoe, Willem, 79

Dai Jinhua, 112

Dalian Wanda Group. *See* Wanda Group

Damon, Matt, 78

Dark Knight Rises, The (2012), 70

Davis, Darrell William, 2, 23

CPSIA information can be obtained
at www.ICGtesting.com
Printed in the USA
LVOW10s0010240917
549718LV00003B/4/P

9 780520 294028